# Praise for *Worlds Apart*

CW01500828

"*WORLDS APART*, the story of
love in Ghana and goes on to create a successful business ——
of her basement in Columbia, MD, while raising a mixed-race
family in race-conscious America, is a compelling read. With
moving insight, Lutterodt shares with her readers how boundaries can be broken, and life can actually be 'win-win' both in
the business world of capitalism and in human relationships."

 —**Frank Sasinowski, M.S., M.P.H., J.D., recipient of
 2021 Pontifical Hero Award for Inspiration.**

"Lutterodt's memoir weaves an exquisite tapestry of her life's
odyssey, reminding us that the quest for identity and belonging transcends borders. As a fellow traveler of diverse identi-
ties, I felt a genuine connection to her story, which she handles
with love, grace, and wisdom."

 —**Josephine Garmen, Executive Director,
 Healey International Relief Foundation**

"*WORLDS APART* is a lovely and inspiring book, full of courage and compassion as the author moves from one world to
another and another, not just coping but flourishing. Lutterodt's
determination to defy the conventional mores about women's
place in society and her reckoning with the enduring influence of one's early life will resonate with readers. Lutterodt
draws on the work of great philosophers and theologians as

she reflects on the big questions in her life, finding peace—but no easy answers—as she lives into her experiences."

**—Joan Neal, Deputy Executive Director,**
**NETWORK Lobby for Catholic Social Justice**

"*WORLDS APART* describes the author's life journey through worlds divided by neo-colonialism, classism, and racism. Lutterodt shares her story with an openness to learning about self and others, and in the process encourages us all to reflect on our purpose and tell our truths."

**—Vicki Cofield Aber, Psychotherapist**

"Lutterodt's brilliant and insightful memoir explores the author's experience living at the intersection between worlds and does so with compassion and empathy. Inspired by the inclusive way of seeing taught by the Franciscan teacher Richard Rohr, she strives to build bridges between people too often separated by lack of cultural awareness."

**—Dr. Tom Eberle, former Director of the Living**
**School, Center for Action and Contemplation**

# Worlds Apart

*A Memoir of Uncertain Belonging*

Sarah A. Lutterodt

*atmosphere press*

*For Clement*
*Together, through thick and thin*

# *Contents*

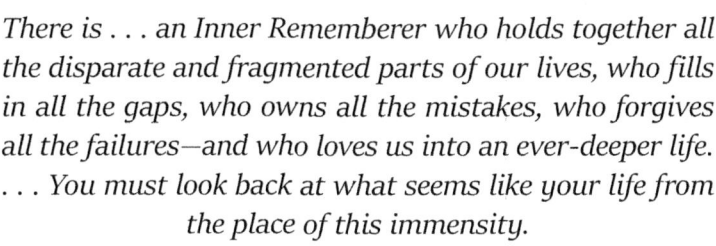

*There is . . . an Inner Rememberer who holds together all the disparate and fragmented parts of our lives, who fills in all the gaps, who owns all the mistakes, who forgives all the failures—and who loves us into an ever-deeper life. . . . You must look back at what seems like your life from the place of this immensity.*

—Richard Rohr, *CAC Daily Meditation, June 2022*

# Introduction

If there is a continuous thread to my life, it runs deep below the surface in places I have found hard to reach. I have lived in many different places. There have been many discontinuities. I have paused—sometimes—to wonder about the common humanity that underlies lives very different from my own. As I grow older, I have paused more often. Sometimes I have sought a deeper connection. Sometimes I have turned away because of fear or ignorance or hubris. I have too often been a prisoner of my own blindness.

Each of us sees the world through the lens of our own culture, education, and belief systems. Each of us lives within a bubble, big or small, be it the life of an African villager whose horizons are limited to a day's walk away from home or the life of an East Coast liberal who has traveled the world yet filters all their experiences through the lens of a seldom-examined American exceptionalism.

I count myself fortunate to have touched different worlds. But each of them, in its own way, has been bounded by its own proclivities and prejudices—some privileged, others much less so. Many times, I have been on the inside, unaware of my own entrapment until I broke out or looked back. More often I have lived on the edge looking in: observing, judging, valuing. Never quite belonging. Once, I jumped right in and had to fight to survive. Over time, my lens has broadened, I hope, but it is still a lens forged in the particular circumstances of my birth and education.

I am a pragmatist. I don't have the eye or ear of a novelist.

My skill has been to adapt, to cope, to find a way through each day and each circumstance, not to uncover deep meaning as I went. Nor to really acknowledge why my accent has always set me apart in the U.S. or to accept the incomprehension my marriage to a Ghanaian seems to provoke.

In this memoir I set out initially to tell stories of my encounters with different worlds, my relationship to each, and my struggles along the way. But as I look back, the search for meaning, for a unifying thread, becomes imperative. I need to see the quilt that emerges when all the pieces are stitched together, when boundaries become places of connection rather than division. The picture is emerging slowly.

My story starts with the sheltered world of my childhood. I grew up on a farm in Surrey, England. Social class and religion defined the world in which we lived. Racial divisions didn't exist; we were simply unaware of different races. People of different skin color, as seen in the pages of picture books or represented by "Golliwog" dolls, might as well have been gnomes or elves.

My parents, our nanny, my three siblings, and I lived in an ancient Tudor farmhouse. The farmworkers lived in cottages across the road from us. The boundaries seemed immutable. From the age of seven I attended a convent boarding school. There, our sense of apartness—not to say superiority—was reinforced by the versions of history and geography we learned in the classroom. We had brief glimpses of other worlds. But these glimpses did little to affect my sense of who I was or where I belonged. My early identity has marked me indelibly, even though I have traveled far.

My story ends—or nearly so—in Ghana. An image is woven into the patchwork of my life. We're sitting in the air-conditioned living room of our house in Accra. The curtains are drawn. CNN is blasting news into the room, thanks to the satellite dish on our roof. The news connects us to the U.S., where we moved when we left Ghana in 1980. Adongo lives with his family in the staff quarters behind our house. The wall that separates our lives from theirs is not dissimilar from the one that separated my family growing up from the workers on my father's farm all those years ago. Now, viewed through a wiser lens, I like to think that the boundaries are less rigid, more porous—places where lives are joined with empathy and understanding. They are boundaries, nonetheless.

No one has the capacity to live in an unboundaried world. The scale is too vast, our need for security too great. But we can live with more awareness of our blinders and with compassion for those in other worlds. We can stretch the fissures in our own containers to learn what lies outside and rejoice at what we find. We can persevere in the search for connection. Maybe it is in the search itself that the pattern underlying the disparate details of my life is to be found.

# Part I

# A Secure Container

*[Children] need boundaries, identity, safety, and some degree of order and consistency to get started. . . . You need a very strong container to hold the contents and contradictions that arrive later in life.*

*—Richard Rohr,* Falling Upward

# Protected

---

M ine was a protected childhood. The container was strong and clearly bounded. I was cocooned in a world where family bonds and the routines of farm and village largely eclipsed the horrors of war that dominated the wider society. As war gave way to the struggles of post-war rationing, the structures of class and religion that defined our family's place in the world were explicit and immutable. Patriotism, at once insular and imperial, was unquestioned. I had few opportunities to see and understand a wider world. Although my life has taken me far from my place of origin and the limits of my early experience, the foundational rootedness—even entitlement—of my childhood has echoed, often unnoticed, through the years. So, too, have the personality traits bequeathed to me by nature and nurture.

## A War Baby

At the beginning of June 1940, men of the British Expeditionary Force were gunned down, or surrendered, or struggled to clamber on board boats that would ferry them from Dunkirk to safety in England. The bombs were falling all around. The soldiers were tired and hungry after their long march to the coast. Many were wounded. They were immersed in the fear and terror of war. My mother listened to the radio from her hospital bed. She had given birth to me on May 31$^{st}$. "It was beautiful June weather," she told me when I was old enough

7

to understand. "I followed the evacuation closely; we all did. Hundreds of small boats stepped in to help. They came from up and down the south coast. Many soldiers were rescued." But many were not. Much later, we learned that our parish priest and a family friend were among those captured at Dunkirk. They both spent five years in prisoner-of-war camp, but we never heard their stories.

In Mother's telling, the evacuation of Dunkirk was an occasion for heroism and pride, illumined by a flat and shining sea. The image she conveyed to me was in stark contrast to the reality portrayed in the eponymous movie that I watched, with horror, in 2017. The thunder of war or the gentle hum of outboard motors? Soldiers, bloody and traumatized, or salt-of-the-earth fishermen calmly going about their patriotic duty? One reality, two radically different portrayals. In her romanticized retelling, Mother protected me—and maybe herself too—from the reality of war that overwhelmed the outside world.

Later in the war, our farmhouse was in the path of the German bombers that destroyed much of London during the blitz. Looking north, over the Downs, we could see the glow of fires lighting the night sky. As a small child, I learned to use a gas mask. A metal air-raid shelter, constructed in our dining room, doubled as a playhouse during the day. During the final days of the war, the notorious doodlebug rockets sometimes cut out just above the house. We rushed out of the house and looked up in the sky, wondering where they would land. One exploded in a field close by, another in a coppice a mile away. Fortunately, there were no direct hits.

I recall experiencing curiosity and a tense excitement but not existential fear. Even though war was all around us, I was shielded from its terror. I knew the purpose of the large searchlight positioned in a nearby field; it was so real to me that I am still reminded of it anytime I see a searchlight piercing the night sky. Yet the memory is not accompanied by the gripping panic of a looming invasion. From news on the radio, I came to think of war as a zero-sum game in which winning involved killing or capturing all the enemy soldiers. I had no mental picture of the blood and mayhem involved. The closest I came to understanding the reality was when my Aunt Lily soothed me by calling me a "poor wounded soldier" as she cleaned my bloodied knee after a fall. Within the confines of our home, I was safe.

Despite the anxieties that surely overwhelmed them at times, our parents gave me and my siblings the blessing of a safe and secure childhood. But the protective shield they provided didn't diminish their relief and excitement when victory was declared. When Aunt Lily stopped by to celebrate, she greeted me as a "war baby." And so I was. When I was born, a German invasion had seemed imminent; now, after many years of vicious fighting, Germany lay in ruins.

## Boundaries

In the world in which we lived, there was no question that Britain won the war. The myth of British superiority was unquestioned. Along with social class and religion, nationality was an essential pillar of the identity bequeathed to me. A birthright if you will. Being British and at the pinnacle of a worldwide empire carried with it a sense of invincibility, not to say superiority. It was a comforting myth for a child. Never mind that the empire was on the verge of disintegration. Our protected childhood was a priceless gift, but it was marred by stubborn blinders. It would take many years—even decades—before I would really confront the myth. Even now—having spent most of my life outside England—I find relics hiding in the deepest recesses of my mind.

During the war, the family made friends with U.S. and

Canadian soldiers stationed in the area, but, as conveyed to me as a child, their contribution was peripheral to the main war effort. I don't recall any acknowledgement of Britain's desperate dependence on American help or of Russia's sacrificial role on the Eastern Front. Pearl Harbor was never mentioned, nor do I remember any talk of the nuclear bombs falling on Japan. These events have left no trace in my memory of those years. America and Russia were bit players, just like Canada and Australia. The contribution of Britain's many colonies was scarcely acknowledged. How different the story looks from the other side of the pond seventy-plus years later!

The occasional visits of Aunt Milly Stanley from the U.S. provided a rare window to a wider world. She came laden with candies and other goodies that were unheard of in the England of those days. Their decorative containers found many uses around the house and were a constant reminder of her generosity. Only later did we learn that she also sent packages to her relatives in Germany because our family had deep connections to the enemy country. Yet these connections did nothing to affect the foundational—largely unspoken—assumption of Britain as the norm and reference point for all our experiences.

Although my mother was born and raised in England and always thought of herself as English, her family was of German origin. For them, the war with Germany—the second in a generation—was a particularly wrenching experience. My maternal grandmother had come from Germany as a young bride, eighteen years old. Her sons fought for Britain in both world wars; one died. Her nephews fought on the opposite side.

My maternal grandfather, too, had German roots. He was born in England to German parents. His business involved importing fine wines from vineyards along the Rhine and Mosel Rivers. His brother had settled in Koblenz, where the two rivers meet.

My mother's family was vacationing in Germany when the First World War was declared; they returned to England on the last train out. She spoke German fluently. Yet, despite her German roots and connections, she clung to her English identity.

When my mother was growing up, her family led a comfortable bourgeois existence in London. Theirs was a proverbial "upstairs-downstairs" household, in which all kitchen activity was conducted downstairs and out of sight. However foreign they may have seemed to their neighbors, my grandparents' lifestyle conformed with that of the British upper middle class. At the time of her marriage, my mother had never even boiled an egg. "We would just call down to the kitchen to tell the cook to serve pureed spinach for dinner," she told me once. "We didn't give a second thought to the amount of work that involved."

The rigidities of Britain's class structure—with its division of the world into those who give orders and those who have no option but to obey; those who have and those who struggle to make ends meet; those who matter and those who don't count for much—have been passed down from one generation to another. From my grandmother to my mother and on to me, albeit, I'd like to think, in a less mindless way. Having encountered many different worlds, I am acutely aware of my advantages in life and struggle with the privilege I enjoy. But I have no recollection of my parents experiencing such a struggle. They seemed to accept the ordering of society as a given. As a child I had no reason to question the boundaried world in which we lived.

Although my mother went to a good secondary school, like most young women of her generation she had no higher education and never worked for a living. When she married my father, she exchanged the relative ease of her life in London for life on a farm. At first there were maids, but when the war came, the only person who remained was our nanny. Over the years, Mother taught herself to cook, tended our large garden with minimal help, and did the family laundry, first with the help of an old-fashioned wringer and later with the aid of a spin dryer and primitive washing machine. Through it all, and into a relatively comfortable old age, she maintained a deep ambivalence about her German origins and a strong attachment to her position in British society.

My father's background was different. He was the eighth son of an impecunious Irish baron and grew up on a large family estate, Frenchpark in County Roscommon. He settled at Brewerstreet Farm in the early 1920's, having earned a diploma in agriculture at Cambridge University. With the benefit of a government loan and financial help from the family, he was able to purchase the farm, along with the fifteenth-century farmhouse in which we grew up. Despite his upbringing, he had no pretension to the life of a gentleman farmer. Far from it. For many years he would get up at 4:00 am each Tuesday to take his produce to the vegetable market at Covent Garden. He didn't hunt or fish or ride a horse, and his shooting was limited to foxes and rabbits around the farm. With his tweed cap and sturdy Wellington boots, he remained every bit the working farmer throughout his life. His aristocratic origins didn't affect his demeanor in any way. When someone came to the farm asking to see "the Honorable Hubert French" and found him in working attire, he told them the "Honorable Hubert" had gone out.

It is commonplace nowadays for people to use DNA analysis and genealogical research tools to probe their ancestry as a way of understanding where they have come from and hence their place in the world. It is a tragedy that many African Americans are unable to trace their origins for more than a few generations because of the cruel separation of families during slavery. I try to empathize with the sense of rootlessness they must feel even as I, somewhat grudgingly, acknowledge what it means to me to have a family history that can be traced back many centuries. As a young adult I was highly critical of the classism of British society and scoffed at my mother's attachment to social position, but in my early teens I eagerly sought out a copy of *Burke's Peerage of the Realm* in the school library, happy to locate my name buried in the smallest of small print on the page devoted to Baron de Freyne and discover the long line of Frenches in the west of Ireland from whom I was descended. It gave me a sense of my place in the world and in the great sweep of history.

My mother, ever protective of the honorific title she had acquired by marriage, was more deliberate than my father in articulating our place in the British class structure. Although she maintained contact with her relatives in Germany, our place in British society was what mattered. She even went to the extent of arranging for my sister, Jane, and me to be presented at court, which required us to get expensive outfits—with mandatory hats—and involved attending a garden party at Buckingham Palace where we had to curtsey to the queen. We even took lessons to be sure we got the curtsey right! Our parents didn't have the financial resources for us to participate in the full panoply of social events that being a debutante involved, but my mother did her best. In retrospect, it is hard to believe I went along with this antiquated "coming out" practice. At the time, I accepted my parents' wishes without question; I wasn't ready to rebel.

To Mother's chagrin, her goal of positioning Jane and me as eligible young women in the debutante marriage market didn't work out as she would have liked. When Jane got engaged to Don, a computer engineer who, though Catholic, didn't check the box for having attended exactly the right type of school, she was distraught. Jane had crossed—by a whisker—one of the defining boundaries of the world in which we'd been raised. I can only imagine the emotional turmoil that my marriage to an African mathematician—not even a Catholic—caused her five years later. My transgression was far more egregious. To her credit, Mother came in time to accept both situations and the grandchildren we gave her.

In addition to nationality and social class, religion was a key definer of the world in which I grew up. My parents were both Catholic. My father, along with his many brothers, attended the Oratory School, founded by Cardinal John Henry Newman. My maternal uncles attended the same school. Despite differences in their backgrounds, my parents had a shared identity as members of the educated Catholic minority in England. ("Educated" was my mother's euphemism for membership of an acceptable social class, irrespective of educational attainment.)

In the 1940s and '50s, Catholicism was still regarded with considerable suspicion in England. Catholics felt a need to be ever ready with an excuse for the church's proclivities; we would never have called them failures or even shortcomings. We felt responsible for defending the church against common challenges such as why the liturgy was in Latin; why the church supported the fascist Franco; why abortion and birth control were sinful even if the mother's life was at risk; why (and when) the Pope was infallible; and on and on. We twisted our minds to remain loyal to the "one true church," and this allegiance enhanced our sense of belonging. It helped to define us.

Our world was divided neatly into "us and them": Catholics and the rest. When a visitor came to the house, my brother Christopher—aged about six—asked: "Are you Catholic or Protestant?" The visitor's answer determined whether the person could be counted as one of us.

It would be wrong to imply that my parents' religious affiliation was purely a matter of social convention or confined to attendance at Sunday Mass and bi-weekly confession. Religion wasn't simply an identifier; it was deeply woven into our lives. We always said grace before and after meals, and night prayers together were part of our family routine. Every evening, when Mother had got us ready for bed, Jane or I would knock on the floor above my father's favorite chair in the sitting room, signaling that we were ready for prayers: a nightly ritual in which both parents joined us.

Although Father went along, it was doubtless Mother who was the primary driver of our religious observance. Into her old age, she prayed the rosary each night, kneeling beside her bed. She kept a stoop with holy water in her bedroom and a crucifix on the wall, and when any of us was faced with an inconvenience or worse, she would always exhort us to "offer it up." Although rarely articulated explicitly, her piety permeated our worldview in significant ways. It certainly influenced my direction in life, even if I now have a more detached view of the Catholic Church with all its strictures and constraints.

## *A Tight-Knit Family Unit*

When we were not at boarding school, my three siblings and I, along with our parents, formed a cohesive family unit. Nanny and Aunt Lily were also—and always—an integral part of our childhood, contributing in no small measure to the stable, nurturing environment we experienced.

My sister, Jane, was the oldest. I came next. My two brothers, Christopher and Richard, followed at roughly two-year intervals. Although Sarah is the name on my birth certificate, the family has always called me Sally. They still do. I never really understood why; the name "Sarah" seemed so much more dignified! Jane tells me it was our nanny's doing: her response to the popular song and movie "Sally in Our Alley." As a young adult, I was determined to be known by the name I was given at birth, so now I have a split identity: I am Sally to old friends and family and Sarah to the rest of the world.

As small children, Jane and I were always together. We were

usually dressed alike, whether in the grey flannel overcoats with matching round hats that we wore for big occasions or the red velvet dresses that were reserved for Christmas parties. We often got matching Christmas presents. One year, it was a small red suitcase for Jane and a green one for me—each marked with our initials; I have mine still. Another year it was matched woolen twin sets. When our parents' friends gave parties for their children, we were usually invited together.

Attending occasional parties was about the limit of our connection to other children in the area, and those connections were strictly confined to those in the appropriate social strata. Neither Jane nor I was gifted socially. We didn't particularly enjoy the parties and mostly would have preferred to stay home. In other ways our personalities were quite different. Jane was a country girl who loved to be outside. Each spring she would scour the woodlands to pick primroses and bluebells for us all to enjoy; she tracked birds' nesting places and knew where to find the hatchling blue tits or chaffinches. At times she would go out early in the morning to watch for badgers when they came out of their setts to feed. She knew many of the cows in our father's herd by name. I read books, played games, and whined when I was bored. Happiest when I was curled up with a book on the old Chesterfield sofa in the living room, I was mostly oblivious to the beautiful countryside that surrounded us. Although I felt safe within the limits of my childhood world, I was always something of an outlier.

As we moved into our late teens and early twenties, I followed an academic path. Jane qualified as an elementary school teacher but always remained adept in the domestic arts, making and decorating the family Christmas cake and crafting beautiful flower arrangements for the living room. Although I did better in the narrow world of school, her gifts were more celebrated at home. Jane's rootedness and constancy were rewarded late in life when she received a medal from the Pope for more than forty years of faithful service to her local parish church.

Similarly, our brothers have very different gifts and interests. Like Jane, Christopher has always been close to the land. One could say he was born to be a farmer. He inherited the farm and lives in the old farmhouse to this day. As an adult he became prominent in national farming circles. Richard was more academically gifted, though less bookish than me, and always keen on sports. He went on to a successful career in civil engineering—a career that took him to many parts of the world. It must have come as a relief to Mother that her two sons both chose partners who met her narrow criteria for social acceptability—both Catholics no less. (Father died before any of us were married.) All four of us have lived to celebrate our golden wedding anniversaries.

Nanny was a constant presence throughout our childhood. She joined the family when Jane was born and stayed until Richard went to boarding school. Other than visiting a few family members on her days off, Nanny had little life of her own. As a nanny all her life, she had moved from one family to another, always close but never quite belonging, in accordance with the class-based hierarchy of the time. One family had taken her to India during the time of the Raj where she was placed in a higher social stratum than that of other household employees. "Never touch a native's hand," her employer cautioned her. Her whiteness gave her status even if it meant living in a social no-man's-land.

During the war, when other household help joined the land army working on the farm, Nanny turned her hand to cooking and other chores around the old farmhouse. Every Friday morning, she got on her knees to scrub the rough, red-tiled floors in the kitchen and passageway. Woe betide any child whose dirty boots muddied her clean floor. Although she could be fierce at times, Nanny held our affection in an undemanding way. She belonged with the family, and we loved her. Yet, given the way social structures were defined, her belonging was incomplete. After leaving Brewerstreet, she never settled in a home of her own. In hindsight, I can imagine the loneliness and abandonment she must have felt.

Aunt Lily, my father's oldest sister, was always there for us. She acted as housekeeper for my father until he married, and when he did, she had a house built for herself a short distance away. For us it was a home away from home. Many are the times we walked with her down the rural lane that wound its way past the farm, whether after visiting her at home, or on our way back from nursery school, or on occasions when we accompanied her on a goodwill visit to one of the farmworkers' families. As we walked, she would regale us with teddy bear stories and her own brand of wisdom. One of her favorite replies when asked a childish question was "Put your thinking cap on." I wondered what such headgear would look like.

In those days there was little traffic on the road, just the occasional farm vehicle or my father's herd of milking cows being driven to their afternoon pasture. The skies were often grey, and damp leaves lay underfoot for much of the year. As summer gave way to autumn, we'd try to catch the leaves as they spiraled down from the trees. "See how many leaves you can catch," Aunt Lily urged us. Each leaf caught before it touched the ground signaled a month of good fortune during the coming year.

Every summer, we'd pack our suitcases and go stay at Aunt Lily's house for a few days. It was a big adventure! Her house was custom-designed in the dying days of pre-war living when she still had a full-time maid. I always slept in the maid's room. It had its own bathroom. I loved having the space to myself. It gave me a sense of privacy that wasn't always available in the rough and tumble of life in a large family. At home, I shared a room with Jane.

During our visits, we went on picnics in an adjacent meadow, taking with us an old-fashioned picnic hamper carefully packed with goodies. To get to our destination, we pretend-drove her car, which remained unused in her garage for many years after the war because she couldn't afford to run it. Mostly, she bicycled where she needed to go, or walked, or took a ride with us. Living on a fixed income as she did, money was always short, but she rarely complained.

Later, when my appetite for games was insatiable, I often walked to her house, hoping for a game of cards. She never disappointed. With Lily, the game was nearly always a favorite version of solitaire. When her sister, our Aunt Moule, was visiting from London, we ventured more widely, playing backgammon, dominoes, hearts, bezique, canasta, and more. I have long since forgotten the rules and strategy associated with each game, but the pleasure they gave me remains, as does the selflessness with which my two aunts dropped everything to indulge my passion.

Both within the immediate family, and in our relationships with the many uncles, aunts, and cousins in our extended family, my siblings and I were tightly held in a web of family affection, an unquestioned place of belonging. The bonds were so strong and ever-present that, as a child, I hardly noticed them; as a teenager, I started to find them irksome and limiting.


## Making Do

Living on a farm in post-war Britain offered little scope for indulgence. The uncertainties of living off the land and the strictures of rationing called for a pragmatic approach to life. Even after rationing ended, my parents were never what my mother would longingly describe as "comfortably off." They were always careful how money was spent. Although we were protected from the worst of their anxieties, my parents' lives—and thus my childhood—were framed by a great deal of prudence in their approach to material possessions. Luxuries were few and far between. Coping, getting by without complaining, making do were the virtues that oiled the wheels of everyday life. These were values that shaped me and have enabled me to weather difficult times.

Although we were not rich, we were not poor either. I never faced real adversity as a child; rich and poor are, after all, relative terms. We lived off the fat of the land: fresh milk and cream delivered to the door by the cowman; butter curdled in our own churning machine; fruit and vegetables in season—or bottled to last through the winter; chickens killed and plucked in time for Sunday dinner; eggs aplenty. But cash wasn't abundant. Mother used her small personal income to buy our clothes and other items we needed that were not available from the farm. When it came time to pay school fees, Father often had to sell a cow. Any expenditures on new linens or furniture were carefully evaluated. Mother seldom bought herself a new outfit; I don't ever remember her buying jewelry.

We only got new clothes when we had outgrown what we already had, and mine were almost always pass-me-downs from Jane. Once, I was treated to brand-new pajamas! They had bold, green stripes and a cord at the waist. Although they were new, they were not really for me. They were boys' pajamas that could be passed on to my brothers when I had outgrown them. Who was I to complain? In our world, the gender hierarchy was simply taken for granted. My brothers would never have been expected to wear girls' pass-me-downs!

A particular shopping trip sticks in my mind. I was about fifteen and now taller than Jane, so inheriting her outgrown clothes didn't work anymore. Mother and I took the train to London, headed for the West End, aka Oxford Street, to shop for a summer dress. On such trips, Jane and I would tag behind Mother, trying to keep up as she wove her way at a brisk pace through the bustling crowds filling the sidewalk. We stopped at each of our favorite stores to see if we could find what we liked: John Lewis, DH Evans, maybe Selfridges, and Dickins & Jones. Because any item we purchased would have to last, we usually did a lot of looking to find just the right one. We might go to four or five stores and back again before making a decision.

Mother always insisted on seeing the fabric in natural light. "Let me just take it to the window?" she'd ask the store assistant, who'd then direct us past the dressing rooms to a spot where light from the grey London skies replaced the bright lights of the shopping floor. "I need to have a good look," she'd say as she held the garment up to the window, turning it this way and that to catch the light at different angles. She didn't want any surprises when we got home.

On the day in question, we were lucky to find two summer dresses that I liked in the same store. One was in a soft sky-blue cotton embroidered with small white daisies. The other was more striking; it was a shirt-waister in a stiffer cotton with bands of pink and black. I had to choose. There was no question of having both.

"The blue one really suits you," Mother said. "The color matches your eyes."

"Yes, but . . ." I objected. "The pink one is really fun."

"The blue one is more unusual. But it's up to you."

Mother had her way, of course. I took the blue. It felt like I was being asked to choose between two versions of myself: mild and conforming or bold and a little outrageous. There is no doubt—in retrospect—that the mild blue suited me better. Beneath some of my bombast as a teenager, I was *au fond* as subservient to authority as any parent could wish for. But there was something about the disappointment I experienced in renouncing the bold version that remains with me to this day. Why else would I remember the occasion so vividly?

Post-war rationing and shortages led to other thrifty habits. If a parcel arrived, we would never think of throwing away the string or brown-paper packaging. Each piece of string was unknotted and wound around our fingers into a simple skein before joining other such remnants in a large tin at the bottom of one of the kitchen cabinets. Similarly, the brown paper was carefully folded, ready for reuse. These habits endured long beyond the time when they were necessary.

Schooled in this way, we were very careful in the way we deployed our meagre pocket money. In the fifties, when biros—ball-point pens—were still a novelty, I spent the princely sum of five shillings—the equivalent of several pounds in today's money—to buy one. It was green and shiny with a hexagonal cross-section. I treasured it for many years.

My childhood experiences of thrift and scarcity were a fore-taste of the much more severe shortages I was to experience as an adult in Ghana. And both sets of experiences put me at odds with the profligate consumerism we encountered when we came to the U.S. I still stifle feelings of guilt if I splurge on two dresses or shirts when, in truth, one would suffice. But then, remembering it is American consumer spending that fuels the world economy, and our purchases provide a meagre living for factory workers in Bangladesh, Vietnam, and elsewhere, I puzzle as to how Western consumers should exercise their economic privilege. To buy or not to buy? There is no simple answer to the enduring moral conundrum of privilege and inequality.

## Earthbound and Lean of Expression

My life as a child was framed by earthy realities, not cultural refinement. Life on a farm—with its annual cycle of planting and harvesting with too much rain or too little, scarcely ever just right—doesn't leave much time or appetite to indulge in the finer arts of life.

During the war, and in the immediate post-war years, the radio was the main source of news and popular entertainment. A British soap opera about the life of a doctor's wife, *Mrs. Dale's Diary*—which ran for fifteen minutes every afternoon—was a favorite of the women in our family for many,

many years. The episodes were filled with small-town events that they could relate to. My father was an avid follower of *The Archers,* a saga that traced the fortunes of a farming family in the west of England and often incorporated up-to-the-minute information about agricultural policies and events. The show started in 1951 and is still running today! Another long-running favorite was Alistair Cooke's *Letter from America.* Discovering it was still airing when we moved to the U.S. in the 1980s brought back memories of my distant childhood with my father glued to the radio, hanging on every word.

*Letter from America* was about as highbrow as it got in our household. My parents never tuned in to the BBC's *Third Programme* with its focus on the arts and more intellectual topics. They read *The Times* but few books. Apart from the annual trip to a Christmas pantomime in London, music and theater were not woven into our lives. Jane and I both took piano lessons but, outside of that, had scant exposure to music. Art and poetry had little place in our lives except in much-treasured books of children's verse such as those by A.A. Milne and Lewis Carroll.

The proverbial British stiff upper lip was a natural corollary to the pragmatism that marked my childhood, leaving me more adept at navigating life at the surface than diving deep to wrestle with existential questions or resonate with fundamental emotions. There is no doubt our parents loved us and did everything they could to give us a good start in life, including— for me—educational opportunities that were rare for girls at that time. But their reluctance to express emotions, combined with the amount of time we spent away from them at boarding school, made it difficult for us to develop an aptitude for intimacy. It just wasn't part of our DNA.

My early memories of my father center around our bedtime routine. I loved the rough see-saw motion with which he dried my back, using one of the large green bath towels that followed me from home to boarding school and back again. I loved the way he tucked me into bed, as tight as could be, until the mattress curled up to meet the sheets. I remember, too, his sense of humor. He responded particularly well to jokes with an Irish flavor, off-color limericks, or lavatory humor, but he was embarrassed by jokes with sexual innuendo. When television arrived, he enjoyed news programs but was visibly discomfited by shows in which kissing or other signs of affection were portrayed, even though such scenes were far more restrained than they are today.

Given that he made his living on the farm, Father was close to home most of the time, but he was always lean of expression. He spoke rarely, if at all, of his early life and the many losses he had suffered. His own father had died when he was in his teens. He lost four brothers in the First World War and three others to illness in subsequent decades. His farming partner had been killed by an avalanche when skiing in Switzerland. Had he suppressed all his sadness, or did he simply want to hide it from us children? During a family vacation in Ireland, we visited the site of his old home at Frenchpark and found the house in ruins. I can imagine how distressing that must have been for him, but all I remember is his silence.

Mother was a more hands-on parent, the organizer. I am told that I have inherited aspects of her personality. She was a devoted mother, giving us delicate treats like Brands Essence Jelly and honey sandwiches when we were sick and preparing our favorite meals when we came home as young adults. She read stories to us as children (*Mary Plain* by Gwynedd Rae was a favorite) and organized outings to places of historical interest during school vacations: Hampton Court, the Tower of London, Greenwich, the Festival of Britain. She was always there for us when we needed her, but she wasn't emotionally close. There was no "birds and bees" talk prior to or during puberty, and when, at the age of twelve, I was having difficulty seeing the blackboard at school, it was our nanny, not my mother, who I told.

Mother may well have been exasperated by my whiny moods in my pre-teen years. When I wasn't engrossed in a book and didn't know what to do with myself, I would ask repeatedly, "What shall I do now?" Her response, more than once, was, "Do the nuns at school tell you that you are 'spineless?' " I'm not sure what she intended me to do with the question. Was it simply that I was being a pain in the . . . ? Was that what her own teachers had called her when she was the same age? Or was I somehow less valued because I hung around indoors while Jane busied herself outdoors? The shelter and protection of my childhood years were jeopardized, albeit briefly, on such occasions. They were precursors of the cracks in my childhood container that were to come.

Beyond the close-in world of home and family, the permanence and regularity of the surrounding environment—its people and its rhythms—contributed to the sense of safety and security I enjoyed as a child. Though separated from us by barriers of class and education, the people of farm and village were a constant presence in our lives. Collectively, they contributed to the stable container that framed my childhood years.

# A Rich Tapestry

W hile home and family shaped the inner container in which I was raised, the people and places of farm and village—Brewerstreet Farm and the nearby village of Bletchingley—provided a secure outer shell. The characters, as I remember them, were as rich in human detail and variety as those of the Bayeux Tapestry. Together they contributed to the secure, dependable world in which I was nurtured.

Within this world, roles and relationships were determined by the stratified social system that was still alive and well in the immediate post-war years. Human connections with all their conditionalities and ambiguities, though tightly framed and largely transactional, were nonetheless real. For me as a child, the regularity and dependability of this wider environment contributed to my rootedness and sense of security. This world with its predictable rhythms was where I belonged. I had no reason to question the structures that sustained it.

## The People of Brewerstreet

As though to epitomize the prevailing class divisions, most of the farmworkers at Brewerstreet lived in cottages across the road from our farmhouse—"on the other side of the tracks," one might say in the U.S. On our side of the road, though further apart than the cottages, were friends and family. Up the street in one direction was Place Farm, where my Aunt Maud and our three older cousins lived. (Her husband, my father's younger brother, had purchased the farm next door to Brewerstreet; he died soon after I was born.) In the other direction was the magnificent Old Rectory with its expansive house and gardens. The Caves, good friends of the family, lived there. A little further round the corner was our beloved Aunt Lily's house.

Together, the four houses formed their own little bubble, a world apart from that of the workers who occupied the cottages opposite. "I call it causerie corner," Aunt Maud used to say, pronouncing the word "cau-ser-ie" carefully to emphasize her appropriation of the French word for chatter. "Causerie, not cosy, because of all the small talk and gossip that bounces around."

Many of the farmworkers had lived and worked on Brewerstreet Farm their whole lives. The large Medhurst family lived in the central unit of a triple-dwelling building that backed onto the cowsheds. The water closet was at the end of the garden. Jack Medhurst had worked on the farm since before my father's arrival in 1921. I remember him as a wizened old man of few words who wore black boots, navy pants, a waistcoat, and—always—a cap on his head. It seemed like he'd looked after the horses since the dawn of time. Sometimes Jane and I would go to the stable yard in the evening so that we could ride the carthorses out to the field after their day's work. Jane rode Turpin; my mount was a beautiful bay, the large and soulful Prince. Jane was in her element. I was terrified.

One of the Medhurst daughters, Daphne—or Daph as we called her—was married to Jack Tinelly, who'd come from Northern Ireland to work on the farm. She cleaned house for us for a while. Although their five children were similar to us in age, we didn't play together. That would have been unthinkable. It was a boundary never to be crossed.

Tinelly was short and wiry, a little bow-legged. After the death of their second son in a tragic bicycle accident, he returned to the Catholicism of his birth, and we used to give him a ride to church on Sundays. As we dropped him back home, it was always the same cheery joke: "Thankssh for the bussh ride." His accent was undimmed by the long years he had lived in England. I never heard of him returning home to see his family in Ireland or of them visiting him in England.

Another of the Medhurst daughters, Barbara, was married to our tractor driver, Bill Broughton. Broughton—for that is how we always referred to him—helped out in other ways, too. One of his responsibilities was to mow the lawns in the summer. We loved to follow him up and down the tracks the mower left in its wake; he tolerated our presence kindly. On rare occasions we were allowed to take off our shoes and wiggle our toes in the cool, freshly mown grass. The sound of the lawn mower and the smell of fresh-cut grass were sure signs that summer had arrived.

Broughton came into the house each morning to polish shoes. If we left our shoes on the old chest in the back kitchen in the evening, he'd clean and polish them the next morning before starting out on the tractor. We took such perks of farm living for granted—part of the natural order of our lives. "Thanks, Broughton," we'd say if we saw him, our sense of entitlement evident in the casual way we addressed him; it never occurred to us that "Mr. Broughton" would have been a more respectful way to address someone who was our senior by far.

Of all the Medhurst siblings, Violet, or Vi, was the longest surviving and the one we knew best. She worked on the farm for many years then came to work in the house after my father died, helping Mother with cleaning, carrying coal, and other chores the old farmhouse required. Many years later she went to work at the village newspaper shop. There she could be found selling newspapers on a Sunday morning into her ripe old age. When vacationing in Bletchingley in the 1970s and '80s, I often stopped by to pick up a copy of the Sunday *Observer* and say hello. The children were usually with me.

It was an opportunity for them to meet someone who'd been part of my childhood and for me to reconnect with my past.

"Hello, Sally," Vi greeted me, using my family nickname, a cigarette dripping from her mouth. "How've you bin? Havin' a good time over there in Africa?"

"Hello, Vi. Good to see you. We're staying with Mother for a month," I replied. Then, indicating the children, "This is Toby, and this is Isabelle."

Looking the children up and down, she continued, "You know little Daph. She lives in Brighton now." She was proud to tell me of the upward trajectory of her niece, her life a far cry from that of her parents and grandparents. "She's doin' real well. Works as a dispenser at a chemist shop."

As she spoke, I caught a look of lingering suspicion behind her friendly words. The radical class divisions that separated us from the Medhursts when we were children had narrowed but not disappeared. I can only imagine what she made of the fact that I had married an African yet still carried the mantle of outdated privilege!

Roy Yielding (whom we knew as Mr. Roy or simply "Roy") was a fixture for the family. Whether driving one of the lorries or busy in the packing shed across the yard, Roy was always around. He had worked on the farm from the age of twelve. When my father considered letting him go as part of a man-power-reduction exercise, we children were indignant. "You can't do that to Roy," we protested. Not aware of our father's underlying financial concerns, we were outraged that Roy's loyalty could be treated so shabbily. He was part of the family tapestry. When I returned to spend vacations in Bletchingley with the family, he was still there doing odd jobs around the farm and garden. He would tip his hat and greet us with a broad smile, probably unsure of where I had come from this time. My brother Christopher tolerated Roy's foibles as he aged and took care of him until the end.

Unlike the rough but solid Roy, his wife—Mrs. Roy, as we

knew her—was sweet and soft-spoken. She had lost her one child at birth and, from then on, suffered a series of mysterious ailments. When she was well enough, she did a little sewing for the family. I took the children to see her whenever we visited Mother in the 1970s and '80s.

"Gillian is doing very well," she told us one time, referring to the niece who was her pride and joy. "She's going to the grammar school now." Like Vi, Mrs. Roy's dreams for a future freed from the boundaries of social class were tightly linked to her niece's success.

When I got married in 1971, Mrs. Roy gave us a set of hand-sewn table napkins, and when we visited in 1980, she sewed two beautiful school dresses for Isabelle. I was touched by these gestures, which spoke of a warm human bond and mutual respect. The family often grumbled that Mrs. Roy had ideas "above her station." While I didn't go along with their critique, I realize now how difficult it was for me to detach myself from the sentiment entirely. Class consciousness continued to infuse my thinking in insidious ways.

Mr. Warby, the farm bookkeeper, also looms large in my early memories. Tall and grey and monotone, he could have come straight out of the pages of a Dickens novel. He was upright and correct; his speech was low and sparse. We children didn't mess with him. We called him Warby. I don't even remember his first name. Dropping the title "Mr." when referring to him—an unsubtle indication of our own status—was so taken for granted that it went entirely unremarked. As a white-collar worker, he occupied a rank somewhat above that of the farmworkers in the social hierarchy of the day, but he was definitely not "one of us."

The farm office, where Warby worked, was a rough-and-ready wooden structure at the back of the house, raised from the ground on what always seemed to me like large mushroom pillars. In winter, a small paraffin stove was the only form of heat; the office always smelled of kerosene. Warby kept the books in large ledgers using ample copper-plate writing. His industrious and time-consuming search for the last penny to balance the accounts was a continuing source of irritation to my father. But his loyalty was unquestioned. After my father died, it was Warby who warned my mother she was being cheated right and left by the farm manager who she had trusted implicitly. He worked for the family for more than forty years and was a fixture of my childhood.

## Bletchingley Village

The people of Bletchingley village are also imprinted on my mind, as are the places we frequented there as children. They were part of the framing of my childhood, lending a sense of permanence and stability to my early experience. Bletchingley was where we shopped for groceries. It was where I attended nursery school.

Dominating the village and standing a little back from the High Street is the Anglican Church of St. Mary the Virgin. Most of those in our family's social circle were Anglican, at least nominally, and it was there that they worshipped. We would often pass friends going to a service at St. Mary's when we were en route to the nine o'clock service at a local Catholic boys' home. When it came to churchgoing, we lived quite separate lives. Then came the Second Vatican Council with its momentous changes in the Catholic Church's thinking and practice. When the council's teachings finally trickled down to the parishes in the 1990s, permission was granted for Catholic Mass to be celebrated at St. Mary's. Even though Catholics and Anglicans still held separate services, a seemingly immutable barrier had been breached.

Miss Hogg's, the nursery school I attended from the age of four, was located in a house close to the church. Most Bletchingley residents of a certain social standing sent their children there. They would never have permitted their children to go to the rowdy village school up the street. Or so we thought until a prominent local family sent their son there in the late 1950s. It was a violation of class norms. "Poor child," wagged the gossips. "How will he cope with all those rough kids?" The fact that his mother was American—and not indoctrinated in the British class structure—wasn't considered a sufficient excuse.

The stores we frequented were located up and down the High Street. Taylor & Bristow, where we shopped for groceries, was at the heart and center. We often glimpsed Mr. Bristow, the owner, doing his accounts in a glass-walled cubicle across from the grocery counter, but it was Mr. Warren, the grocery manager, who Mother normally dealt with. A large white apron encircled his ample frame and a kindly smile twinkled behind his heavy moustache. He always made us feel welcome. We perched on high stools at the counter as Mother gave him her weekly order; as she did so, he painstakingly entered each item in his order book—the carbon paper securely in place so that he could keep a copy. Butter was cut from large slabs on the counter behind him; bacon was sliced to order. Biscuits (cookies)—which our family consumed in considerable quantities—were stacked in large tins on the steps leading to the upper floor of the store. "Come and see what we have today," Mr. Warren would invite us. With luck, we got a sample to taste.

Mr. Selmes was the village butcher. At the center of his shop was a large wooden block on which the meat was cut; it was worn and blood-stained. Carcasses hung on hooks from the ceiling. Sawdust covered the floor to absorb the drippings. The bookkeeper sat in a small office at the back, separated from the blood and smell of the shop by a glass window. Mr. Selmes, with his small head cocked sideways on his robust body, was always anxious to please. Our order of a joint or chops—occasionally liver or kidneys—was prepared as we waited, then wrapped in newsprint or brown paper. Plastic bags—a clean and anodyne alternative—hadn't yet left their trail of pollution across the globe. Our Sunday lunch was almost always a joint from Selmes. If needed, Mother could always order the meat to be delivered, confident Mr. Selmes would provide high-quality cuts. In a small village, news travels fast, and he couldn't risk having dissatisfied customers.

In the 1940s and '50s, every small village still had a baker, and Bletchingley was no exception. (Sliced bread wasn't yet invented.) Mr. Grice baked all the bread on the premises. The heady smell of baking flooded his small shop on the High Street and the smell lingered in his delivery van, which made twice-weekly deliveries to the farm. When the van arrived we'd run out to greet Ted, the genial driver, clamoring for our favorite items. We loved the twist loaf, freshly baked. Whenever we stopped to buy one at the bakery, the twisty ends were usually devoured surreptitiously before we got home. Penny buns or the smaller ha'penny (half-penny) buns—slightly sweet and with a few currants sparsely distributed in the dough—were standard fare for birthdays. On Good Friday—and Good Friday only—we had spicy hot cross buns. I was horrified to learn that hot cross buns are now available year-round in England!

There were other shops too. There was Longhurst's, the newsagent, where stationery items, candies, and a miscellany of goods were to be found in addition to newspapers and periodicals. Barclays Bank, open two days a week, stood on the other side of the High Street. It was there that my father cashed money to pay the farmworkers every Friday. We often accompanied him. I was impressed by the heavily frosted glass that separated the cashier from customers. It told me that banking was serious business—and not a little mysterious!

At the top of the High Street, Mrs. Marsden had a small general-purpose store that occasionally had bananas to sell; they were a rare treat in post-war Britain. We used to go in expectantly, scrutinizing her expression for clues.

"Any bananas this week?" Mother would ask.

"Sorry, ducks! Not today. Maybe next week" was her usual answer, and we'd have to make do with a few items bought with our minimalist post-war "sweets" ration.

Just occasionally, we were in luck. "Come, see what I have for you today!" Mrs. Marsden would whisper conspiratorially, as she led us to the back of the store where we could select a few precious fruits to take home.

The people and places of farm and village are so firmly etched in my memory that if I had any artistic talent, I believe I would be able to render them on paper in minute detail. They were reliable pillars of my childhood, their permanence and dependability contributing to a deep-rooted sense of trust in people that I still retain despite the inevitable disappointments of life. Encountering others with less stable childhoods helps me appreciate the significance of the gift.

Inevitably change has now come to my childhood world. Most of the people have passed on. The shops are long gone, but the ancient buildings remain, presenting an English village of enduring charm. Christopher and his wife, Sacha, still live in the old farmhouse. When farming in the area became unsustainable, Christopher converted the farm buildings into a business park—one of the first of its kind in England. There are no cows being driven to pasture, leaving a messy trail in their wake. Carthorses have vanished from the land. The farm cottages have been converted into tony residences, much sought after because of their rural setting and close proximity to London. Increased social mobility has softened, though not entirely erased, the rigid class stratification that marked my childhood and defined my worldview for more years than I like to admit.

I visited frequently when Mother was alive and still do so from time to time, thanks to Christopher and Sacha's generous hospitality. Driving down Bletchingley High Street and visiting the old farmhouse evoke memories of an earlier time. They put me in touch with my beginnings, remind me of my journey.

The boarding school I attended from a very young age provided a parallel set of experiences. It, too, was tightly contained and timeless in its way, sheltering those within from the turbulent reality of the world outside.

# The Angelus on the Stroke of Twelve

Vivien Leigh had been a pupil at the Convent of the Sacred Heart school in Roehampton in the 1930's. The nuns used her as an example of the horrible fate that awaited us in "the world" if we didn't hold fast to the moral values they taught us. I was a pupil at the school in the 1950s when Princess Margaret renounced her romance with Peter Thorneycroft, a divorcé. The good nuns rejoiced at her decision as an answer to prayer. Good had triumphed. No matter that Margaret's life thereafter descended into a spiral of depression and failed relationships. Being a good Catholic meant holding fast to dogma and the rigid moral code emanating from the Vatican. This was before Pope John XXIII's *aggiornamento* and the Second Vatican Council breathed new life into the ancient institution, and long before Pope Francis's joyful embrace of human nature in all its complexity gave hope to the faithful.

Jane and I went to the Convent of the Sacred Heart when it opened at its post-war location in Woldingham. The school's arrival, just a few miles from Brewerstreet, gave our parents the opportunity to give us an education they considered appropriate. Jane, at eight years old, had outgrown Miss Hogg's nursery school. I was six and went along, too.

Although our life at school was very different from the life we knew at home, there was an underlying convergence. The values of nationality, class, and religion that defined our identity at home were powerfully reinforced. Though bounded and blind in many ways, the education we received was guided by fundamental principles and an enduring wisdom that have served me well throughout my life.

## A Cloistered World

The school property is nestled in a valley near the North Downs, surrounded by woods and meadows with two long driveways connecting it to the nearby communities. We went as day girls at first, but my parents hadn't reckoned with the terrible snowy winter of 1946/47. Even though the school was only a few miles away, the twice-daily drive proved too much for my mother. The driveway we used was accessed via a narrow lane that wound its way uphill from the main road. Our car often broke down or failed to start and had to be hand-cranked. We carried a shovel to dig us out of snow drifts if needed. By the time I was seven, Jane and I became weekly boarders, transitioning to full boarders a few years later.

From an early age, home and school became two quasi-independent strands in my life, sharing the same sociocultural boundaries but quite distinct in terms of relationships and daily routines. Although homesick from time to time, I fitted relatively easily into school life and enjoyed my success as a student. I wonder now at the ease with which a child of seven could have been absorbed so easily in the life of a residential institution, however benign. I wonder, too, at the strength of the social obligation that led so many British parents to send their children away to boarding school as young as six or seven years old. Jane and I lived close enough to go home for lunch almost every Sunday. Most pupils lived much further away and rarely saw their parents during term time. Maybe because of this, and because each class unit stayed together for many years, we formed close bonds. Friendships forged over the years in classrooms and dormitories have stood the test of time.

The main school building was a large mansion, built in the style of a French chateau. It had been requisitioned by the army during the war, and a great deal of refurbishing was needed when the nuns purchased the property. Nissen huts used for storage remained on the grounds for many years. The former cowsheds became the chapel. While the main section of the shed was reserved for nuns and students, visitors were relegated to pews in the adjacent bullpen! A large quadrangle, home to the stables in former years, housed classrooms and the nuns' quarters while chimes from the clocktower marked the hours. At the strike of noon every day, the nuns stopped in their tracks to pray the Angelus. A relic of medieval piety? Maybe, but one that still framed the community's routine.

Behind the main house was a beautiful garden that we enjoyed in a taken-for-granted sort of way. A pergola with climbing roses bordered a sweeping lawn presided over by a huge weeping beech tree. It was ideal for playing hide-and-seek and provided ample shade when the teacher gathered us as junior school pupils to listen to *The Hobbit* and other stories. Close to the house was a small pond with goldfish to amuse us in our idle hours, and immediately beyond it, flights of steps rose to a series of terraces used as tennis courts and for athletic competitions.

The property also included a working farm. For many years, my father came once a week to advise the nuns on its management. Seeing his parked car in the driveway on Friday afternoons was a reassuring sign of his presence, but I rarely saw him to exchange a greeting.

A deep hollow in the woods a little distance from the house fascinated us; it could have been a crater formed by a doodle-bug. It was filled with dry leaves that crunched and crackled as we walked—or rolled in when the nun in charge wasn't watching. We called it the Congo Basin. That was about as close as we got to thinking about Africa, other than the pictures of sick or starving children that were the currency of returning missionaries.

As pupils, we were strictly confined to school property. The school grounds were expansive with plenty of room to roam, emphasizing our distance from what the nuns ominously referred to as "the world." Occasionally, older students took a path behind the house that led through the woods to Woldingham village, which was strictly out of bounds. I did so once and considered myself very daring.

There was no television—of course—but there was no radio either, and it was only toward the end of my time at the school that a few selected newspaper articles from *The Times* or *The Telegraph* would be posted on a bulletin board for us to read. The boundaries that defined our life at school were strictly enforced.

If you can win the heart and mind of a child by the age of seven, he or she is yours for life. Or so the Jesuits claim. The nuns certainly tried. Our lives at school were immersed in the rituals of traditional Catholic observance. There were novenas and rosaries and medals, first Friday specials, bi-weekly confessions, and indulgences galore. Chapel was a central part of the school routine. When Jane and I went home for lunch on Sundays, we always had to be back by 6 pm for Benediction. I can still feel the lump in the pit of my stomach as we reached the school just in time and rushed to the chapel, grabbing our veils on the way. (A head covering in church was still mandatory for women and girls.) Despite the initial feeling of dread, I had no difficulty fitting back into the school's routine.

Alongside the many religious practices that I have long abandoned, the convent environment enabled genuine moments of spiritual awakening that have remained with me. We were encouraged to visit the chapel in our free time for private prayer. I particularly recall evenings when I crept quietly into the small organ loft which could be accessed from one of the dormitories. From the loft I had a bird's eye view of the dimly lit chapel with the sanctuary light flickering in the tabernacle, a few novices kneeling in silent prayer. I was entranced by the quiet intensity of the moment, the sense of a pervading presence. It was an experience of the numinous that I still treasure.

## Women of Their Time

The classism within British society was reflected in the ranks of the good nuns. The professed nuns, referred to as "Mother," were from the "educated" classes. They were the teachers and administrators. Lay sisters, mostly from Malta or Ireland, performed the menial work. Vestiges of the British Raj lingered on in the form of two girls' schools in India that fell within the province governed by our own Reverend Mother. Although she visited Bombay and Bangalore regularly, no effort was made to introduce us to the rich cultural traditions of their country. Nor did we have any idea of the massive displacement of populations that took place when Britain summarily withdrew from its former "Jewel in the Crown" in 1947 and the chaos and bloodshed involved. We lived in a different world.

Beneath the externalities of Catholicism with which they surrounded us and the elaborate habits that disguised their individuality, the nuns were genuinely good women who had given their lives in service of a higher cause. I don't remember any bad apples among them. Many had entered the convent in their late teens or early twenties and hadn't so much as left the convent grounds since then. They didn't know another life. Yet, they were preparing us for lives as wives and mothers as best they could, and they did so with love and dedication.

From time to time the nuns dropped subtle hints that some of us might want to follow their lead into the convent, occasionally using Francis Thompson's poem "The Hound of Heaven" to amplify their message. The poem's message echoed ominously in the "labyrinthine ways of my own mind" for many years.

Mother Shanley was the administrative head of the school for most of the ten years I was there. She addressed the student body every morning from a landing halfway up the sweep of the former chateau's magnificent staircase. From there, she looked down on the assembled students with her penetrating eyes and beaklike nose, her nun's hood—we called it a pie frill—fitted close around her face, the veil trailing behind her. Shan—as we referred to her—embodied the mores she had left behind when she entered the convent. Her message was one of being true to God and our place in society. "It all reflects on your home training" was a frequent rebuke to girls who had stepped out of line. We had the responsibility to uphold the good name of our families.

"Some of the girls actually eat in the kitchen at home," she remarked once in disbelief to my aunt, whose daughters also attended the school. My aunt didn't let on that we often did just that.

On another occasion, we were returning for the new school year when she confided to my mother, "There was a girl recommended to us; when she arrived, we found out she was Chinese!" Shan was incredulous but continued reassuringly, "Fortunately, we were able to find another school that would take her."

I don't remember how my mother reacted to Shan's remarks, but they must have lodged deep in my psyche or I wouldn't have remembered them so clearly all these years later. White entitlement was alive and well—without a hint of shame!

In the evenings, students had the opportunity to sign up for individual conversations with Shan. From time to time, I would sign up even if I had no particular agenda. I craved the attention of an adult who could look into my soul but lacked the vocabulary to express my need. Shan, with her steady gaze, seemed to understand.

Shan lived to be over a hundred years old. After the nuns shed their veils and enclosures in the 1970s, she reentered the world with gusto, visiting students' families in their homes and welcoming them to her home in London. Former students sought her out for advice or solace and found her to be wise beyond their reckoning.

## An Improbable Launching Pad

During my ten years at Woldingham school there were never more than about 120 students, ranging in age from five to eighteen and covering the full gamut of abilities. Though mostly focused on preparing girls for life in society, the school recognized and nurtured our diverse talents. I was a dud at sports and lacked any artistic skill or imagination; academics were my forte. A few, like me, went on to study at university. Improbably, given that it was still unusual for women to have careers, members of my small year group went on to serve in a variety of professions: lawyer, nurse, secretary, economist, business owner, physical therapist.

The course of study the nuns provided was unremarkable for its time. English literature and language; math and general science; Latin and French; history and geography. And, of course, religion, or "doctrine" as it was called. Religious truth was conveyed as the unshakeable Word of God to be studied in the same way as historical events or scientific theories. Dogma was infallible. No ifs or buts. The nuns said nothing to suggest that religious teachings were a different genre of truth altogether. It was only much, much later that the teaching of Richard Rohr, a Franciscan priest, finally liberated me from the tenacious grasp of Catholic orthodoxy.

In doctrine class, we delighted in engaging our teachers in "how many angels fit on a pinhead" type of conundrums and agonized over how long children who died without being baptized would remain in Limbo—a place that was as real to us as far-flung continents. Mother Wheatley, who I later got to know as a wise and loving human being, was quite unable to satisfy our curious minds. The church taught that, in extremis, any of its members could administer the sacrament of Baptism. The only requirement was water poured over the head of the candidate with the sign of the cross and the requisite words.

"In an emergency, any water can be used, even muddy water from a puddle," Mother Wheatley explained.

"What about lemon juice?" asked a class pundit.

"Definitely not!" was her unhesitating reply.

The geography we were taught was still deeply influenced by Britain's recent imperial past. We really believed in our role in the world. Similarly, history was viewed strictly through a nationalistic lens, and one that was strongly influenced by English Catholicism. Thomas More and John Fisher, who were hold-out Catholics during the Reformation, were celebrated as glorious martyrs, while Bloody Mary's Protestant victims, if ever they got a mention, were roundly condemned as apostates and sinners.

An unusually enlightened practice was the challenging essay that the sixth-form teacher required us to write every Saturday morning. She gave us a topic and two or three hours to get our thoughts together. Then we read our essays to each other somewhat in the style of an Oxford tutorial. One week, unaccountably, the topic was the desirability of interracial marriage. I was one of two students who argued against!

Mother Binney, a historian, was responsible for the curriculum. She was small and intense with bushy eyebrows. One day, about a year before we would be sitting for the Ordinary Level (O-Level) exam, I ran into her in the quadrangle. She said she wanted to have a word with me. I was surprised and a little intimidated.

"We need to decide what subjects you'll be taking for O-Level," she said, fiddling with the cross around her neck as she spoke. "It depends what you want to study later." I was fourteen years old. Although I was a good student and had vague thoughts about going to university, my future had never been discussed explicitly.

"Have you thought about history?" she asked. I was surprised again. Surely, she knew I wasn't really into history. Unlike my friend Caroline who read every historical novel she could get her hands on. "What about Latin?" she went on.

"Not really." I wondered why she hadn't asked about mathematics. Math was my best subject, but I knew it got really difficult at university. I assumed she had a good reason for not suggesting it and lacked the courage to question her.

"Maybe physics," I said, eventually. I had enjoyed the few physics topics we'd studied in general science, and it seemed the closest I could get to math. It was a purely intellectual interest. I wasn't a hands-on person who enjoyed building things, nor did I have any great curiosity about natural phenomena, but Mother Binney latched on to the idea immediately. There and then my future was decided. I was to be a physicist! There was no further discussion, no parental conference, no aptitude testing . . . nothing. She simply informed my parents of my choice. (We recently came across her letter, which was addressed to my father only!)

I am still amazed by the consequences of what seemed like a casual conversation in the school quadrangle one spring afternoon. Yet it turned out to be a pivotal moment; my choice that day determined my future career with its many unconventional twists and turns.

There is no doubt that my convent school education marked me indelibly. It reinforced the boundaries of class and religion established at home while preparing me for a future beyond any my parents or the school could have envisioned. However far I have traveled, the benefits of secure Catholic roots and the confidence resulting from my class-based entitlement have remained anchored in my psyche. Though blind and limiting in many ways, they provided a firm ground for my future endeavors. I can say that with hindsight. But first I needed to break loose from their constraints. Just as a chick, as it emerges into life, must crack open the shell that has protected it thus far, so the very principles in which I was grounded led me to question the boundaries they upheld.

# Cracks in the Container

Although the warp and weft of my childhood held me close, providing a safe environment for me then, and memories that I treasure now, the cracks started early and widened as I grew.

I was bookish in a way that my family was not. Not that I aspired to anything highbrow. I survived on the works of Arthur Ransome and other popular children's authors. My parents read *The Times* and the *Daily Mail*. In *The Times*, my mother's first stop was always the notices of births, deaths, and engagements, which she referred to as "hatches, matches, and dispatches." For my father, there was also the *Farmers Weekly*. In the dentist's waiting room, Mother opted for *The Tatler*, filled with society gossip and an occasional photograph of someone she knew.

As a family, we had little exposure to the fine arts. It was up to me, as I prepared to write the General Paper for university admission, to cultivate an interest in literary and artistic matters. Neither home or school had given me a framework of understanding and appreciation. Intent on correcting the deficiency, I became something of a culture vulture, putting me at odds with the rest of the family.

When I would have preferred to listen to Handel's *Messiah* at Christmastime, the family tuned the radio to popular carols. When, during a family vacation on the Norfolk Broads, I would have liked to make a stop in Norwich to see the cathedral, the rest of the family vetoed the suggestion. And when, much later, we were returning by car from a vacation in Italy and

I suggested a short detour to visit the former concentration camp at Dachau to witness the horrors that Hitler had perpetrated, no one else in the family favored the idea. More amusing, as I think of it now, was my stance when the family's very first TV arrived in 1957. The dinner table was set at a slant for a better view of popular early evening shows, such as *This is Your Life.* My three siblings sat on one side of the table to view the show. I sat with my back to it to indicate my disapproval!

My parents responded to my success at school with surprise and a degree of caution. What to make of a girl with academic leanings? Was I fated to become a bluestocking? I wasn't encouraged to take my scholarly achievements too seriously and always felt Jane's home-based skills were more highly prized. When, as a teenager, I complained to my mother about the pervasive class snobbery in our social circle, she countered that intellectual snobbery was just as grievous. She was right, of course. God forbid that I would get a swollen head!

Though rarely voiced, my parents' pride in my success was nonetheless real. I will always be grateful to them for enabling my education. Grateful, too, to my father's cousin, Winifred Lamb, for her support. Winifred, a noted archaeologist of ancient Greece and Turkey, was an outlier in a family whose concerns were mostly centered on the land and the practicalities of daily life. She relied on my father for help in managing her very substantial estate in Hampshire, while my parents looked to her for advice on educational matters. At a time when many parents vetoed higher education for their daughters, Winifred's influence and support was critical.

My brother Richard was also a good student, but being a boy, his academic promise wasn't considered unusual or problematic. Besides, he didn't challenge the family's conservative values as I did.

Douglas Houghton, a respected member of the House of

Commons, had made his home in a converted cottage just up the road from Brewerstreet. The family considered him to be "quite a nice chap" despite the cardinal sin of being a member of the Labour Party. I was at home on one of the rare occasions when he visited my parents. We got into a lengthy discussion about the ethical implications of the hydrogen bomb. It was the time of Bertrand Russell, the Campaign for Nuclear Disarmament, and protest marches to American bases in England. He was surprised to discover I was further to the left than he was!

My parents were shocked at my outspokenness but confident I would outgrow my outrageous opinions. I didn't. The walls of the container that offered me such a secure, if bounded, childhood were cracking. At Oxford the fissures would grow wider.

# Part II

# Emerging Possibilities

*What is it you plan to do with your one wild and precious life?*

*—Mary Oliver, "The Summer Day"*


*Leave your country, your family and your father's house for the new land that I will show you.*

*—Genesis 12:1*

# *Transitions*

The boundaries of my world expanded during my years at Oxford, but I was not in open rebellion against the core values of my childhood. Paradoxically, I realize, looking back, that it was these values that nurtured my growing interest in what were then referred to as "underdeveloped countries" and hence, gradually, my embrace of a very different world-view. At the time I could never have imagined how the years would unfold, culminating in my out-of-the-box engagement to a Ghanaian mathematician, and the start of our long life together.

## *Oxford*

My years as an undergraduate at Oxford were pivotal in many respects, but not in the way an easily impressed American might expect. My time there was not one of great academic achievement; my performance as a physics student was mediocre at best. Nor were they times of extraordinary teaching by brilliant scientists. The curriculum was badly planned, the famed tutorial system being ill-suited to the scientific disciplines. At least, that is my opinion now, after a career in curriculum development. Physics professors delivered carefully crafted lectures with little regard for what students were learning and made little attempt to weave connections between university-wide lectures, college-based tutorials, and the laboratory exercises at which we toiled for many hours a week.

Nor, for me, were my undergraduate years a time for great romance. Socially, I struggled. Ever the wallflower, I defaulted to the Catholic chaplaincy community as a center for social activity. Rather, it was shifts in Catholic thinking that accompanied the Second Vatican Council, as well as my exposure to a diverse group of fellow students and long conversations on topics of existential significance lasting well into the night, that broadened my horizons, cracking me open—bit by bit—to a wider world.

Although the undergraduate body at Oxford was predominantly White and largely educated at English public schools, I mixed freely with students from different class backgrounds and from other countries.

"Do you meet students from grammar schools?" one of my mother's friends enquired with some anxiety. As part of the state education system, grammar schools were outside the experience of her social circle. For them, the privileged, fee-paying public schools were the norm.

"Yes, of course," was my glib response.

What I hadn't fully understood then was that it was often the former grammar school students who held me at a distance, rather than vice versa. It is clearer to me now. Students from less privileged backgrounds were almost certainly more worldly-wise than those of us who had been cocooned at private boarding schools. They understood us far better than we understood them. The phenomenon is repeated in many environments where social barriers are firmly entrenched: in the colonized person's superior understanding of the colonizer's world or the enslaved person's unsuspected insight into the master's thought processes.

It was at Oxford that I first got to know people from other countries. Rajani—an Indian student who lived in the same hostel for all three of my undergraduate years—stands out. She has remained a lifelong friend. She visited me at Brewerstreet after graduation, and we met up again in Mumbai in 2016—

after more than fifty-five years! My Ghanaian husband, Clement, was with me. Like her, I had married outside my "caste," and she was intrigued to meet him. She and Clement had shared experiences of growing up in the shadow of British imperialism. While I had had no exposure to India's rich history and culture, Rajani understood all too well the cultural forces that shaped her British peers. How ignorant we were by comparison. Yet I don't remember Rajani ever expressing any bitterness or harsh feelings toward our country or chafing at the sense of entitlement that many of us must surely have exuded, albeit unconsciously. After my many years in Ghana and in a cross-cultural marriage, I was better positioned to appreciate what she had experienced when we met again so many years later.

During my time at Oxford I gradually became aware of needs beyond England's borders and my blinders slowly started to lift. Europe was still suffering from the disruption caused by the war, and the colonies were pressing for independence. It was the early days of the Oxford Committee for Famine Relief—now the influential organization Oxfam—whose modest offices were a short distance from our lodgings. And student activities such as World Refugee Day—which we recognized with bread-and-cheese fundraiser lunches in the days when New Zealand cheddar was still a poor man's food—alerted us to the needs of the wider world.

My interest in issues of economic development was strongly influenced—largely at secondhand—by a Belgian priest, Père Yves Nolet, who attached himself to the Catholic chaplaincy for several years. I say "at secondhand" because I wasn't one of his chosen inner circles of students. (In the lingo of the day, I would have been categorized as a "grey" student—definitely not one of the intellectual elite.) I nonetheless participated in a group called Ad Lucem that Pere Yves introduced to the university. The organization was founded in France with the goal of preparing young people for work overseas with a focus on development activities. I went to several of their summer camps at magnificent aging chateaux buried deep in the French countryside. Mingling with people of different languages and cultures challenged my childhood boundaries. Inspired by the stories I heard there, a future of exciting possibilities stretched before me. It was as a member of Ad Lucem that my resolve to spend time working in a developing country grew and matured.

In my last year at Oxford, Père Yves brought a young Jordanian to stay at the Catholic chaplaincy, much to the chagrin of the chaplain. His name was Atta Abu Rumi. Père Yves, who had met him on a pilgrimage to the Holy Land, brought him to England, and landed him in Oxford. Atta was probably one of many thousands of young Jordanians desperate for the chance to emigrate to a first-world country. Other than the fact that Atta had in some way fallen foul of the Jordanian authorities, Père Yves's reason for singling him out to bring to England—and the plan once he arrived—was never clear. What I remember all too well is that when Pere Yves left Oxford, Atta remained.

The chaplain wasn't happy! He likened Atta to Tigger of Pooh Bear fame, who didn't like anything his host offered him for breakfast. I was president of the students' Newman Association at the time, and the chaplain hinted it was my responsibility to help Atta decide his future. I had no idea what to do. My youthful idealism, with its focus on the needs of developing countries, had in no way prepared me for this reality: a displaced Jordanian in a foreign land with no discernible skills and little interest—or so it seemed—in earning a living.

At one point I invited Atta to stay at Brewerstreet for a few days. He left a trail of miscomprehension in his wake. My brother Christopher still loves to tell stories of his outrageous habits. Father had died about a year earlier, and my Uncle

Freddy—Mother's brother—cautioned her, "You can't take this on, Mary. Sally has really crossed a line."

I approached a few organizations for help, to no avail. Eventually the White Fathers—a group of priests dedicated to missionary work in Africa who I knew through Ad Lucem—came to the rescue. They provide Atta with a temporary home at their house in London in exchange for help around the house. When Atta failed to settle there, the Fathers helped him emigrate to Algeria. There he would at least understand the language.

Sadly, Atta was a loser wherever he found himself. In Algeria, too, he had difficulty settling. For two or three years, he wrote occasionally. Cards or short letters, always in search of a future beyond his grasp. Then there was silence. I never found out what happened. There had been no easy solution to his plight.

Atta was the first person I encountered whose life circumstances differed so radically from my own. I'm not sure what I learned from the experience other than a painful recognition of my inability to make a difference. As for Père Yves, he had vanished from the scene!

## *Whither?*

Some months before graduating from Oxford in 1961, I made a mandatory visit to the Oxford Appointments Board—what today would be called career services. I'd explored the possibility of graduate work at an African university, but their research focus on geophysics didn't appeal to me. I needed to broaden my search. Ever since I'd opted to study physics, the question "What can she do with a physics degree?" had reverberated in my parents' circle. "Maybe she could become assistant to a physicist," some opined, always with the assumption that the physicist would be a man. That a woman scientist might have an independent career was unthinkable.

The official at the Appointments Board had a similar mindset. After I'd explained some of my own thoughts and aspirations, he jumped quickly to a conclusion.

"I can see that you're a do-gooder," he said, not unkindly. "Have you thought of teaching?" Apparently, he saw no need to help me think outside the box.

"What about industry?" I ventured, wanting to explore my options more thoroughly.

"Industry is no place for a woman," he responded immediately. His words have rung in my ears ever since.

We were both wrong. He was blinded by the prevailing male hegemony, while I was too timid to challenge it head-on. Neither of us foresaw the changes that would enable me to make my way eventually in an overwhelmingly male business environment.

At the time, I took the path of least resistance. I completed a postgraduate educational diploma and taught for a year at a secondary school near London while continuing to explore opportunities for working overseas.

Still haunted by Francis Thompson's poem and the direction in which "The Hound of Heaven" seemed to be nudging me, yet intent on working in a developing country, I compromised. In addition to Ad Lucem, Pere Yves had introduced students at Oxford to a Brussels-based organization of women committed to serving as lay missionaries in developing countries. The Auxiliares Feminines Internationales (AFI) sent small teams to far-flung places across the globe. They included teachers, doctors, nurses, social workers, and the like. I admired their spirit of service, their international ethic, and their openness to the changes the Vatican Council was promoting. Joining the organization meant envisioning a lifelong commitment. I decided to give it a try.

And so, with a mixture of purposeful anticipation and lingering uncertainty, I took the train from Victoria Station to join the Dover-Ostend ferry in September 1963. I was twenty-three years old. I was transitioning to an environment where, while remaining securely within the institutional church, boundaries of class and country would no longer apply. The AFI would provide me with a structured environment, a container if you will, but one that was very different from that of my childhood.

After a year's training at the headquarters in Brussels, where my fluency in French increased to an acceptable level, I returned to London to complete a master's degree in nuclear physics. On graduation, thanks to connections within the AFI, I got an appointment as *assistante* in the physics department at Université Lovanium in the Congo (now the Democratic Republic of Congo or DRC.) There I joined a small team of AFI members—Italian, German, Belgian—working within the university community and beyond.

It was as I prepared to leave for Lovanium that I decided to revert to the name I had been given at birth, Sarah. I would no longer be Sally. The name Sarah, with its Biblical roots, had always seemed much more dignified to me. Besides, I'd now be in a French-speaking environment. "Sally" sounded too much like the French words *salé*, meaning salty, and *salis*, dirty. Since then, I've always been known as Sarah, except by my immediate family and childhood friends. I've learned to live with what sometimes feels like a split identity.

## Lovanium

At Lovanium we were in Africa, but only barely! The very name signified the university's relationship with the mother university of Louvain in Belgium and the newly independent country's dependence on its former colonizer. (Every year the university chartered planes to take the largely expatriate staff back to Belgium for their annual summer vacation.)

The university campus, complete with its own church, hospital, and residences, was built on a hill a few miles outside the capital, Kinshasa, fenced off from the surrounding communities. When I arrived in 1966, Mobutu had just come to power and the country was still on edge after the post-independence disturbances. On campus we lived in an isolated bubble, largely sheltered from the surrounding turmoil. Soldiers manned the gates; beyond the campus young, trigger-happy soldiers were everywhere. Our occasional trips to the city were undertaken with considerable caution.

Other members of the AFI team were immersed in the life of the community. One was in charge of the residence for female students; another taught sewing and other domestic skills to local women; a third worked in the administrative offices of the Bishop of Kinshasa. Belgium had left the Congo with no educated elite at the time of independence. Université Lovanium was helping the country play catch-up, but nearly all senior positions were occupied by Europeans. In the science faculty only two members of the academic staff were Congolese. It was a neocolonial environment but one with a strictly Belgian flavor. The educational system differed in many respects from what I knew. My British sense of imperial entitlement could only take me so far.

I count it as one of my more unusual achievements to have taught physics in French for two years. I got by somehow. Though I was more or less fluent in everyday French, operating professionally in the language was a challenge. The students laughed—not unkindly—when I stumbled over the gender of nouns, and I always needed someone to check problems I set the students to be sure they were grammatically correct. In many ways it was a humbling experience.

At the time, I thought and dreamed in French, but there was a price to pay. The quality of my thinking started to reflect my facility with the language—or lack thereof. Brené Brown quotes Wittgenstein as saying, "The limits of my language mean the limits of my world." Subtlety of meaning is often lost as one struggles to express oneself in a language in which one has a limited vocabulary or command of idioms. Moreover, operating in a foreign language necessarily puts one at a disadvantage in interpersonal communications. The power dynamic changes.

French was the mother tongue of only one member of our small AFI team. At home, we managed well with French as the lingua franca, but in the halls of academe, it was more of a struggle. I often felt isolated and "less than." Looking back, I am grateful to have experienced the diminishment that comes with operating in a foreign language. There were lessons to be learned. Living securely in an English-speaking environment now, my experience at Lovanium helps me to empathize with the struggle of refugees and immigrants for whom English is a foreign language. I try to remember to reach for the meaning behind their paucity of expression.

Students at Lovanium generally came from poor backgrounds with inadequate secondary education; a year of catch-up was needed before they could begin the four-year licentiate program. I taught physics to these pre-university students. One of them—Cyrille Mukendi—stood out for his brilliance. Always sitting just in front of me, he almost took the words from my mouth, anticipating exactly the explanation I was about to provide.

Years later, as I was working on my master of education program in England, I thought of students like Cyrille when talking to one of the lecturers, Bill, about different ways to present a physics concept that students often find difficult.

"Many of the students I taught in Africa caught on quite quickly," I remarked. I was deliberately being provocative.

"Really?" He was incredulous.

"When I was in the Congo, I taught some really brilliant

students," I went on. I could see Bill was having difficulty getting his head around what I was saying. "In Africa, students who reach secondary school or university are part of a highly select group," I continued, perversely enjoying his discomfort. "It's different when there is universal secondary education—like in England."

I left Bill to connect the dots. I wonder if he ever did. Even now, for a host of reasons, the intellectual capital on the African continent is largely unrecognized and untapped.

After two years in the Congo, I was ready to leave the AFI. I valued the mission of the organization and appreciated the time I had spent with them, but I wasn't ready for a lifelong commitment. It had provided a safe structure within which I could take my first small steps on the African continent. With them I had experienced living and working in a different culture using a different language. It was a wonderful, formative period in my life. Now I was ready to venture out on my own.

I considered applying for a school teaching job in Congo, but eventually opted to work in an English-speaking country. I was fortunate to land a job that was more rewarding than any I could have imagined. From Kinshasa in Congo, I moved to Cape Coast in Ghana. In truth, I moved from one expatriate bubble to another—but it was one with more familiar contours. Cape Coast was to be my home for many years.

# *A New Beginning*

The year 1968 was a momentous one at home and abroad. In the U.S., it was the year Martin Luther King and Bobby Kennedy were assassinated. In Prague, the Czech uprising was ruthlessly suppressed as Russian tanks rolled in. In Vietnam, it was the year of the Tet Offensive. At Brewerstreet, an epic storm brought rain pouring into the backyard and down the front path. We waded around in the driveway with water up to our calves. Christopher, now married and living in a small house on the property, took charge using sandbags as best he could to prevent water entering the house, but the floodwater prevailed, much to Mother's distress.

Most significantly for me, 1968 was the year when I left my two-year stint at Université Lovanium in the Congo and accepted a "joint appointment" in physics and education at the University College of Cape Coast in Ghana. When the flood came, I was with Mother at Brewerstreet, anxiously awaiting news of the appointment, not sure what the future would bring. I couldn't have guessed then how big a part Ghana would play in my life. Nor did I realize the extent of the baggage—both of privilege and purpose—that I carried with me. I was to join a university community—another bubble if you will —where I was able to thrive personally and professionally, despite the many attributes that marked me as a foreigner. More importantly, it was in Cape Coast that I would meet Clement, my future husband.

## Town and Gown

Mr. Smart French from the university administration met me at the airport in Accra. He was intrigued that we shared a last name. "I had to come and meet my sister," he told me, using "sister" in the Ghanaian sense.

From the airport he drove me directly to the university campus, two hours away, and to my flat in Block 40. Flat 3 was the first home of my own and I loved it. There was no air conditioning, but with fans in every room and louvered windows on either side, the air circulated freely. The flat felt fresh, even on the hottest days. The university provided bare-bones furniture; the rest was up to us. Once settled, I used local cloth for drapes and to cover the cushions of the university's standard-issue easy chairs. To me, the choice of strong, contrasting colors added interest to the space, but the use of deep-red cloth, usually associated with funerals, probably surprised Ghanaian visitors.

That first evening, I wandered through the rooms wondering which bedroom I would use as my own and which would serve as a study. I tried to imagine how my new life would unfold. Who lived in the flat across the hall? Would we get along? Would I make friends—Ghanaian or expatriate—I could invite to a meal? What would my teaching load be? Would there be opportunities for research? There were many unknowns.

The following morning, I walked up the hill to the staff club, where Mr. Smart French had told me I could get breakfast. The humid tropical air embraced me. The campus was ablaze with flowering shrubs, and when I reached the brow of the hill, I caught a breathtaking view of the ocean. It was a thrilling moment. Maybe I should have been apprehensive, but I remember only the excitement of arriving in a new country and keen anticipation of the job that awaited me. Ghana seemed welcoming and free of the tension that was so pervasive in the Congo. No doubt, there were still undercurrents of the struggle against British colonialists—it was a mere eleven years since Ghanaian independence and just two years since the coup that overthrew the country's first president, Kwame Nkrumah—but the tensions didn't bubble to the surface as they did in the Congo. They could easily be overlooked by a newly arrived expatriate. People were relaxed and welcoming.

The university is situated on a large campus on the main Accra–Takoradi road, which bypasses the town of Cape Coast. The university buildings are located on two sites about a mile and a half apart. In 1968, the old site, formerly a teacher training college, housed the administration building and the faculties of arts and education, as well as the library and student residence halls. The new site had yet to be developed; only the science faculty was located there. My flat at Block 40 was situated on the road linking the two sites. The traditional village of Apewosika was just across the road. By day, many of the villagers worked for the university. By night, their drumming and singing often lasted into the early hours.

Thus, right there on campus, three worlds were joined: the colonial past represented by the old training college buildings; the future of independent Ghana vested in the science faculty and other yet-to-be-constructed university buildings; and the enduring local traditions rooted in the life of Apewosika. How did I as a foreigner fit into the dynamic relationship between these three realities? This question is important for me now as I reflect on the significance of my early years in Ghana. On my first day in the country, it was far from my mind.

I was pleased to have a job through which I believed I could assist Britain's former colony in realizing the full potential of its independence. I didn't give much thought to the fact that I would be part of lingering neocolonial systems and structures. In hindsight, I realize how little I understood of Ghana's relationship with its colonial past or what it meant to be part of an institution that was still reaching for its Ghanaian identity.

My first stop after breakfast was at the office of Professor T.L. Green, dean of education. It was TL, as the staff usually called him, who had interviewed me in London and was the architect of the idea of joint appointments. The college's mission was to train secondary school teachers, and all students were required to study both an academic subject and education, so having faculty members with cross-disciplinary qualifications made sense. I was the first joint appointee. The position offered me an intriguing professional challenge. I would have to reach beyond the confines of physics, with its universally agreed laws and theories, and train students in teaching methodology, a field where adaptation to the local environment would be required. Although I had a postgraduate certificate of education and some teaching experience, this would be less familiar territory.

TL was the quintessential British colonial: competent, fatherly, and a little patronizing, with a wry sense of humor. His deep ambivalence about the country that hosted him, an ambivalence he shared with many expatriates, was epitomized in an unguarded remark he made when referring to a company that made preserves using local fruits. "They call the company Ghana Can. My wife and I call it Ghana Can't," he quipped.

On that first morning, TL greeted me cordially, a little surprised that my arrival had been arranged so quickly. Although he hadn't informed—let alone consulted—my future colleagues about my appointment, neither he nor they seemed to regard the omission as the grave lack of respect it surely was. Did they view it as a norm of ex-colonial behavior? I wonder. Whatever they were thinking, they nonetheless welcomed me warmly in the Ghanaian spirit of *akwaaba*—welcome.

From the education department, TL took me to the new

site to meet Professor de Sa, the Indian dean of science. Both deans were expatriates, but the vice chancellor and registrar of the college were Ghanaian as were many faculty members, including the chair of physics. For me, the fact that the university was firmly set on the path toward Ghanainization, albeit within the setting of a Western-style institution, was a definite plus and a welcome contrast to what I'd experienced at Lovanium. I looked forward to working alongside Ghanaian colleagues and under their leadership. I had no interest in being part of a neocolonial extension service.

That afternoon, Mrs. De Sa, the dean's wife, came with car and driver to take me shopping, allowing me to glimpse the long history and cultural importance of the town I came to know so well. Still today, whenever we visit Cape Coast, its streets evoke deep and resonant memories of the years when I made my home at the university on its periphery.

A dominant feature of Cape Coast is the castle. It was built and expanded over the centuries by successive European powers for whom it served as a point of commerce, including, most infamously, the trans-Atlantic slave trade. Rising magnificently out of the ocean, its physical presence dominates the coastal part of town, even if the impoverished fishermen mending their nets in its shadow seem mostly untouched by the horrendous human story it represents. Not so the many overseas visitors—including President and Michelle Obama in 2009, First Lady Melania Trump in 2018, and Vice President Kamala Harris in 2023—for whom tours of the castles in Cape Coast and neighboring Elmina are a mandatory, albeit salutary, part of any visit to Ghana.

Across the street from the castle is the Anglican church where—as I learned later—my future father-in-law served as parish priest for many years. Until recently, a plaque inside the church recognized his contribution in building the church's spire. Close by the castle, in an ironic twist that is so typically Ghanaian and so endearing to the visitor, is Victoria Park, a small patch of green that still boasts a bust of Queen Victoria, now largely ignored by the townsfolk. Less easily ignored, and directly across the street from the park, is the recently renovated palace of the paramount chief.

Beyond the castle are houses, schools, and other structures, many of which date back several centuries to the time when Cape Coast was a hub of trade, a point of entry for successive colonizers, and—later—the first capital of the British colony. Substantial colonial dwellings are tucked away out of sight. So, too, the Koranic schools whose chanting provided one of the few indications of a Muslim presence in the late 1960s. Now, in contrast, mosques and Islamic dress are ubiquitous in Cape Coast and throughout the country. The European—mostly Christian—hegemony, which subtly undergirded our presence as expatriate faculty and on which we relied in unspoken ways for our teaching authority, can no longer be taken for granted.

I was jolted into awareness of the transitory nature of that authority many years later. Clement and I were visiting Cape Coast and had invited two former colleagues and their wives to join us for dinner. We talked about changes taking place in the country, including the more conspicuous Muslim presence. Joe, a retired professor of classics, remarked, "Let's not forget. The Muslims were here in Ghana long before the Christians." Of course! European domination had been short-lived. Islamic traders had crossed the Sahara to reach the west coast of Africa well before Columbus stopped in Elmina en route to the New World in 1480. Obvious as it was when Joe said it, the fact had never occurred to me until then.

On that first trip to town, I needed to purchase food supplies and essential household items. Mrs. de Sa took me first to Kingsway Stores, a small general-purpose store, such as one might find anywhere in the world. It was the go-to place for expatriates to shop for meat, groceries, and other household items. When I first arrived in Ghana, choice was limited, but supplies of basic commodities were ample. The shortages were yet to come.

From Kingsway, we went to Kotokraba market; it couldn't have been more different. Kotokraba overflowed with local color. Market women wearing brightly colored cloth and wide-brimmed hats sat behind large wooden platters of produce. The lanes threading their way among the stalls were narrow and crowded; we had to jostle to get through while carefully avoiding the open gutters. Mrs. de Sa was an able guide.

All the vegetables used in local dishes were to be found there: tomatoes, garden eggs, okra, *nkontomire* leaves, cocoyams, yams (of the West African variety), peppers in many different varieties, beans, gingerroot, onions, palm nuts, plantain. Fruits, including pineapple, pawpaw, oranges (green on the outside), and mangoes in season, were available too, but not so plentiful. If you were looking for *oborɔnyi*[1] foods, such as cabbage or green peppers or potatoes, you were out of luck. They were only available in Accra or, just occasionally, from an enterprising local grower.

The market women arranged the fruit and vegetables in small parcels on their platters: three tomatoes or six fingers of okra. The prices were usually negotiable. When the price had been agreed, it was customary to ask for a "dash;" the seller would then add an extra finger of okra or garden egg to your basket as a way of concluding the deal. Later, I became proficient in navigating the lanes and bargaining for what I needed, proud of my successful enculturation.

After our trip to town, Mrs. de Sa dropped me back at my flat, replete with everything I needed. I was excited at the promise of the new life ahead of me. Town and gown were much closer in Cape Coast than they had been at Lovanium. Moreover, there were no soldiers in sight. I had a good feeling that this was a place I'd be able to call home. And so it proved to be, despite the town children's annoying habit of always calling out to remind me I was an *oborɔnyi*. This was their boundary, not mine.

---

[1] *Oborɔnyi* is the term used for foreigner or White person in Akan languages.

## A Job That I Loved

I settled easily into my teaching responsibilities. I enjoyed the opportunity to work in two different departments, tootling frequently between the two sides of campus in my hardy VW Beetle. It was an exhilarating time. As one of the grey students at Oxford, I lacked the personality or confidence to make a mark. At Lovanium, I was constrained by language, by an unfamiliar educational system, and by the isolation of the university with its largely expatriate faculty. At Cape Coast, despite the large cohort of Ghanaian staff, the university still leaned heavily on British traditions, enabling me to leverage my own education as I immersed myself in my job, confident in what I had to offer. Too confident maybe. Although I was deeply committed to giving my best in the cause of Ghana's development, I was largely oblivious to the ways in which my privilege separated me from those I wished to serve.

In the physics department, the curriculum and methods of instruction were conventional, much as one would find in higher education institutions anywhere. My responsibilities included teaching a nuclear physics course and running a lab course for "prelim" students preparing for admission to the degree program. Most of the physics faculty were Ghanaian. The chair was a clever scientist and well versed in university politics. Although he always treated me with respect, I could never make out whether some deep postcolonial angst—an unease in the presence of White people that is the enduring legacy of years of British rule—lay behind his Cheshire cat grin.

In the education faculty, I taught physics teaching methods. This included supervising methods essays—capstone projects to be completed by students in their final year. In the essay, students fleshed out an approach to teaching a particular topic, often including detailed lesson plans. I was a stickler for a structured, logical approach; I'm sure there was a lot of grumbling behind my back! One student I supervised went on to an academic career in physics, returning to Cape Coast as dean of science after earning a Ph.D. from the University of Bologna. When we met many years later, he reminded me with wry amusement and a touch of lingering resentment that I had denied him distinction for his essay.

As a member of the education faculty, I was also tasked with monitoring students' performance during their two periods of teaching practice (internships) each year. The students were assigned to secondary schools all over the country and faculty traveled widely to monitor their progress. My VW stood me in good stead as I made my way to schools that were sometimes quite remote from major towns. I passed through villages where women tended the crops and children carried buckets of water on their heads, their way of life little changed for centuries.

I loved the freedom and sense of adventure, embellishing the stories I told myself—and those I told the family back home—with a little derring-do to enhance the narrative. In reality, although I was often alone in the Ghanaian countryside, I was never concerned for my personal safety. If I needed to change a tire, I could manage on my own or benefit from the help of a passing stranger, and if I got lost, there was usually someone who spoke a little English, ready to help.

We were responsible for supervising all the students assigned to each school we visited. This meant observing lessons in subjects as disparate as French, mathematics, and history. I particularly enjoyed the French lessons. The students had learned the direct method of language instruction from faculty who were part of the French Assistance Technique program. Right from secondary form one (with students aged eleven or twelve), the student teachers used French as the medium of instruction, conveying their meaning with the help of objects and gestures.

"*Voici un crayon,*" the teacher would say, holding up a pencil.

"*Voici un crayon,*" the pupils responded.

*"Qu'est-ce que c'est?"*

*"C'est un crayon."*

And so the dialogue continued back and forth. The lessons were lively and fun; they provided a benchmark for me as to how foreign languages should be taught. I was bitterly disappointed when my own children at school in the U.S. years later were taught languages using rigid traditional methods focused on grammar and the written word.

My closest colleague in the education faculty was George Collison. Prior to my arrival, George had been solely responsible for teaching physics methods, a responsibility we then shared. George had a Ph.D. from Harvard School of Education and knew more than he liked to let on. I learned a lot from him, including, importantly, how local phenomena exemplified scientific principles.

"Watch how the women bunch up the cloth they put on their head when they are carrying a load," he'd say, to exemplify the elementary formula for pressure. This was a situation familiar to every student.

George gave me a lot of latitude to innovate and grow. "Why not ask publishers to send us sample copies?" he suggested when we were searching for textbooks to recommend to schools.

I did just that, assembling a mini library of books for the department as a result. When it came to equipping a small physics teaching lab, we worked together. He never imposed his ideas but was unfailingly kind and respectful. It could well have been otherwise. After all, he'd had no say in my appointment and had every reason to resent this uppity young British woman who'd suddenly appeared on the scene. I will always be grateful for his openness to my ideas and enthusiasms, however impractical they may have seemed. Sometimes, a faint smile hovering around his mouth was sufficient to tell me that I risked overstepping the mark. I valued his friendship and advice and was sad to learn a few years after leaving Cape Coast that he had succumbed to an inherited form of dementia and died an early death.

Another valued colleague was Kwabena Awuku, who taught biology methods. Kwabena was hardworking and dedicated to his job. He, too, had qualified in the U.S. but was more wary than George in his relationships with expatriate staff. He appreciated the services of Peace Corps volunteers, who he rated as among "the best the U.S. has to offer," but could be trenchant in his criticism of foreigners who didn't pull their weight. At one point, TL appointed a retired educational administrator from the UK to a senior position in the education faculty. To everyone's surprise, TL sent him to represent Ghana at a conference in Kenya. On his return, he regaled us with stories of the wildlife he had seen. "Does he think he has come here on a post-retirement vacation?" was Kwabena's icy comment. I knew I had to earn Kwabena's respect and was always apprehensive that I, too, might be exposed to his devastating critique.

By happenstance, the teaching of chemistry methods was, for many years, in the hands of expatriates: a succession of British Council and UNESCO appointees with varying degrees of competence and commitment. None stayed more than two years. A Holy Child nun, Sister Clarita, took the position at one time. She was excellent while she lasted, but barely had time to settle in. After just one year, she was moved to Nigeria as the Superior of her congregation's West African province. To me, it seemed that the congregation had used the university for their institutional advantage. I was angry, but my Ghanaian colleagues didn't show the same surprise or disappointment. "What else do you expect?" they seemed to be saying. They knew that expatriates were unlikely to stay around for long. Our "belonging" was transitory.

Outside the university, I became actively involved with a group promoting integrated science as a way of introducing the study of science in secondary school. It was part of a global movement, and I was fortunate to attend international conferences on the topic in Nijmegen (1978) and Halifax (1979).

The program we worked on was the forerunner of the integrated science curriculum still used in Ghana's junior secondary schools today. Developing the curriculum had been a collegial experience, and issues encountered in implementing the program became the focus of my Ph.D. thesis. Sadly, as foreshadowed in my research, the impact of the curriculum on the scientific literacy of the population has been far less than we hoped.

One of our curriculum planning meetings took place in Takoradi in Ghana's Western Region at the time of the moon landing. We learned of this amazing scientific achievement by radio without the benefit of television coverage. (The U.S. seemed as far away as the moon!) Although the moon landings were not addressed explicitly in the curriculum, an underlying goal had been to generate interest in science and technology more generally. Fast forward several decades. We were chatting with two girls from our Accra neighborhood one evening in 2018 or thereabouts; both girls had completed their secondary education. There was a full moon overhead.

"Just look at the moon," I said to them. "Do you know that some years ago, men walked on the moon's surface?"

The girls gasped.

"Did no teacher ever tell you that in school?" I went on.

"Well, maybe I read it somewhere once," one of the girls said, her voice trailing off.

It was disappointing to realize that the science learned in school had done little to kindle their curiosity. They remained ignorant of the world outside their immediate surroundings other than what little was contained in their school textbooks and required for the official examinations. I am similarly disappointed that our efforts to train a cadre of secondary school teachers at the university didn't have the desired outcome. Many of the students went on to successful careers in fields other than education but Ghana's education system, though vastly expanded, remains deeply troubled.

## *Expatriate*

As I understood it, my role at the university was to contribute to Ghana's largely unquestioned thrust toward economic development. I believed I had useful knowledge and skills to share and enjoyed working cooperatively with Ghanaian colleagues toward a common goal. Looking back, I realize that as an expatriate faculty member I was inevitably a purveyor of Western culture and, having been born and bred in England, held a position of power and privilege. I was all but blind to conflicts with traditional values that may have simmered beneath the surface. It's not clear to me even today how they should be resolved. Just as Westerners struggle with the impact of capitalism on the well-being of humanity, so too Ghanaians must figure out how to reconcile Western models of development with their own deeply held traditions.

Most Ghanaian faculty members were immersed in family situations that required their time and attention and had no hesitation in prioritizing them over their job responsibilities if necessary. For them, the Western credo of "leave your personal problems at home" was simply unworkable. Expatriate faculty were not subject to family pressures to the same extent and, with a different mindset, were often critical of our Ghanaian colleagues' work ethic. James was lab assistant for all those who taught science methods. He had participated in several training programs in the UK sponsored by the British Council and knew his job well. Unfortunately—as I saw it—his good-will was exploited by colleagues who often used him to run personal errands, such as picking children up from school or driving their wives to market. They seemed to consider his services a perk of the job.

"Where's James?" I asked a colleague, as I was preparing for a lab class and needed his help.

"He's taken Kweku's wife to town," was a typical answer.

"He knew I had a lab class coming up," I muttered to myself, boiling inside but careful not to say too much, given my status as a foreigner.

Although my annoyance was most probably communicated nonverbally, it did nothing to change the situation. For Kweku, the demands of life and work were all of a piece. I was the one trying to build fences between them.

Later, a promising student, Jophus, was appointed as a graduate assistant, teaching chemistry methods. At that time, the senior chemistry methods lecturer was a good friend, Bob; he had taught chemistry at the University of Ghana for many years and was now on a UNESCO appointment at Cape Coast. Bob complained that Jophus was often absent and didn't take his responsibilities seriously. His family was from Cape Coast, and as a salary earner, he was probably experiencing family pressures of which we were oblivious. His later career proved he was far from incompetent. After one or two years as a graduate assistant, he went to Canada for his Ph.D. On his return—and long after we'd left the university—he rose to become the dean of education and subsequently the first vice chancellor of a new University of Education. Jophus's time in Canada had allowed him to take distance from family pressures and find culturally acceptable ways to manage the competing demands of work and family when he returned home.

There may well have been some complaining behind the scenes—most likely shared in a local language in which our counterparts could communicate the subtlety of their feelings better than they could in English—but for the most part, my relationships with Ghanaian colleagues were very cordial, forged in mutual respect and the pursuit of common goals. In the ten years or so I taught at Cape Coast, I remember only one occasion when I encountered overt hostility and disrespect. It occurred in the context of the prelim lab course that I had taught for several years on my own and was now teaching with the help of a young graduate assistant, Kojo. In the course, I liked to emphasize concepts of measurement error and significant figures in interpreting numerical data. The concepts are epitomized by the statement, "Don't state a weight to the nearest microgram if the instrument you are using is only accurate to the nearest milligram." Obvious as it may seem, this simple maxim is frequently ignored and easily leads to unsupported claims for lab results.

Kojo had just graduated with first-class honors from the Kwame Nkrumah University of Science and Technology in Kumasi. Apparently, no one had exposed him to the topic, and he failed to recognize its importance. Emboldened by his success as an undergraduate and—very probably—irritated by my expatriate presence, he would often contradict me in front of the class. Not only was his behavior offensive, but in contradicting me he betrayed his own ignorance. I wondered what I could say to preserve my authority without humiliating him. To say nothing or expose his ignorance to the class were not desirable options. I remember talking to him on the side but without success. It seemed that as a foreigner—and a woman to boot—I didn't merit his respect.

When I first arrived in Cape Coast, the University College was still in transition from a structure established by the colonials to the fully Ghanaianized institution that it would become. Professor Boateng, the vice chancellor, was an eloquent orator. He, along with other senior Ghanaians, proved themselves to be savvy politicians who could easily outsmart naïve and unsuspecting expatriates if the need arose. Having received most of their own education at the hands of expatriates, our Ghanaian colleagues understood us far better than we could ever understand them.

Expatriate staff weren't always aware of the tricky waters to be navigated as Ghanaians gradually took their rightful place as guardians of the university's future. In most cases, any resentment Ghanaian faculty may have felt toward expatriates was shielded from view. Provided we minded our P's and Q's, it remained an undercurrent rather than open hostility.

Although there was a good deal of grumbling among expatriate staff—bordering on an "us vs. them" mentality—most recognized that, as foreigners, our best policy was to keep our mouths shut. Not so, a Baptist minister from North Carolina who served for a while as Protestant chaplain. Rich thought it was his business to criticize some aspect of university policy from the pulpit and also publicly at an all-hands faculty meeting. He hadn't reckoned with Vice Chancellor Boateng. Rich soon learned his contract wouldn't be renewed.

In retrospect, I wonder how Rich came to be at the university in the first place. Ghana had no shortage of pastors who could have served as chaplains. Although pleasant enough, he seemed even more out of place in the burgeoning Ghanaian institution than those of us who were there to teach secular disciplines.

Though relationships were occasionally strained, collaboration between local and expatriate faculty was for the most part genuine and constructive. The boundaries were more clearly drawn when it came to social life.

Arriving on my own at the university, it was a priority for me to get to know people and make friends. My early attempts to immerse myself in the university community included eating from time to time at the student dining hall and inviting groups of students over for drinks at my flat. I stopped when I realized my attempts at openness were being misinterpreted by some of the male students. In another effort at outreach, I befriended the family of a colleague, taking his children to the beach and buying them the occasional treat. Later, I provided the family modest financial support to allow the colleague to complete his university degree. The family was grateful for my help, but looking back, I have no doubt that I was the chief beneficiary of the relationship, which burnished my self-image and satisfied my deep need for acceptance. It is difficult to say whether connections or boundaries prevailed.

I formed more authentic connections with my fellow residents in Block 40. My neighbors in the block were mostly expatriates and mostly single, but there were a few Ghanaians newly returned from overseas and a few married couples. Across the hall from me was a young English couple, both of whom had recently joined the Department of Economics. They were more radical than me in their embrace of '60s'-style values, but we became good friends and remain so to this day. On the top floor was Joyce, also from England. Like me, she married a Ghanaian, and with children of similar ages, our families became close, celebrating several Christmases together. When luxuries were hard to come by, we often shared afternoon tea, treating ourselves to homemade shortbread. Joyce stayed in Ghana long after we'd left, experiencing the dire economic conditions that prevailed in the 1980s. Much later, after moving back to England, she visited the U.S. many times to work with me on business projects. Our shared experiences have formed an enduring bond.

Clara, a Ghanaian faculty member in the French department, had recently returned from many years of study overseas. The daughter of a judge who held an important position in the Nkrumah government, she returned to a Ghana she hardly knew and to a family that was no longer in a position of influence. Clara was familiar with Western ways and became good friends with Joyce and me, sharing valuable insights into Ghanaian culture with us. We accompanied her as best we could through the angst of her reinsertion into the country and the emotional turmoil of two romantic relationships with expatriate faculty members. She, in turn, supported me through moments of doubt in my developing relationship with Clement.

Another young Ghanaian lecturer lived in Block 40 for a short time. She'd just returned from studies in California. With her Afro hairstyle, she seemed to exude the spirit of Angela Davis and was more guarded than Clara in her relationship with White expatriates. In contrast, Ama Atta Aidoo, a published author, blew caution to the winds. She was expansive with all comers, fiercely and unabashedly critical of humbug and pomposity wherever she found it, including of course in colonial rule and its legacy. As a trailblazer among African women literary figures, she went on to national and international prominence.

Beyond Block 40, the expatriate community—both faculty members and those who were teachers at the many secondary schools in town—was mostly but not exclusively White and British. Several represented technical assistance programs: the British Council, UNESCO, Peace Corps, France's Assistance Technique. Most were solid citizens who wanted to do a good job for Ghana and for their countries of origin. Some were simply looking for a first step on the academic ladder; others were motivated by idealism or a desire to see the world. A few, freed from the restraints of home, were notorious sexual adventurers. Most were happy to experience life in the tropics and be exposed to another culture. Some dug deeper, but for most, appreciation of the culture was superficial at best. Inevitably, we—and I include myself—brought with us the entitlement and assumptions of our upbringing. I am more aware now of the cultural baggage that accompanies me—still—wherever I go.

Many expatriates would have liked more social contact with their Ghanaian counterparts and made good-faith attempts to do so, but it wasn't easy. Dinner invitations were seldom returned. The differences in financial and family situations created barriers that were difficult to circumvent. Many of us were beneficiaries of some form of aid that set us apart from our Ghanaian colleagues. (When I was hired in 1968, all British faculty at the university received a salary supplement from the UK government allowing us to achieve parity with our counterparts in UK universities.)

Most of the senior Ghanaian faculty were established citizens with responsibilities to their church communities and extended families that absorbed their energies and resources, leaving them with little time or appetite for socializing with expatriate colleagues. Many were former schoolteachers. They enjoyed their relatively well-appointed campus houses, adapting them to familiar lifestyles and often supporting several less privileged relatives in addition to their own families. Every evening, a thud-thud reverberated around the campus as the women pounded *fufu* for their husbands' evening meals; it was a reminder of the traditional gender roles and lifestyles that still prevailed. The wives of Ghanaian faculty members had little in common with fly-by-night foreigners who were spared such onerous domestic duties. It was difficult for us to get to know them beyond a smile and a friendly greeting.

A small group of single faculty members, both expatriate and Ghanaian, unencumbered by family responsibilities and less tied to cultural norms than their older counterparts, formed a sub-community of their own. They did not identify fully with the expatriate community or with the more settled Ghanaian families on campus. I moved in and out of this group, not participating fully in the more liberated aspects of their lifestyle, but joining them for major social events. Several mixed-race marriages, including my own, were the result.

When their efforts at outreach failed, members of the larger expatriate community tended to withdraw into their own familiar circle. There were dinner parties, games of bridge, trips to the beach, and meet-ups on Sundays at the Elmina Motel, where a tasty curry lunch was served, very much in the colonial tradition.

Regrettably, there was always an undercurrent of criticism of the many ways in which Ghana fell short of their (superior!) standards, with the unspoken assumption that the university should be run the same way as it was in the home country. When things didn't happen as expected, the grumbling began. Meetings should start and stop on time, lectures shouldn't be canceled when it rains, faculty shouldn't take time off to bury relatives who passed away in remote locations, and a full-time appointment is not simply a prize to be enjoyed, but carries with it a responsibility to work at least forty hours a week. The tone was that of small-town gossip anywhere.

"Have you heard what Kofi said?"

"Can you believe what happened to Matt?"

"Do you know that Dr. B is having a baby out of wedlock? They say his wife can't conceive."

"The admin building was deserted after the rain on Friday. No one in sight to process the paperwork!"

Even those most committed to Ghana's development carried with them elements of the White entitlement that is noted so often in today's racial discourse but was largely unrecognized at the time. I tried to avoid joining the cacophony of gossip and complaints, but my silence didn't extinguish my own internal critique; the values imbibed during my British upbringing were alive and well. Indeed, I still wonder whether it's more respectful for foreigners to speak or stay silent. What does belonging require? Is it even possible? However far we might have ventured from our place of origin, most of us would never be fully integrated in the country where we were living. The most we could do was acknowledge our differences and respect those who played by a different rule book.

Despite the ambiguities and apartness of expatriate life in Cape Coast, I look back on that period of my life as halcyon years. The sun shone, the country was benign and welcoming, I flourished professionally, I felt I was pursuing a worthy goal. Although I remained closely in touch with my family in England—or as close as snail mail allowed—I had emerged from the strict boundedness of my upbringing to a new freedom and openness to the world. Or so I thought.

In retrospect I can see the defining contours of the new bubble in which I was immersed with greater clarity. The university community provided me with shelter and a sense of belonging, albeit of a different sort than I had experienced growing up. But it beckoned me to a different future—one in which I would need to examine the boundaries more carefully. It was in Cape Coast—at the intersection between the expatriate community and the small cadre of young, single faculty members—that I met Clement.

# *Clement*

---

lement was different. That became clear very soon. He
mingled more fluently with the expatriate community
than most of his countrymen, even those who had studied
overseas for several years. He had wider horizons, showed
more interest in the world outside. Indeed, our shared desire to
reach beyond the confines of our respective traditions helped
spark our relationship, which quickly grew and matured.

To Westerners who encounter him in Europe or America,
Clement is easily labeled simply as "Black," or "from Africa,"
with no apparent need to look further. "Not so fast," I feel like
saying. "Don't think you can box him in so easily."

Clement's character defies easy stereotyping, formed as he
has been by a confluence of circumstances: his family's status in colonial Gold Coast, an education steeped in Western
values, and the cerebral life of a professional mathematician.
Clement's family background and early life shaped the man
he has become; they form an essential background to our life
together.

## *An African Family with a Difference*

In Germany, Hamburg's Lutterothstrasse is named after a former deputy mayor of the city whose descendants are wealthy
bankers and live there still. In old-town Accra, Lutterodt Street
and Lutterodt Circle are well-known landmarks. Same name,
same family—with a minor difference in spelling.

Clement's ancestor, Georg Lutterodt, came to the "Coast"—present-day Ghana—as a child in 1802. Because of difficult family circumstances, he had been entrusted to the care of his aunt, wife of the governor of Christiansborg Castle. The castle, still standing in Accra today, was an important trading fort, then in Danish hands. (Georg's uncle was instrumental in implementing abolition of the slave trade from the castle in 1805 at the direction of the Danish government.)

The West Coast of Africa—or Guinea Coast as it was called—was known as the White man's grave. Traders, colonialists, and adventurers typically died an early death or returned home after two or three years. Unusually, Georg remained there until his death at the age of sixty-one, becoming a successful businessman and trader and learning the art of survival in the presence of widespread disease. All the Lutterodts in Ghana today, many hundreds in number, are Georg's descendants.

Clement's father, Samuel Augustus Christian Lutterodt (Sammy), was Georg's great-grandson. Trained initially as a teacher, Sammy went on to be ordained in the Anglican Church as one of a very few Indigenous priests. In the late 1940s, he was sent to Liverpool, England, to serve as priest for the burgeoning immigrant population. Although clerical politics blocked his path to a bishopric, he was a respected figure in the church. His last post before retirement was as archdeacon at the interdenominational Ridge Church in Accra.

Clement's mother, Olaoni, was one of twelve children of S.O. Akiwumi (known as SOA), a wealthy Yoruba businessman who had settled in Ghana, pursuing a range of interests including diamond mining, cocoa farming, and banking. Photos of SOA show him dressed immaculately in three-piece suits, even in the heat of the tropics. He was so concerned about maintaining a proper appearance that he shipped his clothes to be laundered in England! As a member of pre-independence Gold Coast's African elite, SOA lived in uneasy alliance with the colonial rulers, absorbing many of their customs yet excluded from full participation in their society.

Valuing the benefits of a British education, SOA sent several of his children, including Clement's mother and her sister, Sodi, to school in England. They left for England after the end of World War l and remained there for six years. School photographs show the sisters as part of the hockey team, melding in an apparently seamless way with their British classmates. We learn they were well accepted by their fellow students, some of whom sent Olaoni lavish gifts when she got married. As the youngest child, Clement was always close to his mother and stories of her time in England stirred his youthful imagination.

After returning home Olaoni and Sodi became teachers. They taught for a while in Kumasi, and it was there that Olaoni got to know Sammy, who was a friend of one of her brothers. They were married in 1933. Their five sons arrived at roughly two-year intervals. As a priest, Sammy and his growing family were moved to parishes in different parts of the country, including Nsawam, where Clement was born, and Cape Coast. But Accra was always home, and that's where Clement's parents settled in their later years.

Both the Lutterodt and Akiwumi families formed part of Accra's elite. This tightly knit group, well-educated and urbane, included the doctors, lawyers, and politicians of late colonial Ghana. It is with this subset of Ghanaian society that Clement identified growing up; this is the Ghana where he belongs. It is far indeed from the stereotypical Western image of a poverty-stricken, "uncivilized" African country, an image he loves to challenge.

As one of the few native-born clergymen at the time, Sammy had frequent contact with his White colleagues, some of whom were regular visitors to the house. With the benefit of her years in England, Olaoni also socialized easily with White people. (An English friend who knew her told me she was one of the few Ghanaians she felt she could talk to.) When

Clement was growing up, his family lived at the intersection between their fellow countrymen, who were clamoring for independence, and representatives of the imperial culture they wished to overthrow. They witnessed at close hand the turbulent times leading to independence in 1957 and the repressive society that characterized Nkrumah's later years in power. Just as my own mother carried deep uneasiness about her German roots, so Clement's family must have lived with considerable ambivalence about their relationship to the oppressive colonial regime under which they lived but whose national church was the source of their livelihood.

Although Clement learned to socialize with White people as a child, the underlying ambivalence—carefully veiled—may well have influenced his relationship with the expatriate community in Cape Coast when we first met; indeed, it still colors his relationship with many White people today. At the interface between people of different races and cultures, there is invariably a barrier to trust and understanding that requires time and effort to overcome.

## *Elementary Particles*

**W**hen we met in February 1969, Clement had just taken a position as lecturer in the math department at Cape Coast. I'd been at the university for five months. As I left the science faculty building one afternoon, I stopped at the bulletin board in the lobby to see if anything new had been posted. Clement— who I hadn't yet met—joined me there. We struck up a conversation about a *Scientific American* article on elementary particles that I was reading.

"What's the latest particle to have been discovered?" we wondered.

"How many particles do we need to make sense of the universe?"

"Is there a unifying theory?"

Even though I was a bit familiar with the topic, my interest was somewhat contrived; Clement's was genuine. The conversation continued over dinner at my place a few days later. We soon started dating, attending parties on campus and an occasional concert or amateur theatrical production together. On weekends, we met at the beach or at my flat for dinner. Sometimes he stopped to visit with his dog, Fizzy. Clement has always loved dogs and Fizzy was his treasured companion.

We rarely met at the house off-campus that Clement shared with Brian, a colleague from Northern Ireland. Brian had a tight circle of bachelor friends and kept me at a distance. He didn't understand how Clement could be dating an upper-class English spinster like me. When his sister came to visit, Brian tried hard to pair Clement off with her. On one occasion, quite early in our relationship, we were all staying at the university rest house in Accra over a weekend. I thought that Clement and I had a date on Saturday evening, but he opted to go out with Brian and his sister, leaving me to fend for myself. I was miffed. When a week or so later a student invited me to visit his hometown over Easter, I accepted. Clement got the message, and our relationship survived.

Clement learned to drive using his father's car but hadn't had much chance to practice. After we'd got to know each other, I was happy for him to hone his skills using my hardy VW. He soon became a bit overconfident. Heading back to the university along the coastal road one day after a heavy rain, there were large patches of water on the road; we couldn't tell how deep they were.

"Be careful," I cautioned. "The road may be slippery."

"It's OK," he responded, without lessening the pace. Sure enough, when the car hit one of the puddles, it went into a nasty skid. Fortunately, the car righted itself and all was well, but we both got a bad fright. I had no need to say, "I warned you." Clement had learned a lesson about driving in wet conditions that has lived on in our collective memory.

## Clement's Family

On one of our trips to Accra, Clement introduced me to his parents, who were then living in the family house in Osu. Sammy, recently retired, had suffered a stroke and couldn't speak. A shadow of his former self, he spent his days sitting outside the house. After I'd visited a few times, he recognized me and smiled in greeting, but I never knew the eloquent preacher he'd once been. Nor did I know the strict disciplinarian and controlling presence he'd been within the family, insisting on extreme habits of cleanliness and hygiene, which all his sons have perpetuated in their own ways.

Clement's mother was always gracious and welcoming but, as I later learned, was wary of our developing relationship. Three of her nephews had married White women; none of the marriages had lasted. She never betrayed her misgivings to me. Through all the years I knew her, she was unfailingly kind and respectful of our marriage, never letting me feel I was an outsider. Although I was no match for her when it came to the domestic arts, I never felt judged.

Like her husband, my future mother-in-law also held the family to high standards, but in a less demanding way. In addition to being a well-loved teacher, she was a superb cook and seamstress and put her talents to work for her growing family. Though at least as well educated as her husband, she was largely subservient to him, in accordance with the gender roles that prevailed at the time. It was he who determined how her inherited money should be spent, had the last word about which relatives they would take care of, and intervened one time to prevent her from embarking on a commercial venture with a friend. It was a rare act of rebellion when she joined her brother in attending Christian Science services, though she never turned her back completely on the Anglican Church in which her husband was a minister. Clement joined her at Christian Science services for a few years in his teens. Traces of their teachings, including a deep skepticism of Western medicine, linger in his worldview.

When I first visited Clement's parents at Osu, his oldest brother, Nii, was also living there. He had an undiagnosed developmental disability and had never left home. In those days it wasn't easy for his parents to identify the help he surely needed. Their instinct was to shelter him from public view, and he rarely showed his face. When I stayed at the house after we were married, I came to appreciate his simple, guileless presence.

On our trips to Accra, we'd sometimes stop to visit Clement's cousin Nicho in Kaneshie on our way back to Cape Coast. Nicho was adopted by Sammy as a teenager because of her own father's ineptness as a parent, and Clement treated her as an older sister. As a student, he made his home with her when he needed to escape his father's overpowering presence. She always welcomed me kindly, but I never really knew what she made of our growing relationship.

Nicholas, familiarly known as Papaa—the second oldest of Clement's brothers—worked for an electrical contractor close to Kaneshie and we often stopped by to say hello. Papaa had recently returned from Ukraine where he qualified as an electrical engineer. He was one of many Ghanaians who went to the USSR for their tertiary education during Nkrumah's time when generous scholarships were offered to Ghanaian students. Their return home wasn't easy. The students' hard-earned credentials were questioned because the system that awarded them was unfamiliar to those trained in the West, who had now regained their influence. After a few years Papaa left Ghana again, this time for the U.S., where his wife, Regina, joined him later. He went on to a successful career with IBM and has remained in America ever since.

Clement's two other brothers, Gresham and Miguel, both studied medicine in Russia. Because of the prevailing attitude toward those trained in the USSR, they were determined not to return home when they qualified. Gresham worked as a surgeon in England, where he and his Russian wife, Natasha, have remained. Miguel took up a research position in Norway. It was there that he met his Danish wife, Ingrid. Together they moved to Denmark, where Miguel worked as a gynecologist until his untimely death from cancer in 2009. Even within our close family circle we cross many borders.

Natasha and Ingrid have both visited Ghana several times in recent years, but I am the only one of the White sisters-in-law to have lived there for any length of time. Despite my longer connection to the country, we have a bond of shared experiences: our global connectedness, the challenge of raising mixed-race children in majority-White countries, and the nexus of relationships in both the Lutterodt and Akiwumi families that stretch further and bind more closely than relationships in a typical Western family.

Moreover, being married to Lutterodt brothers creates a special type of bond between us, given the attitudes and strict behaviors drilled into them in childhood. I understood all too well when Ingrid described how Miguel's suspicions were aroused to a fury when he couldn't locate a garden hose and immediately blamed a neighbor. Or when Natasha told how Gresham always travels with a spare pair of socks to put on after walking through the airport security scanner. God forbid that he would put on his shoes wearing the same dirty socks! Thankfully, we can laugh together at some of the typical Lutterodt excesses!

## Early Experiences

Just as my family prided itself on its upper-class connections but was far from wealthy, so too Clement's family belonged to Accra's educated elite yet had a modest middle-class lifestyle, befitting the circumstances of a clergyman. Like me, Clement benefited from a protected childhood. The children suffering from *kwashiorkor*—a condition that takes its name from Ga, his mother tongue—were no more part of his immediate family circle than the slum dwellers of London's East End were part of mine. And yet Clement wasn't completely shielded from the hardships of the surrounding environment. He had experiences as a child that have left him cautious and risk-averse as an adult: a house on fire, a near-drowning, sickness and death among those close to him. He often tells me I am not careful enough.

Clement's school experiences also left their mark. For the most part he excelled at elementary school, except for one year when his class teacher took a dislike to him and lost no opportunity to berate him. The teacher's oppressive behavior set him back badly and was part of the reason for his delayed admission to secondary school. The disappointment lingered for a long time. When he did start in Form 1 at Adisadel College—the Anglican Church's flagship secondary school in Cape Coast—he was determined to prove himself and, laser-focused on his studies, became something of a recluse. His efforts paid off when he placed first in his class that year. Unfortunately, some of his classmates resented his achievement, and their subsequent rejection reinforced his tendency toward withdrawal and overly competitive behavior.

In the 1960s, the curriculum in Ghana still followed the British model, with little regard for local context or culture, so the content of what Clement and I studied in school was very similar, even though its impact was surely very different. What was a Ghanaian schoolboy in recently independent Ghana to make of the vast expanse of Britain's crumbling empire, which was still a source of misplaced pride to the average schoolchild in England? In geography Ghanaian students learned about Lancashire coal rather than Ashanti gold, and in history they studied the Tudors and Stuarts rather than the West African

93

empires of old. In primary school, they had been taught songs about daffodils: never mind that none of the students had ever set eyes on one.

Many of Clement's secondary school teachers were British, products of public schools and Oxbridge. They held out the professions as suitable goals for their most able students: law, medicine, academia. The arts weren't so highly valued. As a result, Clement had little opportunity to develop his artistic talents. (In matters of aesthetics—whether in dress or decorating our home or musical appreciation—I nearly always defer to Clement.) Hobbies centered on these talents would have provided a good balance in his life as a mathematician and been invaluable gifts to share with our children.

After six years at Adisadel College Clement went on to study math at the University of Ghana. As a student of the sciences in the Nkrumah era, he got special privileges, including a financial incentive. While others spent their money on hi-fi radio systems and other luxuries, Clement saved his stipend to travel to the UK during the long vacation. Impressed by the many stories his mother had shared about her time in Britain, he wanted to see for himself. Like me, he was interested in finding out what lay beyond the boundaries of the society in which he grew up and his own youthful experience. Our many travels together have always been times for shared excitement.

## An Unlikely Match?

The period from February 1969—when we first met—to July 1970, when Clement left for graduate school in England, seems in retrospect little more than a blink of an eye. Yet it was enough time for our relationship to blossom. Now, more than fifty years later, I ask myself what drew us to each other initially. What kept the relationship going? And what has sustained it through all the vicissitudes of life?

At the time, I was looking for a partner. I enjoyed Clement's company, and he soon became the emotional anchor I craved. We shared an interest in education and were both immersed in the life of the university. Yet our growing attachment surprised me in some ways. I'd always thought that deeply shared interests were an essential ingredient for a lifelong partnership, but notwithstanding our initial conversation on elementary particles, this wasn't really the case. Despite my physics background, I didn't share Clement's deep thirst for scientific knowledge, and he had little understanding of the idealistic concern for developing countries that had brought me to Ghana. For him, concern for the country's advancement was instinctive; he had no need for an assumed intellectual posture.

When it came to religion, Clement's ideas, formed by his upbringing in the Anglican faith (which he had firmly rejected by this time), his subsequent association with Christian Science, and his more recent reading of Freud, baffled me. He had little or no understanding of the liberal Catholicism following the Second Vatican Council that had played such an important part in my life. In hindsight, I realize that the three defining boundaries of my childhood—nationality, class, and religion—were all challenged by our relationship. It didn't seem to matter. Though I didn't fully acknowledge it at the time, it was a way of definitively breaking free of the "container" in which I had been raised.

As for Clement, he was an eligible young man with options. Our courtship and marriage foiled the designs of many an Accra mother who would've been glad to welcome him as a son-in-law. Was it that he had experienced the unreliability of at least one local girlfriend, where I was solid to a fault? Or that the local women didn't understand his single-minded focus on mathematics, while I was also a serious academic? Maybe he thought our relationship would allow him to break free from what he saw as the backwardness of many elements in his own society, providing him with a bridge to the English culture that had so thoroughly permeated his education. In a sense, we were both looking for an escape.

As our relationship became more serious, Clement chose a quiet moment in my apartment to tell me about his daughter, Linda, now two years old, the result of a youthful misadventure. At first, I thought he was joking. When I realized he wasn't, I took a deep breath as I tried to process what this meant for our future. I appreciated his honesty and didn't allow the information to derail our relationship. I got to meet Linda at Osu on one of our many visits to Accra. By mutual agreement, she continued to live with her grandma throughout her childhood, joining us in America when she had completed her secondary education. She has remained in the U.S., where she qualified as a nurse, but retains strong ties to Ghana where she hopes to start an at-home nursing service for elderly people.

Mother visited me in Ghana for Christmas in 1969 and had the opportunity to meet Clement. She pronounced him to be "rather a nice young man" but never guessed we were dating. Like any mother, she would certainly have been alert for any boyfriend on the horizon, yet she didn't see Clement in that role. It never even occurred to her that he might be a future partner for her daughter. Did he seem too young? Or too foreign? Or not sufficiently aligned with my idealism and religious identity? Or was it quite simply—to put it crudely—a question of race? It seemed that my involvement with a Black man was beyond her possible imagining.

The following summer, I was on home leave in England when Clement arrived to start his Ph.D. program at the University of Birmingham. We saw each other in London, and he visited me at Mother's home. Christopher, sensing that he wasn't just a friend, alerted Mother and she confronted me, "This is just a physical attraction. It can't last."

Her reaction didn't surprise me. I'd witnessed her concerns when Jane got engaged to Don, who came from a respectable Catholic family. Clement wasn't Catholic, not even British, let alone from the right social class. Worse still, he was Black! Even though her words echoed some of my own hesitations, I was in no mood to listen.

Shortly before leaving England at the end of the summer, I took Clement to visit my brother Richard with his wife and baby daughter at their home in Epsom, clearly indicating to them—and the rest of the family—the seriousness of our relationship. I hoped they might help allay Mother's concerns and be our allies within the family. That Clement was studying for a Ph.D. in mathematics at an excellent British university might have impressed some people, but it meant little to most of my relatives.

I was glad to return to my job in Ghana, but leaving Clement in the UK was difficult. Who knew where his new experiences would lead him or what interesting young women he would meet? We hadn't yet made a definitive commitment to each other. A lot could happen in a year. Telephone communication wasn't possible, so we had to rely on snail mail. Back in Ghana, I tried to read between the lines of his letters for any emerging friendships. Meanwhile I applied for a Ph.D. program in education, also at the University of Birmingham, for the following academic year. Being together in the UK, I thought, would allow us more time to figure out our future.

After I'd returned to Ghana, Christopher wrote a letter strongly encouraging me to break with Clement. Fond as I have always been of my family, they were not close to the details of my life. I saw no reason to be influenced by their opinion or accept Christopher's advice, which was certainly well-intentioned. I was already living outside the framework of my childhood years. If I were to take a further, more definitive step into a different world, it would be up to me to accept responsibility for that decision.

When Clement's father died in April 1971, his mother sent word to me in Cape Coast, informing me of the funeral arrangements. Encouraged by my friend Clara, I hastily got an outfit made in the traditional "*kaba* and slit" style, using a beautiful black and green batik cloth, and drove to Accra for the funeral. When I arrived at the church, I was astonished to see Clement sitting in the front row with his family. He had persuaded the university—which was funding his graduate program—to give him a ticket home on a compassionate basis. There'd been no way for him to let me know ahead of time. It was a wonderful surprise!

After the service there was the opportunity for me to meet other family members and for them to meet me. We didn't explain our relationship, but our connection was there for all to see. Most were welcoming, but one close cousin did little to disguise her disdain. "What's Clement doing messing with this English woman?" a slight curl of her upper lip seemed to be saying. I knew I would have to win her trust.

Because Clement's brothers weren't able to travel home for the funeral, I expected he would play a significant role in the extended activities. I hadn't understood the custom. All the arrangements were handled by family elders. Clement was little more than a spectator. That suited me well, as we were able to spend much of his short visit together. It was an opportunity for me to learn about his life in Birmingham and for us to strengthen the bonds between us after several months apart. It was a relief to find that no other woman had laid claim to his affection!

By this time, my plans for attending graduate school had been finalized, and Cape Coast University had agreed to let me take a leave of absence. I would be returning to the UK in

July. We agreed to meet in Paris and take a road trip in Europe before returning to England. Paris was to be our "fork in the road," the start of a new life together.

# Stepping into a
# Different Identity

There are times in one's life when the rhythm of events is unchanging, when little happens to challenge one's assumptions, shift one's boundaries, or redirect one's life in any significant way. Such times of relative calm may last for many years. And then there are times when change comes rushing at one. Times that are life-changing, setting one on a different trajectory and significantly altering one's stance in the world. The months of July through September 1971 were like that for me. In those brief months, everything changed.

## Paris

The academic year was over. I'd completed my assignments. When July came, I packed up and prepared for departure. I sold the VW that had served me so well and vacated my flat in Block 40, the site of many happy memories. Knowing I'd surely return, I left many of my household belongings with trusted friends. My leave-taking was "*au revoir*" not "*adieu.*" Cape Coast still felt like home.

From Accra, I took the Air Afrique flight directly to Paris. Clement came from England to meet me at Orly Airport. The luggage from the flight was delayed, and it was a long time before I emerged from customs. The baggage handlers grumbled, "*Ces pays sous développés. J'en ai marre.*" I understood who they were blaming for the long delay. "I'm fed up with these underdeveloped countries." Us and Them. There was no mistaking I was back in the first world.

I was concerned that Clement and I might miss each other since, foolishly, our rendezvous arrangements didn't include any contingency plans. There were no cell phones to help us connect. Fortunately, he found me in the arrivals hall. I breathed a sigh of relief. We were happy to be together again.

Once we'd found a hotel and settled into our room, Clement handed me a small package.

"What can this be?" I wondered aloud, not knowing at all what to expect.

I sensed Clement's excitement as I slowly and carefully opened the wrappings; he said nothing. When at last I saw the contents, I exclaimed, in amazement, "An engagement ring!" My surprise was unfeigned. I hadn't expected him to move so quickly and was caught off guard for a moment. My mind raced to grasp the significance of what was happening. I hesitated, but not for long. Wasn't this the outcome I had been hoping for? The doubts and uncertainties that had hung over my future melted away. Clement had cut through all the back and forth, the ifs and buts, that might have preoccupied us for weeks or months. His decisiveness had saved us a lot of uncertainty. We were now engaged and could enjoy our European vacation as an engaged couple.

The next day, we picked up the rudimentary Renault 4 that I'd ordered from Ghana and embarked on our travels. From Paris, we drove to the Jura Mountains and into Switzerland. There, we enjoyed a visit to the Rhone glacier and stopped briefly with a friend in Freiburg before crossing into Germany. From the border, we headed north to Hamburg where Clement had arranged for us to stay with members of the German Lutteroth family.

Our journey together had started. Together we'd have to forge a new entity, one we would build for ourselves, one with boundaries and barriers we were yet to discover. We didn't give too much thought to what lay ahead. We were happy to have settled our future as a couple. We would deal with any challenges when the need arose. We barely noticed the stares or microaggressions that were probably directed our way at a time when mixed-race couples were far from the norm. But, to the contrary, we were always alert to the few couples like us who crossed our path. Even now, when interracial marriage is no longer a rarity, our antennae are tuned to notice others who have embarked on a similar journey. "Did you see them?" Clement will say of a mixed-race couple who we have just passed in the street. I nod in agreement. How could I *not* have noticed? I think, as I wonder about the circumstances that brought their lives together. How did they meet? What drew them to each other? How have they handled the difficulties they, too, must surely have experienced?

## "My Name is Spelled L-U-T-T-E-R-O-D-T"

Once in Hamburg, we drove directly to the home of Ascan Lutteroth, the elderly scion of the German Lutteroth family. Some years earlier, Ascan had reached out to the German embassy in Accra, asking whether embassy personnel could put him in touch with any Ghanaian Lutterodts. He had reason to believe there was a branch of the family in Ghana and wanted to make contact. The embassy approached Clement's father, who was then archdeacon at the Ridge Church, which was attended by many diplomatic personnel. Sammy, a committed anglophile, didn't want anything to do with his German ancestry and handed the contact information to Clement. Clement was only too happy to pick up the trail and immediately got in touch. He had been in correspondence with Ascan for several years prior to the time of our visit.

Ascan and his wife welcomed us warmly to their beautiful

home overlooking the Elbe River. They had recently added a substantial annex to their house to accommodate the Lutteroth family archive: a large collection of documents and other memorabilia that had been bequeathed to Ascan by a reclusive relative. The archive included written records dating back to the twelfth century and a family tree on which Georg, Clement's ancestor, appeared as a stump. Curiosity about what grew from that stump had led Ascan to see if he could find any Lutterodts in Ghana.

It is hard to know what Ascan and his wife made of my presence during the visit. They were probably expecting a radical cross-cultural experience with their exotic, but distant, Ghanaian relative—an experience that would require them to reach out from their German roots and assumptions to communicate with him. A relative, for sure, but not "one of us." And there was I, his fiancée, a regular English woman, not exotic at all. I can imagine how disconcerting it must have been. Nonetheless, after what may have been an initial regrouping, they were gracious and welcoming. But—and there was a but—I was lodged in the annex, quite apart from the main building where Clement stayed. And, when it came to delving into the family archive, the conversation took place between Ascan and Clement while I was left to my own devices.

Fortunately, I did get to see a few letters from the archive that were of particular interest. The letters had been sent from what was then Gold Coast by two Lutterodt brothers, thought to be Georg's sons. Addressed simply to "The Lutterodt family, Hamburg," they had found their way to Ascan's collection.

"We don't know where our brother is," one letter bemoaned. "He left on the 'Hamburg steamer' and we haven't heard from him since."

"Please rescue us from these inhospitable shores," another letter begged, complaining of the heat and insects and disease.

A third letter took a very different tone: "We invite you to come and visit us on this beautiful coast. We have houses and farms and can make your visit very enjoyable."

I was fascinated by the window into Clement's family origins that the letters provided. The story of the Ghanaian Lutterodt family the letters revealed would soon be my story too.

During our visit, Ascan —Ascan Alfred to be precise — invited his son, Ascan Herman, and several other family members for dinner to meet Clement. It was an evening for information sharing, laced with curiosity and amazement on all sides at the surprising family connection. That dinner was a precursor for the Lutterodt/Lutteroth family reunions that have taken place regularly in recent years, initiated in Hamburg by Ascan Herman in 2004. At these gatherings we've got to know distantly related family members from many different countries, happy to celebrate their common name and family ancestry.

One frequent attendee was Helga, who had been at the original dinner party in Hamburg. Years later, she confided to us that she never thought our relationship would last! It didn't surprise me that behind the polite welcome I'd received in Hamburg lay a deep-seated unease about my presence.

Helga's concern was not, in fact, predictive of my future. I soon became—and have remained—a Lutterodt. In marrying Clement, not only was I joining the large Lutterodt family in Ghana descended from Georg, but I was also joining an extended international family all bearing the same name, albeit with minor variations in spelling: Lutterodt or Lutteroth in Germany; Lutterotti in Italy; Lutterot in Holland; and Lutteroth in Mexico. It is my privilege to belong to a family whose records date as far back as the eighth century in the German diocese of Mainz.

Always spelled Lutterodt in Ghana—and pronounced looter-ot—the name is unfamiliar in the U.S. and in England. Many is the time I have spelled it out for the benefit of tradespeople or dentists or a host of others: L-U-T-T-E R-O-D-T. The question "Where does the name come from?" often follows. If time and occasion permit, I am happy to share the unusual story of the first Lutterodt's arrival at Christiansborg Castle in modern-day Ghana.

From Hamburg, we drove to Ostend and thence to Dover on the cross-channel ferry. Once in England, we went straight to my mother's new home in Bletchingley. Christopher and his young family were now living at Brewerstreet, and Mother had purchased Stychfield, a smaller place close by.

We didn't waste time, or spare her feelings, in telling her we were now engaged. I steeled myself for her reaction, but she took the news calmly. She must have known it was coming. I wasn't in a mood to provide detailed explanations or justifications. I'm grateful she didn't ask or, indeed, create any great drama about our decision. I sensed what she must have been experiencing, but didn't dwell on it. I suppressed any need to extend empathy or understanding. Hopefully, family members and her circle of close friends provided the support she surely needed.

Once we'd announced our engagement, my mother and siblings, to their credit, seemed to accept the situation. They may have wondered how long our marriage would last but didn't express any further opposition. It was a *fait accompli.* I was concerned there might be a lot of negative rumbling behind the scenes but was reassured by an innocent comment by my nephew, Phillip, then about three years old. Clement and I had stopped by at Brewerstreet and found Phillip playing outside.

"Do you know who this is?" I asked him, pointing to Clement.

"It's Clement," he answered, "and he has a chocolate mouth." A chocolate mouth! The connection Phillip made between Clement's skin color and a valued treat spoke volumes.

Our plan was to get married quickly so we could move into a home together before the start of the academic year in October. It was already the end of July and there was a lot to do: purchase a home, furnish it, secure a marriage license, make wedding arrangements, etc. All at lightning speed. Fortunately, everything fell smoothly into place.

We were married at St. Dominic's Church in North London on September 25th, 1971, followed by a luncheon at Clyde's Hotel. Only close family and a few friends from our Cape Coast circle were invited.

I didn't want a large, traditional wedding. I had no intention of decking myself out in white lace or being given away by my younger brother, as Jane had been. I found such practices demeaning, treating women as trophies rather than equal partners. Yet, paradoxically, I was quite happy to take on the Lutterodt name without even hyphenating it to my maiden name. Today, I would have certainly done it differently.

Many relatives, though not invited to attend the wedding, sent gifts and wrote to wish us well. My aunt Winnie in South Africa, immersed in a country where apartheid was ascendant, sent me a beautiful yellow leather suitcase with a blue silk lining. She emphasized it was for my personal use. Even that gesture must have been costly for her, given the pervasive racism of the environment in which she lived.

After the wedding, we had a brief weekend honeymoon in Aberystwyth before heading to our new home in Birmingham. We had embarked on our life together. Gradually, we took on the mantle of our new identity.

# Part III

# Back and Forth Across Three Continents

*Fare forward, you who think that you are voyaging;*
*You are not those who saw the harbour*
*Receding, or those who will disembark.*
*Here between the hither and the farther shore*
*While time is withdrawn, consider the future*
*And the past with an equal mind.*

*—T. S. Eliot, "Four Quartets"*

# Birmingham

We moved a lot in the decade from 1971 to 1981. Three continents, five homes, and many stops along the way. At first there was one small child to care for, then two, then three. There was a lot of planning and packing, saving and storing as we navigated each transition. Many lingering goodbyes, grateful reconnections, and uncertain beginnings. Above all, there was a lot of coping. Except for a few significant decisions requiring careful deliberation, we did what had to be done: took one step at a time, got on with the job. As I think back, that's the only way I could have survived the many changes. I had little time to reflect on the meaning of it all.

Military families also move a lot. They understand what it is to move from base to base, from country to country, but they move within an institutional framework. They are tightly held. We were on our own, adapting as best we could to the different circumstances in which we found ourselves. I was, by turns, excited, challenged, and anxious; always methodical, often lonely. The experiences that formed us as a family were unique and different. We had to invent our own identity. We had few role models or people we could rely on in emergencies.

Our situation as an interracial family has varied from one environment to another: Birmingham, Cape Coast, Bletchingley (intermittently), Tampa, and finally Columbia, Maryland. The process of settling in has varied in each place, but everywhere there have been boundaries to recognize, then navigate. Even now, people find us difficult to understand. The questions recur constantly: "What did you say your name was? Where are you *really* from?"

111

## Graduate Students

I had met Clement in Ghana and it was there, within the mixed-race community at Cape Coast University, that our relationship had developed, but our life as a married couple began in England, as graduate students at the University of Birmingham. I would be living in England for the first time in several years. In a way it was a return to my roots, yet there was a radical discontinuity. I was embarking on a new life with Clement. If gossip swirled around our marriage, I didn't let it concern me. I wasn't about to let English chauvinism define us.

By the end of September 1971, we'd settled into our new home in Birmingham. Clement had already completed one year of graduate studies. He had overcome the initial hurdles of acceptance and was well integrated within the small group of Ph.D. students in the Department of Mathematical Physics. Our social circle during our two years in Birmingham consisted primarily of these students and their partners. One colleague had spent many years of his childhood in Ethiopia. Another was from India. A third—with an English girlfriend—was from Lebanon. They may have been surprised when their Ghanaian colleague returned after the summer vacation with an English wife, but they welcomed me into their circle.

We met up almost every weekend for drinks or a meal. Conversation centered on the men's shared interest in mathematical physics or departmental gossip. One of the other couples had a baby shortly before our own child, Toby, was born, so issues of pregnancy and childbirth were also part of the conversation. This was Clement's circle; if they didn't share many of my long-standing interests, that was fine by me. They have remained lifelong friends. Focused on adapting to married life and immersing myself in my studies, I put my personal interests on hold. I was now on a different trajectory, living in a different bubble. My lingering idealism was now vested in my marriage.

Before registering for a Ph.D. program, the university required me to complete a master's in education (M.Ed.), and this is what I did. The other students in the program were a rather homogeneous group of schoolteachers whose goal was to advance to administrative positions in their respective school systems. Many of them lodged in Birmingham during the week, returning home to their families at the weekends. Birmingham is in the heart of the British Midlands, and—with my lingering class consciousness—I condescendingly thought of them as products of "middle England." They were people of solid values and attainments, but our worlds did not intersect. While most of them would return to their school systems at the end of the program, I would return to Ghana.

For their part, my fellow students probably regarded me as an anomaly, partly because of my accent, which betrayed my origins, but more importantly because of my marriage to a Ghanaian. My situation may well have been a puzzle to them. Was I to be pitied, or envied? Resented or scorned? Being the only woman in the class also set me apart. (It was a source of perverse gratification when I won the academic prize awarded to an M.Ed. student each year.) Despite a few tentative efforts to reach out socially, we didn't form any lasting bonds.

During the years we were in Birmingham—1971 to 1973—Enoch Powell was busy stirring up racial hostility in the UK, but I don't remember encountering overt racism at the university or in the surrounding community. Maybe I was just too blind to notice. I had made the choice to enter a mixed-race marriage and didn't feel I owed the world an apology. Clement's antennae were more finely tuned. He recalls incidents of racial animosity when traveling outside the city and felt demeaned by faculty members on occasion, but this didn't affect the attitude of his peer group, who continued to treat him with affection and respect.

Clement's main struggles at the university arose out of a disconnect with his Ph.D. supervisor. Following a graduate seminar he attended—and urged on by a Ghanaian classmate who was then doing his Ph.D. at Cornell—he formulated a research problem for his dissertation on his own. His supervisor was unfamiliar with the math techniques required and left him to fend for himself. Fortunately, faculty in the mathematics department were prepared to read and critique his work.

Toward the end of the Ph.D. program, Clement presented his research at a conference, only to find later that another participant had coopted his ideas as their own, denying him credit for work that he had originated. While such practices are all too common in the cut-throat world of academia, it is possible they were—at least in part—the result of what we would now call unconscious bias: an unarticulated reluctance to acknowledge that an African could make a serious contribution to mathematics. The White person who had stolen the ideas was simply more credible. We will never know the person's intentions for sure. What is certain is that Clement experienced a barrier to professional recognition that was deeply hurtful. While I empathized with his pain at the time, I may not have appreciated how deeply it affected him. Unfortunately, the bitter aftertaste of this event was reinforced by other episodes later in his career.

Looking back, I am surprised that one of the more lasting bonds we formed at the time was with a modest but insightful Birmingham woman who came to clean for us once a week. Mrs. Ellis related warmly to both of us. Because her own daughter was dating a West Indian man, she seemed to understand the delicate place we occupied in British society as a mixed-race couple. She felt that by keeping her boyfriend at a distance to protect him from racial slights, her daughter was preventing him from developing a healthy relationship with the family. I wondered whether I had unwittingly fallen into the same trap. Had I set up a protective shield around Clement that reinforced the difficulties my family had in relating to him at first? It's possible. It's also possible that any attempt

I might have made to cut through the polite acceptance that marked their relationship would have had the opposite effect and resulted in a lasting rupture. I will never know.

## Married Life

At home, Clement and I each brought our own assumptions and expectations to the marriage. For Clement, these were undoubtedly colored by the model his parents offered: a controlling father and a mother who quietly assumed multiple roles. This wasn't much different from the norm in my own family, but as a woman with a career I had different expectations. One of my mother's elderly friends offered us advice, "Start as you mean to go on." I tried, but I wasn't good at holding a line. I expected us to share domestic responsibilities and made it clear that Clement should iron his own shirts. But when the shirts piled up un-ironed week after week, I was the one who blinked.

For the most part, we had a thoroughly Westernized lifestyle. I simply assumed this would be the case, and Clement didn't ask for anything different. We were in England, after all. We didn't have the newlyweds' proverbial disputes about which end to squeeze a tube of toothpaste or whether the toilet seat should be left up or down. And when Clement wanted the bedroom windows closed at night, while in my home the windows had always stayed open, I readily complied.

If there were differences between us, it was in what Clement liked to call my search for convenience. It reflected our different temperaments more than our cultural backgrounds. It was a puzzle for both of us. To me, it was obvious to look for the easiest—or quickest or most convenient—way to accomplish simple goals, like organizing weekend errands to avoid both of us having to make separate trips; or keeping one's boots close to the front door rather than buried in the coat closet. For me, convenience oiled the wheels of daily living. To Clement, it seemed lazy or self-serving to look for the least demanding way to accomplish a task if there was a more elegant or less messy way it could be done.

There is no question that my search for convenience leads me to cut corners, especially if I am in a hurry to move on to something else. Clement doesn't cut corners. For him, as a mathematician, rigor and precision are always paramount, no matter the time involved. While I might have been content to clean the kitchen at a superficial level to be sure it all looked respectable, he would focus intently on one corner or a single item, such as the toaster, and polish it to a perfect shine. "How do you expect the rest of the kitchen to be cleaned to that degree of perfection?" I'd complain, but to no avail. Once Clement has embarked on a task, he always completes it to perfection, even if it leaves me to complete the remaining tasks in my own get-it-done fashion. I have often thought we exemplify Jack Spratt and his wife of the eponymous nursery rhyme. When this aspect of his personality is on full display, I call him Spratty.

Closely related to our respective approaches to household tasks are our attitudes to risk. Clement is extremely risk-averse. Doors are double-checked to be sure they are locked securely before we leave home. Any house we ever considered buying was always carefully investigated to be sure there was no risk of flooding. Investments are studied to minimize risk. From Clement's perspective I'm often careless and imprudent, overly trusting, rushing to decisions before adequately evaluating the options. These differences—my impatience and penchant for action, his preference for precision and careful reflection—are matters of temperament, not culture, but influenced no doubt by our respective childhood experiences. It has taken long years of marriage for me to celebrate such differences as complementary rather than cause for disagreement.

While we've almost always respected the constraints imposed

by each other's work commitments, finding a mutually accept-able balance between home-based activities and our respec-tive leisure interests has challenged us in different ways over the years. During the early days of our marriage, Clement liked to watch professional boxing matches on TV in the uni-versity common room on Saturday evenings. I wasn't inter-ested in going with him but didn't like his frequent absences. We solved the problem by getting our own TV. Although dif-ferences in our interests remained, we had a common focus for our nonwork activities and concerns once the children arrived.

## Motherhood

Toby was born in April 1973; it was our second year in Birmingham. When I told my mother I was pregnant, she expressed surprise, commenting, "I thought you weren't going to have children." I never knew where she got the idea. Was it a matter of wishful thinking? Maybe she couldn't face the idea of having mixed-race grandchildren. Maybe, like a member of the Royal Family prior to the birth of Harry and Meghan's first child, she asked herself apprehensively, "How dark will the child be?"

Our preparations for the baby's arrival were minimal com-pared to those of other parents-to-be. There were no baby showers in England in those days, and because we would be returning to Ghana very soon, we had no incentive to prepare an elaborate nursery. In fact, none of our children had a lov-ingly decorated nursery such as one finds in a typical U.S. or British home when a baby is on the way. We were always on the move. In Birmingham, we made do with an ancient family crib used when Jane and I were babies. By the time we left for Ghana, Toby was a robust six-month-old and more than ready for something bigger.

Toby chose to arrive in the wee hours of April 1st, making him a good target for predictable jokes. Prior to the birth I was asked whether I wanted an epidural injection. We decided against, given the treatment was still somewhat experimental. While I was in labor, the anesthesiologist came to tell me she was going home and asked once again whether I'd like the shot. "You're not so young, obstetrically speaking," she cautioned. I wavered but didn't give in. Fortunately, all was well, and Toby arrived safely—a big, healthy baby. Setting aside her fears, Mother came to help when I got out of hospital and embraced him as her grandson. Clement and I registered each smile, each cry, and each small developmental step with awe and amazement. We were now a family!

After the excitement of my time in Cape Coast, I'd settled into the very different life of a graduate student in Birmingham. In Cape Coast, I'd lived as an expatriate in a well-defined community, albeit in a foreign land. In Birmingham, I lived as part of a small, self-contained community of Ph.D. students. Though England was home in a way, the culture and environment were unfamiliar. Being married to Clement set me apart; the arrival of a baby changed everything.

Professionally, I was still committed to the goal of economic development, which I was pursuing through efforts to improve science education in Ghana. Indeed, that was the whole purpose and thrust of my graduate studies. But the exigencies of my new role inevitably caused a shift in the balance of my time and attention. The baby always came first. When I returned to Cape Coast with Toby, the thread of my life had a different texture. Inevitably, my earlier idealism was put on the back burner. It would be further eroded in the ensuing years, but never entirely forgotten.

# Return to Cape Coast

In September 1973, after completing the preparatory work for my Ph.D. dissertation, I was ready to resume my appointment at Cape Coast University. Clement stayed in Birmingham for a few months to complete some research papers, so I returned to Ghana with Toby on my own.

Fifty years on, the decision to return to Ghana without Clement seems somewhat foolhardy. How could I have chosen to return to Ghana alone with a six-month-old baby? Why didn't I wait until Clement was ready? Did my restless impatience get the better of good sense? Whatever the case, I don't recall giving the decision a second thought at the time. Alongside my concerns as a new mother, I retained a deep commitment to my job. My funding had run out, and Clement's student grant couldn't have sustained us for long. Moreover, I had a professional responsibility to my employer. Why would I not go back in time for the start of the academic year? For me, Africa was not the place of dark foreboding that it was for many. I would be returning to a job I enjoyed and a university community where I belonged. Now, as a member of Clement's family, I had more reason than ever to feel a deep sense of connection to Ghana.

## A Nexus of Belonging

I was met at the airport by Clement's mother, happy to greet her new grandson. Several relatives had assembled to welcome us at the family home in Osu. One of Clement's cousins was concerned. "She can't stay here. The place is not suitable," he told my mother-in-law. She, in turn, asked me gently whether I'd rather go somewhere else. I was puzzled. I was more than happy to be staying in the family home. It had all the amenities I needed to care for the baby. Where else would I go? I didn't recognize then the deep cultural ambivalence prompting the cousin's concern: the sense many people of color have had thrust on them that they are in some way second class or not good enough. The cousin's father had once been a prominent lawyer and at the forefront of opposition to British rule; he had fallen foul of the colonial regime and lost most of his wealth and status—a condition that his son has spent much of his life trying to regain.

Doubtless the cousin's recommendation for me to stay elsewhere was well-intentioned, but his response to my presence at Osu was the exact opposite of my own. While he felt I was out of place, I wanted to be included. I was grateful to be welcomed in the family home and had no desire to be set apart and placed on a pedestal or— to change the metaphor—to be fenced in by my British upbringing. Fortunately, I didn't yield to the suggestion. I couldn't have lived with myself later if I'd turned my back on the many kindnesses that Toby's grandma had shown us.

The next day, a university driver came to take us to Cape Coast. We'd been assigned a house in a newly developed area of the university campus. That evening, an old friend—the English wife of an American lecturer—stopped by.

"I wanted to see if you needed anything," she said. "We heard you were arriving with your baby." News traveled fast on campus.

"Thanks so much, Janet. It's good to be back. This is Toby," I said, picking him up to show her. Toby smiled engagingly, not too disturbed by his long journey and change of environment.

After some "baby talk," I continued, "I'm trying to figure out where on campus we're located!" It was dark when we arrived, and I hadn't yet got my bearings.

"Our house is just up the street," she said. "The road running past your house—that's new. It connects to the science faculty. You'll see in the morning. I'll come round and take you to town so you can get what you need."

I was home!

Clement joined us in January, and we reimmersed ourselves quickly in the life of the university; it was there that our life was centered. I had the same sense of belonging I had enjoyed during the years before I married. We socialized most frequently with the expatriate staff and the increasing number of mixed-race couples. Friends in our immediate circle came from England, Sweden, Bangladesh, Denmark, Russia, Hungary, America, and more. With them, there was no explaining to do.

Even now, I find it difficult to understand why my relationship with families in which both parents were Ghanaian had a different quality. Was it that they had less free time to socialize, were more absorbed in their own extended families, didn't pamper their children so much? Or was it that invisible, seldom acknowledged barrier of race and culture that we have encountered so often as a couple and as a family? I still ponder these questions. When we meet up now with Ghanaians from our Cape Coast days, they are happy to see us both, but they relate to Clement best.

We also maintained close contact with Clement's family in Accra, making regular trips there for work or family functions. We often stopped by to see Clement's cousins—Nicho, Akiwusi, Gerhard—and sometimes met up with his school or university friends. By mutual agreement, Linda—now of school age—remained at Osu with Grandma, but they both visited us in Cape Coast for Christmas and other holidays. They were always welcome. When we went on a road trip to Nigeria during the long vacation in 1974, Grandma came to Cape Coast to look after Toby, now a year old. On our return, he pretended not to know who we were! Such is the way that children learn to defend themselves against feelings of abandonment, even at a very early age!

Before we got married, my friend Clara had cautioned me that all Ghanaians have poor relations in their extended families. We would surely be expected to help out financially, and if we weren't careful family demands would be disruptive to our marriage. Others had sounded similar warnings. As it was, Clement didn't succumb to family demands; he protected the boundaries of our nuclear family well. Grandma, too, was almost always respectful. Just once, there was a near miss.

"Linda and Willie will be going with you to Cape Coast," Grandma told me as we were getting ready to leave Osu to return home after a visit. She spoke as though it was all decided. Willie was Clement's nephew, who was staying with her. She and Clement must have agreed that we would take the two six-year-olds with us without consulting me. I was puzzled.

"Linda is ours. She can come," I said. "But I can't ask Comfort"—our nursemaid at the time—"to take care of them both while I'm working." Willie, a rambunctious little boy, overheard the conversation and started wailing at the thought he'd be left out. Grandma quickly intervened, "Of course. I understand. Better they both stay here."

And that was that. No more was ever said. I had drawn a line in the sand to protect myself from what seemed like family overreach. I was grateful that Grandma had got the message; I hoped it hadn't created a barrier between us.

My second pregnancy was perfectly timed; the birth coincided with my home leave in 1975. Mother generously hosted Toby and me at Stychfield for a month leading up to the birth and for several weeks afterwards. She never complained. She tolerated the disruption to her normal routine and the growing pile of baby clothes and other accoutrements of Western life that I had accumulated under the staircase in preparation for our return to Ghana.

Clement spent the summer pursuing research at UNESCO's Center of Theoretical Physics in Trieste, Italy, arriving at Stychfield shortly before my due date in August. He cried out, "It's a girl," when Isabelle entered the world. We were both thrilled that Toby now had a sister. Our small family was complete . . . for the moment.

During the weeks before and after the birth, we had many occasions to visit Christopher's family at Brewerstreet, conveniently within walking distance of Mother's house, and met up with Jane's family quite often, too. (Richard and his family were living overseas at the time.) The cousins were anxious to meet Toby, now two years old, and they had many good times together.

In subsequent years, we had several lengthy stays at Stychfield, whether during overseas leave from the university, as a stopover during our many tos and fros between continents, or as a place for brief—but precious—holidays once we'd settled in the United States. Stychfield became a home away from home, and Brewerstreet, where the children enjoyed playing with the animals and swimming in the pool, a place of happy memories. Beyond our close bonds with Clement's family in Accra and the campus community in Cape Coast, my family in England provided a third strand of belonging. The children learned to navigate different cultures from a very early age.

## *Working Mother*

**A**lthough the life of a working mother was easier in Cape Coast than it would be later in the U.S., it still presented challenges, not the least of which was finding a nursemaid to look after the children. Despite widespread unemployment, many of the local girls were unreliable or didn't like the isolation of a job on campus or already had babies of their own to take care of. We had numerous disappointments.

Comfort, who was with us for a while, was very amenable and took good care of Toby as a baby. Unfortunately, her winning smile soon attracted the attention of young men in the area, and it wasn't long before she got pregnant and had to leave. Other girls came and went, often preferring to commute from town by day rather than live in our staff quarters. I had many anxious moments wondering whether our current nursemaid would arrive in time for me to leave for an early morning lecture. The question of whether Clement or I would stay home if she didn't turn up never arose. That responsibility invariably fell on me, but I don't recall complaining. I must have accepted the traditional female role unquestioningly.

The situation improved when Sophia and Charlotte came to work for us soon after Isabelle was born. Sophia looked after the children; Charlotte cooked. The two shared the room in the staff quarters and kept each other company. They remained with us for several years, providing much-needed stability at home. We gave both of them an opportunity to acquire vocational skills. Charlotte took sewing lessons from one of the faculty wives on campus, while Sophia attended a secretarial school nearby. Sophia was able to put her training to good use. Sadly, Charlotte relapsed into a life of poverty after we left.

For the most part, the children were raised according to Western norms, as were the other mixed-race children. Most expatriate parents considered items such as books and construction toys essential for children's development and managed to procure them for their children regardless of their financial circumstances. It was more difficult for Ghanaian parents.

Our approach to discipline was generally more relaxed than in typical Ghanaian homes, but Clement did enforce some of the strict measures learned from his parents. If one of the children had a cut that was taking a while to heal, they got the hot-water treatment Clement had known as a child: a cloth soaked in very hot water pressed repeatedly against the wound. The treatment was effective in stemming the spread of infection, which is all too common in the tropics, but was extremely painful. The children were expected to endure stoically. I tried not to interfere.

While cleanliness and insect control were a concern for both of us, Clement took the precautions to extremes. We always had to wait several minutes before entering the house. "No, no. Don't open the door yet," he would tell us as he energetically waved away any mosquitoes hovering around the entrance. Inside, no piece of furniture could touch the walls lest an insect find its way there. Any insect unlucky enough to emerge from a hiding place in the house was ruthlessly eliminated with an overdose of insecticide. And so on. While burdensome, these precautions were effective in protecting the family from major sickness.

Clement has always been fascinated by animal behavior and adept at outsmarting any critters that might cause us harm. If ever we had a snake on the premises, he was in his element. One time, a green mamba raised its beautiful, shiny head very close to the house, waving from side to side as it peered through the grill that barred its entry.

Charlotte screamed in terror, "There's a snake. It's looking at me."

Clement quickly took charge. "Be quiet," he chided her, then calmly went outside to kill the curious mamba. Word of his prowess spread, and he was called in by neighbors to help if ever a snake came to visit.

In addition to our family responsibilities, we were both fully engaged in our academic careers during these years. As a lecturer, Clement was always dedicated to his students, motivating them to set ambitious goals for themselves. He corresponded with many of them for several years after we'd left the university and one of them followed him to America for graduate school.

Clement's ambition for his students translated into a conviction that the curriculum at the university should offer a mathematical education second to none. He had no patience with expatriates who argued that a less rigorous approach would be more appropriate for "these students." The implication that Ghanaian students should be relegated to a second-class education angered him. Interestingly, the very same issue surfaced years later in the often-bitter discussions about the curriculum during Clement's long tenure at Howard University in Washington, DC. Assuming the students were incapable of meeting widely accepted standards seemed to him to be condescending in the extreme.

Clement also worked hard on his research, always with the goal of publishing in recognized mathematical journals. He spent several summers at the UNESCO Center in Trieste on research grants, and we pooled our resources for him to attend the International Mathematical Congress in Helsinki in 1978. It turned out to be a great investment because it was there that he met Professor Donaldson, chair of the math department at Howard University—his future employer.

Meanwhile, I was busy working on my Ph.D. dissertation. I was studying how the integrated science curriculum we had worked on was being used in practice by different teachers. Fortunately, it was easy to combine the fieldwork involving detailed observation of science lessons at local secondary schools with my other academic responsibilities. I did most of the writing during work stoppages at the university, due sometimes to faculty strikes and sometimes to student walkouts. Whenever classes stopped, I put away my lecture notes and got out the dissertation. Word processors were not yet available and, although I had a good typewriter, editing was slow and laborious. Fortunately, I found a skilled typist at the university who prepared the final manuscript using an IBM Selectric typewriter, which was the best technology available at the time.

I presented the dissertation to Birmingham University in 1977 and was gratified to receive the School of Education's George Cadbury Prize, even though the honor carried minimal financial reward.

While encouraging me in my career, Clement struggled with protective instincts I found difficult to understand. I returned home one afternoon after observing student teaching at a school in Saltpond, a small town twenty miles away.

"What were you doing there all morning?" he asked.

"I observed four classes and then debriefed each of the students. One of them—"

"I mean, who did you see? Who else was there?" He interrupted the story I was about to tell.

"You mean apart from the students? I spoke briefly to the regular class teachers."

He complained I was being "reticent" and not giving him the full story. I didn't know what he wanted. No matter how much I tried to tell him, picking out key themes or tidbits of information, it didn't seem to be enough. I was emotionally dependent on Clement and found his constant questioning distressing. I didn't understand why he was so anxious. Was it driven by some deep-seated insecurity? I ask myself now.

At the time, I was focused on coping, getting the job done and was probably insufficiently tuned in to emotional needs—his or mine.

Differences in our understanding of professional responsibility became an issue when Isabelle was about two years old. Toby attended the university kindergarten in the morning. Isabelle stayed home with Sophia and got upset when I left for work. I didn't worry because I trusted Sophia and, because we always came home for lunch, I was rarely gone more than a few hours. Clement thought otherwise. He complained I was neglecting her and wanted me to stay home. I was confused.

"How can I do that and keep my job?" I asked. "I have responsibilities as a faculty member beyond just teaching my courses. Do you expect me to resign and be a full-time mother? Could we afford to live on one salary?"

When Clement persisted, I compromised, arranging with a few friends to run a playgroup that we would each host once a week. This arrangement seemed to satisfy him and only encroached marginally on my working life. I wasn't prepared to let family duties override professional obligations any further. Our Ghanaian colleagues may have felt differently.

To my surprise, I have observed a similar tension between professional and domestic responsibilities playing itself out in the U.S. quite recently. Having achieved tenure, some university faculty feel they can sit back and enjoy their hard-earned job security while doing the minimum to get by on the job. In strongly rejecting this position myself—both then and now—I wonder whether I am blinded by the cultural assumptions of my upbringing. Somehow, I have always felt that professional obligations should be primary, but I realize the rules may be shifting. When so many women in the workplace must juggle professional and domestic responsibility, is greater flexibility required? Was I being way too rigid then? I ask myself. Am I hopelessly old-fashioned now?

## Scarcity

**W**hen I returned to Cape Coast as a married woman, the British government decided I no longer qualified for the salary supplementation I'd previously received. As the Ghanaian economy deteriorated in the early 1970s, the value of the supplementation increased substantially to maintain parity with university salaries in the UK. To contain costs, the British government decided to limit recipients to those in disciplines judged important for development. My field was science education, so I thought my benefit was secure. I hadn't reckoned with the men who ran the British government!

Once married to Clement, I was considered to be domiciled in Ghana, my husband's country; as such I was no longer eligible. I fought hard to have the benefit reinstated. It was a matter of principle. There was no interruption of aid to British men who had Ghanaian wives. Their domicile wasn't deemed to have changed, and they remained beneficiaries of the scheme without question. Women were being treated as though they were chattel of their husband.

"British law now requires employers to treat men and women equally," I pointed out to the folks at the Ministry of Overseas Development (MOD). "You are discriminating against me as a woman."

"You are employed by the University of Cape Coast, not the British government. The law doesn't apply in this situation," they responded.

I hassled representatives from the MOD—all men—on their occasional visits to Cape Coast, but they wouldn't budge. Fortunately, the university didn't consider my marriage to have changed my status as an expatriate employee and continued to give me home leave to England every two years. During one such visit, I engaged a lawyer to write a letter to Sir Geoffrey Howe, a prominent politician at the time, who happened to be the member of Parliament for my mother's constituency.

The letter was copied to the MOD. Finally, unexpectedly, they yielded! The supplementation that the UK government then provided made a world of difference in our lives.

After the 1973 oil crisis in the West, the global financial malaise had spread to African countries and to Ghana in particular, where its effects were magnified by incompetent military rulers. Even basic consumables such as margarine, sugar, and toothpaste were difficult to find. When there was a sudden shortage of toilet rolls in the U.S. in the early days of the Covid pandemic, I was reminded of the time in Cape Coast when I was down to my last roll. After that it would have been newspaper, as it already was for many families. The children remind me how I rationed the number of sheets they were allowed to use.

It was impossible to buy bread. We learned to bake our own, but flour was only available occasionally. "They're expecting a delivery of flour," the word went round the expatriate community. "But you need a chit from the regional commissioner's office." I dutifully made the trip to the former colonial villa perched on a hill outside town to get the required scrap of paper.

As soon as I learned the flour had arrived, I rushed to the depot in town, joining crowds of townsfolk all clamoring for access to the limited supply. In those days, a White person in the crowd attracted favorable attention and I was usually able to procure a sack that would provide us with bread for many weeks. The opposite would probably be true today. As a White person, I might well be overlooked altogether.

For meat, we relied on beef carcasses imported from Argentina. When we heard of a delivery, we would quickly go to the cold store in town and triumphantly haul home a side of beef. Clement became adept at carving the carcass, while I bagged and froze the portions, the children helped, and Charlotte and Sophia cleaned up. I enjoyed the teamwork involved and the luxury of being able to plan for a Sunday roast from time to time. Later, that source also dried up and frozen fish, sold in large cardboard cartons, became our main source of protein. We learned to rely increasingly on Ghanaian staples: *kenkey* and fish, palm soup, beans and rice, *palava* stew, *banku*, fried plantain. The children and I developed a taste for these dishes. Enjoying them together now is a special treat.

We were privileged in being able to import many basic foodstuffs from the UK, thanks to the salary supplementation I was now receiving. Unfortunately, what became a lifeline for us set us apart from colleagues who didn't enjoy the same advantage. Focused as I was on work and family, I had little bandwidth to worry about what others were thinking. Looking back, however, I realize our situation may well have aroused considerable resentment, creating barriers that I didn't intend or even recognize. While I was never one to brag explicitly about my privilege, it must have oozed from every pore. I am more than ever grateful for the few good friends who didn't hold it against me.

During these times of scarcity, life was difficult for all of us, even those who benefited from overseas aid. The search for food and other necessities came to dominate our lives. It was an experience I've never forgotten and one that, hopefully, has made me more sensitive to the plight of the millions of hungry people in the world today. Conversations in our social circle were dominated by the latest information about expected deliveries of flour or fish or meat and the paperwork needed to get one's share. Work was often interrupted by the need to wait in line for some basic item that had just been delivered to the university store, shattering my cherished professional work ethic.

As shortages became more acute, it got more and more difficult to function at work. Social life was stifled. The distance between those who did and didn't have access to supplies became more evident. Many of our colleagues started looking for an escape route. It was the ever-worsening economic situation that led us, eventually, to decide to move permanently to the United States. But first there was Tampa.

# To Tampa and Back

O ur flight from London was delayed, and we had to spend the night in a hotel in Miami before continuing on to Tampa. Toby and Isabelle were with me; I was pregnant with Justine.

As we headed to our room, I asked the Latino bellman whether it was safe to drink water from the tap. His reply, "You are in America now," surprised me. My intention had been to ask a very practical question. Did he feel insulted by the implication that the water might not be potable? Or had he launched a mild insult of his own by implying that this place was different from whatever god-forsaken place I might have come from? What was the meaning behind his words?

It is said that English speakers are often divided by their common language. I wondered what that would mean for us. What did America hold in store? It was our first night on American soil: another environment, a different piece of the patchwork.

## Our First Taste of America

Clement was already in Tampa. He had been awarded a Fulbright fellowship, which he arranged to spend at the University of South Florida (USF). I took sabbatical leave from the University of Cape Coast to join him for a term, starting in April 1979, attaching myself to the education department at the university while writing up my Ghana-based research for

133

publication. My sabbatical morphed into maternity leave as I stayed on for the birth of Justine that October.

Given the difficult economic conditions in Ghana, we planned to use our time in Tampa to decide whether America was somewhere we'd like to settle. Unlike many would-be immigrants, our question wasn't so much "Will America take us in?" as "Will we be happy living there?" One of our main concerns was how we would be received as a mixed-race family. Although we were familiar in general terms with the struggles of the Civil Rights Movement, we were quite ignorant about how racial issues played out in day-to-day life; moreover, we were largely unaware of our own naïveté.

On the surface, we experienced curiosity but little outright negativity. It may well have been a source of cognitive dissonance for the math team at the university to learn that the wife of a visiting scholar from Ghana was an Oxford-educated English woman. Nonetheless, the professor who had sponsored Clement's fellowship received us kindly at first, as did his family and the head of department.

White Americans outside the university showed ill-disguised relief when our accents told them we were foreigners. "It doesn't sound like you folks are from around here," they commented jovially. "Where y'all from?"

"We're visiting," we replied, dodging the question.

Since we weren't American, it seemed we could be forgiven our mixed-race situation. We didn't fall within their normal frame of reference, so our presence invoked surprise and incomprehension rather than hostility.

One Sunday, when I was heavily pregnant, I waited with Toby and Isabelle for Clement to pick us up after church. A woman engaged me briefly in conversation. "Will this be your first?" she asked.

"No," I replied, indicating the children playing together under a tree close by. "Those two are mine."

I didn't understand her failure to configure the scene in

front of her. The children were clearly in my care; there was no other adult around. Surely, I thought, any observer would conclude that they were my children. Why would they not? Had she never encountered biracial children before? Her lack of awareness shocked me, and her remark struck me as grossly insensitive.

Now, after many years of living in the U.S., I realize my reaction revealed my own ignorance as much as it did hers. I hadn't fully grasped the extent of the racial divisions that marked American life. Most likely it was outside her range of experience for a seemingly respectable young woman with an English accent to have a partner who was Black.

The gulf of misunderstanding between the woman and myself was wide and deep. It wasn't just differences in use of the English language that set us apart, but rather differences in the lens of experience through which we viewed the world. I understood I might be rejected because of my interracial marriage, but it never occurred to me that such a union wouldn't even exist as a possibility in someone's mind.

Most of the time when racial animosity lay thinly disguised just beneath the surface, I preferred not to look too closely. The children couldn't avoid it. Because children don't filter what they say or do in the same way as adults, they were more exposed to the sharp edge of racial aggression than we were. At the daycare-cum-primary school the children attended, Toby, whose racial identity is somewhat ambiguous, was accepted quite easily at first. Isabelle, whose hair and skin tone more clearly reveal her parentage, had a more difficult time. When it became clear that Isabelle was his sister, Toby also became a victim of other children's kicks and punches. We lacked the hard-earned wisdom of African American parents that would have prepared us to teach our children how to defend themselves against such types of aggression.

The most overt instance of racial animus we experienced in Tampa occurred about a year later. After returning to Cape Coast for a short period, we'd moved back to the United States and were settling into a new life in Maryland. During the Christmas break we drove to Tampa to collect household effects left in storage. While staying with a friend, one of the few people who had warmed to us during the months there, we awoke on New Year's Day to find our car covered with broken eggs. Our hostess tried to brush the incident aside. To us, the racist intent was unmistakable.

## A New Arrival and a Planned Departure

My mother visited us in Tampa for two weeks the summer that we spent there. She worried about how we would manage the upcoming birth, just two months away; we had no support systems close by. Fortunately, all was well. Justine arrived on October 30th without incident, albeit nearly three weeks late. The arrangements we'd made to take care of Toby and Isabelle held up, allowing Clement to attend the birth and even travel to a conference in Ohio a few days after the event.

Because our insurance didn't cover a pre-existing condition such as pregnancy, we'd arranged for the delivery to take place at a public hospital, Tampa General. When Toby and Isabelle were born in the UK, we used the National Health Service, just as everyone did. We didn't realize the stigma the public sector carries in the U.S. or how use of a public hospital may have diminished us in the eyes of Clement's colleagues. When Clement's mentor and his wife kindly visited me in hospital, they were probably appalled by the fact that I was in a room with three other mothers and one bathroom between us.

While I was still in hospital, Toby and Isabelle stayed a couple of days with a family who had children of similar ages and were unusually open and accepting of our situation.

Toby—just six and a half years old—surprised them by wanting to watch the news on TV rather than the cartoons their own children preferred!

When I left hospital with Justine and we were all back together at the apartment, Toby and Isabelle were delighted to welcome their new sister. While Toby continued in school through the end of the term, Isabelle was glad of the opportunity to stay home many days to help look after the baby. We were happy and grateful to now be a family of five.

Following his Fulbright fellowship, Clement was offered an appointment to teach at USF for the 1979/80 academic year, providing him a base from which to look for a more permanent job in the U.S. if conditions in Ghana didn't improve. Our plan was for him to stay in Tampa through June while I returned to Ghana with the children in time for the second university term. Although the College of Education at USF had accommodated my request to spend my sabbatical there, I had found little common ground with members of the faculty and saw no reason to stay on after my maternity leave.

The decision to return to Ghana on my own—this time with three children—may seem a bit reckless, but my sabbatical carried with it a requirement to complete at least two academic terms back in Cape Coast. I didn't want the obligation hanging over me if we ended up moving to the U.S. permanently. Besides, living in Tampa on Clement's meagre salary wouldn't have been easy. Returning to my job in Ghana with the children seemed the best option.

I prepared for our departure methodically, one step at a time, trying to anticipate any problems or eventualities. To help me out while I was on my own in Cape Coast, we looked for someone to come with me who could help run errands, including fetching and carrying the children from school. Our advertisement for someone interested in an "African adventure" got only one serious response. The respondent, Andrea, was a graduate student in anthropology; she had been to Ghana before and that was a definite plus. When we interviewed her, I explained in no uncertain terms the difficult economic situation she would encounter.

"There are a lot of shortages," I said. "Basic stuff like flour and toilet paper. Meat is difficult to find."

"I don't eat meat," she said helpfully. "Only chicken."

"Even chickens aren't always easy to get hold of," I went on. "Mostly, we eat fish. We can usually find fish to buy."

"I like fish." Andrea seemed anxious to adapt to whatever reality I described.

"That's good," I said. Not sure she had really grasped how grave the shortages were, I added, "Sometimes bread is not available either. When you were in Ghana before, did you get to eat local foods?"

"I love groundnut soup," she replied.

Groundnut soup is a Ghanaian dish most foreigners enjoy, but it's something of a luxury. I wondered whether she was familiar with the more everyday items. "That's a good start," I said, still not sure she had really understood. "How about *kenkey* or *gari*?"

Mother, who was staying with us at the time, said nothing during the interview, but remarked afterward, "You really laid it on a bit thick. All those shortages! It's enough to scare the poor girl off." She thought I'd exaggerated. I hadn't. I knew it was important to be upfront about the reality of the situation. I didn't want Andrea telling me later she hadn't been warned.

I realize now how difficult it must have been for her to absorb what I was saying. Her previous visit to Ghana had been in better times. She may well have thought my complaints were just one more example of a privileged White person with a negative attitude to Africa, upset that I didn't have access to all the amenities I was used to. She would see for herself.

We left Tampa in December. We had shipped all the baby

items and books and toys we thought we might need ahead of us. As the only U.S. citizen in the family, Justine needed her own passport; her passport photo shows her lying on my lap in the photographer's studio. Like Isabelle, she took her first flight when she was only a few weeks old.

I wasn't sorry to leave Tampa. In Ghana, for all its economic woes, we were part of a small campus community focused on the educational betterment of the country. In Tampa, the vast network of avenues and highways separating people from each other seemed antithetical to healthy community life. Moreover, we couldn't relate to the general pleasure-seeking ethos and the apparent insouciance for the rest of the world. Cape Coast was no cultural mecca, but at least we had BBC World Service, while the radio programs we tuned into in Tampa were filled with consumer ads and jingles that I found endlessly repetitive and annoying. I hadn't ruled out returning to the U.S. one day, but I hoped it wouldn't be to Florida.

## Cape Coast Again—without Clement

We arrived in Ghana just before Christmas after spending a few days with Mother. Andrea was with us. Clement came to help us settle back in. I knew it wouldn't be easy. As it happened, the trouble started immediately. The batteries in both cars were failing, with little hope of replacing them locally. What to do? I needed a car for work and Andrea would need the second car for fetching and carrying the children. Clement would only be with us a few days before returning to Tampa. We felt we had no option but to make a day trip to Lomé, where goods of every sort were widely available.

Lomé is situated on the Ghana-Togo border, about five hours from Cape Coast by car. We'd made the trip several times in the past and knew the road to be in reasonable condition, but we had none of the paperwork normally required at the border. We decided to risk it anyway. I would go with Clement, taking Justine along and leaving the two older children at home with Andrea. If we couldn't take the car across the border, I could stay with it on the Ghana side while Clement headed into Lomé to get the batteries.

We set off early and made it to the border in good time. The Togolese immigration officer seemed amused seeing the two of us with Justine. "That be your baby? *C'est à vous?*" he asked, turning from me to Clement and back again with a doubtful smile. Justine was a very fair baby; his look told us he didn't believe she was Clement's child. Did he think I was escaping from the natural father? Whether for his private amusement or some other reason, he waived the normal entry requirements and let the three of us into Togo, along with the car. We were duly grateful.

Our sense of relief was short-lived, however. We soon learned that Lomé was shut down for the New Year's holiday. It was December 29th, and the official auto suppliers weren't scheduled to open again until January 2nd, the very day Clement was due to return to America. Thankfully, however, the back-street economy was still functioning, and with a bit of luck we located a fitter's yard with batteries for sale. Content that our main goal had been achieved, we stopped at a grocery store to get a few items currently unavailable in Ghana before heading back to the border. By this time, it was late in the afternoon.

Our day had gone quite smoothly, all things considered, but there was trouble ahead. The border guard refused to stamp my passport to let me back into Ghana. I had a residence visa, but not the required reentry permit. We pleaded and argued, but she wouldn't budge. Rules are rules. What to do? We wouldn't be able to get any documents from the embassy in Lomé until after New Year, and Clement had to return to the U.S. before then. Moreover, Andrea—new to the country—was at home in Cape Coast alone with the two older children, unreachable by phone. Eventually we decided to take the law into our own hands. "Let's just go," I said to Clement.

The customs office stood a little back from the road and, inexplicably, there was no physical barrier to pass through after stopping at customs. We got in the car and drove. I held my breath as we waited for the border guard to raise the alarm; fortunately, she didn't. As I look back, I realize she probably empathized with our situation and, unable to give us the official OK, simply looked the other way. In typical Ghanaian style, she opted for decency over strict adherence to bureaucratic rules.

We made the long drive back to Cape Coast without further incident, arriving home about 10 pm to find Andrea in a state of panic.

"I didn't know what could have happened," she complained, her concern spilling out in anger at what must have seemed our lack of care. "What was I to do alone with Toby and Isabelle?"

"We had no way of contacting you," I explained. "We got stopped at the border."

"But, but . . ." her pent-up anxiety was palpable.

"Fortunately, we made it," I tried to reassure her. "We got what we needed."

I understood Andrea's angst; I'd got used to expecting the unexpected in Ghana, the need to manage without easy communications. For Andrea, newly arrived in the country, the uncertainty had been agonizing.

After Clement's departure, I slipped easily back into the routine of my job and life on campus. It was a more difficult adjustment for Andrea.

"I feel boxed in," she complained to me after a week or so. "I'm alone in the house most of the day. Everyone else is at work."

"Just give us a chance to get settled," I said, trying to empathize with her situation but feeling stretched myself with all that I was doing to pick up the threads of my job and make sure basic household needs were met. "I'll talk to a few people and see if something can be arranged."

Fortunately, within a couple of weeks, one of the lecturers hired her to do some part-time teaching; this gave her a purpose outside the home and an opportunity to participate in the life of the university.

It soon became apparent, however, that she hadn't understood the full extent of the shortages we were facing. To start with, she complained that a breakfast of bread and margarine—with jam if we were lucky—was insufficient. She needed something more substantial. Eventually we settled on a Ghanaian staple—rice water—that seemed to satisfy her. Later, she asked whether it would be possible to eat chicken from time to time. "I'd love that, but . . ." I answered.

It wasn't easy to find chicken to buy. I gave her cash and the car keys and told her to see what she could find. After some hours, she returned empty-handed. Not only were there no chickens for sale in the market or the local stores, but she'd visited several poultry keepers in the area. None had a bird they were willing to sell. They were keeping the few they had for sale at Easter when the prices would be higher. Finally, she seemed to grasp the reality of our situation!

Although life was difficult for us in Cape Coast, we were in a supportive community. Clement, on his own in Tampa, had a worse time and I wasn't there to help him process the negativity he experienced. He got on well with the students he taught, but his mentor in the math department—the one who'd welcomed him kindly when he first arrived—far from supporting his research work, chose to demean and humiliate him. I never properly understood the reason for what seemed such an abrupt change in attitude. What I do know, all too well, is that mathematicians, who are used to pursuing truth in a highly abstract form, can be trenchant in their criticism of each other's work and blind to how their words are received.

Clement's unhappiness bubbled over in extreme concern for the family. His letters were filled with anxious questions about my life and how I was caring for the children. When Justine, though perfectly healthy, stopped gaining weight for some unexplained reason, his worries increased. Given our dependence on snail mail, it was normally at least two weeks before he received my answers to his questions, which only served to increase his worry. Our anxieties ricocheted back and forth across the ocean in a mutually reinforcing feedback loop.

On a few occasions we were able to talk directly by phone, but the circumstances were unconventional, to say the least. A group of Franciscan missionaries newly arrived in the country had a ham radio that allowed them to communicate directly with their monastery in Massachusetts. From there, the operator was able to patch into the U.S. phone system. From time to time, a group of Americans eager to talk to friends or relatives in the U.S. gathered in the friars' living room. Once contact with the U.S. was established, the operator dialed in to our respective friends and family members. All those in the room listened in. From his apartment in Tampa, Clement couldn't envision the scene at our end as he spilled his angst into the friars' living room for all to hear! It wasn't the private conversation we so badly needed.

I eagerly awaited his return at the end of June.

Toby and Isabelle went with me to Accra to meet Clement. From the roof of the passenger building, we had a good view of aircraft coming and going and waited excitedly, scanning the sky as the 747 bringing him from New York gradually emerged from the clouds. First a pinprick of light, then a small grey object growing steadily as it approached, until finally the huge Pan Am jumbo jet with Clement on board came fully into view, gradually gliding down onto the runway, then bumping a little on the uneven surface as it taxied to a halt. We scrutinized the passengers as they exited the plane.

Toby spotted Clement first as he walked across the tarmac and called out to him, but it was impossible for Clement to see or hear us as we called and waved in welcome. After he had completed immigration formalities and collected his luggage, we drove straight back to Cape Coast, where Justine and Andrea awaited us.

Clement needed time for all his pent-up unhappiness to unravel, and the family needed an opportunity to reconnect and rebuild as we envisioned our future. We decided to spend a few days in Lomé, where we could enjoy the relative luxury of the Sarakawa resort, free of the pervasive shortages in Ghana.

## To Go or to Stay?

While in Tampa, Clement had applied for several jobs. On his return, he had offers pending, but nothing definite. In Lomé, he called to follow up with Professor Donaldson of Howard University, who he'd first met at the mathematical congress in Helsinki. When he returned to our room after the call, I searched his face for news. It gave nothing away. In typical fashion, he kept me guessing.

"Well, did you get through? What did he say?" I asked impatiently.

"Hmm, yes. I spoke to Professor Donaldson."

"And?" His prevarication was driving me crazy.

"Well, um . . ." He was enjoying winding me up, but I noticed his face softening and a faint smile emerging.

"So?" I pressed my advantage.

"One year at most," he said grudgingly.

"They're offering you a one-year appointment?" I asked. "Is that what you're saying? Is that true?" I was starting to get excited.

"That sort of thing," he mumbled.

Finally, bit by bit, the good news emerged. Donaldson had offered him a one-year appointment as visiting assistant professor in the math department. The appointment carried the possibility—but no certainty—of renewal. The salary was at the very bottom of the scale—but it was an offer, nonetheless. Wow!

Excited as we were about the job offer, the decision to accept wasn't a slam dunk by any means. We agonized over it. Should we leave or should we stay? We were settled in Cape Coast and shielded from the worst of the scarcities thanks to the overseas aid I was receiving. The salary offer wasn't great, and the long-term prospects were uncertain. But it was a job offer nonetheless, and a one-year appointment would give Clement a foothold in the U.S. job market. Many of our friends were leaving with no certainty of employment. With or without foreign aid, daily life in Ghana was challenging. When so much time was spent hunting for basic food supplies, it was difficult for any of us to do our jobs effectively. If we couldn't do our jobs what was the point in staying? I asked myself. Moreover, we had three children to educate. Given the way things were going, what sort of future could Ghana offer them?

We debated the issues back and forth as we waited for the official appointment letter to arrive. When it did, we were ready. Despite our ambivalence about America, we decided to pull up our roots and go.

Once the decision was made, we had no time to spare. It was already the beginning of August. The academic year at Howard started at the end of the month, and Clement needed to get there on time if possible. I had to give in my notice and prepare for departure. I buried my sadness and concern for the future in the myriad tasks to be accomplished, including the disposition of our belongings. Should we ship, sell, donate, or discard?

I didn't take time to grieve; I was all business. Clement responded differently to the pressures of departure. In my mind's eye, I see him now sitting in our living room, surrounded by trunks and unsorted documents. The shippers were expected at any moment, but he was engrossed in reading articles from ancient copies of *The Times* he found lurking in one of the trunks! He wasn't to be hurried! We ended up stuffing many books and papers, unsorted, into our boxes, regardless of their value, and shipping more mildewed documents than we'd ever need! They remained untouched for many years.

And so it was that we left Cape Coast for good. I was leaving a place I'd been glad to call home and a job that I loved. The town and university felt safe and familiar. We'd been part of a connected community. The move meant yet another change of environment for the children, another leap into the unknown. There would be new frontiers to navigate.

From an American perspective, we were immigrants joining "the tired, the poor, the huddled masses," but in no way did we see ourselves as the "wretched refuse" of the famed inscription. Far from it. We left Ghana in search of a different future, but with our heads held high. What we saw when we looked at ourselves in the mirror was quite different from what Americans would see when we arrived. There we would be viewed through a different lens.

# America Again, This Time to Stay

Clement went ahead of the family to settle into his job and find a place for us to live; I took the three children to stay with my mother once again. This time we were there for almost two months. Toby went to the village school in Bletchingley for a while. For me, it was an opportunity to strengthen family bonds. We hoped our move to the Washington, DC, area would be permanent, so future visits to England would be shorter and less frequent, contact with family more distant.

It was October before Clement was ready for us to join him. On the descent into Washington, the British Airways pilot announced our impending arrival at "Dewls" (pronounced to rhyme with "mules") airport. Toby, aged seven, knew better. "Dull-less—not Dewls." The pilot's mispronunciation has been a family in-joke ever since. In the baggage area, our luggage was on the same belt as luggage from an Air Japan flight. While I struggled with the baby and paperwork, Toby pulled our bags from the belt. One of the Japanese passengers remarked that I had an able helper. Yes, indeed!

Clement was at the airport to meet us along with Joe Tetteh—a family friend from Osu with whom he had been lodging since he arrived in August. Joe, a bear-hug of a man, welcomed us as warmly as he had welcomed Clement.

## The Valencia Motel

Clement had arranged for us to spend our first week in a suite at the Valencia Motel on Route 1 in Laurel for the princely sum of $80! The motel was a seedy venue if ever there was one, but we could never have anticipated the notoriety it would achieve when it was learned that the 9/11 terrorists lodged there immediately prior to their attack on New York City.

When I drive down Route 1 now, I am reminded of those first days in Maryland. The motel looks smaller and less desirable every time, but it served its purpose. There was space for us all, with cooking facilities into the bargain. During the day, alone with the children and with Clement at work, there was little to do. We walked beside the horse-racing track that abutted the motel and looked through the fence. The lady in the room next door peered from behind lace curtains. Perhaps she sensed how lost we were!

By luck, Bob and Carrol Pearson, colleagues from Cape Coast days, were living not far away in College Park. Bob had a one-year teaching assignment at the University of Maryland. They, too, were trying to find their feet in the U.S. after many years in Ghana but, since Bob was American, knew their way around better than we did. I valued their presence close by and the link to our old life they provided at this time of new beginnings and great uncertainty. On Justine's first birthday Carrol fetched us from Laurel and we celebrated at their home. They also invited us for our first Thanksgiving dinner, prepared by Bob's mother. For many years, I adhered strictly to her protocol in cooking dinner for this unfamiliar all-American holiday.

After the Valencia Motel, our next stepping stone was to be a rental apartment Clement had found in Columbia, a few miles away. The apartment was unfurnished, and we had no furniture of any sort. All we had with us was the luggage we were allowed to bring on the plane, 20 kg per passenger. The household goods we'd shipped from Ghana were in London awaiting forwarding instructions. What we'd used in Tampa remained there in storage. Every evening when Clement returned from the university, we went out in search of the basics: beds, chairs, a table, pots and pans, silverware, etc.

In addition to the Renault Le Car that Clement had just purchased and was using to commute to work, we had the old Dodge we'd used in Florida. Clement had left it at his brother's place in Poughkeepsie when he rejoined us in Ghana; unfortunately, the paperwork got lost in the shuffle and it wasn't registered in Maryland. In my impatience to get started on our new life—and bored with our confinement in the motel—I risked driving it once or twice to scope out our new environment.

One time I ventured to Columbia to register the children at the school they would be attending. The road from Laurel to Columbia seemed windswept and dreary. It was a gloomy November day, and the scene was desolate. I missed the warmth and sunshine of Ghana. I hated having to dress the children in layers of clothing before heading out. More than once, I wondered how I would survive in this new place. But we'd made our decision, we'd cut ourselves loose. We were committed to moving forward, to building a future for ourselves and our children. I tried not to look back.

When we got to the school, the secretary greeted us kindly. "Well, hello, what can I do for you?" she asked. She even smiled. It was a rare gesture of welcome amid the hassle and uncertainty of our arrival. I nearly wept. I hadn't realized how close I was to breaking.

Later, after we'd moved to the apartment, I would often wake in the morning with my fingers frozen in a clasped position. I had to slowly pry them open one by one. A symptom of the stress we were under no doubt. The stressors were real: Would I find a job? How would we manage financially until I did? Would Clement's appointment be renewed? Would we be able to adjust our immigration status? And these long-term concerns were in addition to the daily tasks of managing the family in a new environment.

The children never complained about the many times they had been uprooted and had to adapt to a new home on a different continent. Toby, an airplane aficionado from a very young age, enjoyed the many long-distance flights and was always my able helper. Justine was too young to notice much of anything. Of the three, Isabelle probably experienced the disruption most keenly. We tried to provide all the love and security they needed within the family unit, but was it enough? While there was no point dwelling on the unsettling effects of so much dislocation, I was determined we wouldn't move yet again if we could possibly help it.

While our own concerns were real, I often told myself how privileged we were compared to other immigrants who arrive in the U.S. faced with the task of navigating an unfamiliar system. As newly arrived immigrants, we may have been nobodies in American society, but we had many advantages: our education, money in the bank, a job (albeit for one year), and—maybe most significant of all—the language of our host country. Our many friends who had, like us, left Ghana because of the dire economic circumstances had a much steeper road to climb. They had scattered widely: Saudi Arabia, Sweden, Nigeria, Libya, Ivory Coast, UK, Papua New Guinea, and on. For those who stayed, the conditions grew steadily worse. Although I'd never heard of the American Dream and shared many Europeans' ill-founded disdain for American culture, I knew we were fortunate to be where we were. Despite all the dislocation we'd experienced and an existential uncertainty about our future, we never seriously regretted our decision to leave Ghana.

## An Apartment Home

Columbia, conveniently located a forty-five-minute drive from Howard University, was where Clement had lodged with the Tetteh family, and he had come to like the place. The entrepreneur, James Rouse, developed the town in the green fields of Howard County in the late 1960s. He envisioned a model community in which those of different races, religions, and social classes could live together harmoniously. All would be welcome; small-scale "village" life would be encouraged; and neighbors would meet at communal postboxes. By all accounts it was a place where a mixed-race family would be welcome. It has been our home now for more than forty years!

We moved into an apartment in the Autumn Crest development one week after our arrival. We were happy to leave the prying eyes at the motel. Happy to have a place we could call home. Happy, too, that Toby and Isabelle would be starting school. For Toby this was to be the fourth school in three continents in under a year; for Isabelle—just five years old—it was the third.

We were unaware of the connotation of apartment living in the U.S. when we moved in. The apartment complex included subsidized housing, and our neighbors were a motley crew. I made friends as best I could. I went strawberry picking with a neighbor who was also in a mixed-race marriage and socialized as best I could with a Japanese family living downstairs. The husband was doing postgraduate work at Johns Hopkins University and the wife stayed home with the children. Unfortunately, she spoke little English, but we nodded and smiled at each other over occasional cups of tea, using gestures and broken English to communicate.

When the family returned to Japan, they left us some dishes, including a Pyrex dish in which the mother had baked a cake for us before she left. I use the dish still. Their dinner set went with Toby to Detroit when he started working for Ford;

remnants are still in use in his home in Seattle. We exchanged Christmas cards for many years. Although we could share only a few words, the relationship was important to both of us as foreigners without connection to the surrounding community.

Getting the family settled absorbed most of my energy at first, but the need to look for a job was never far from my thoughts. My identity had always been linked to my work. That link had been severed when we left Cape Coast, but I wasn't ready to relinquish my professional life for long. With my education and experience, I hoped to be able to rebuild my career. I had no idea how difficult it would be.

Soon after our arrival, Joe Tetteh's wife, Avis, asked whether I could take care of their youngest child during the day. She probably thought of it as a win-win situation: I'd help her out with childcare and earn some money while staying home with Justine. I was mortified. Childminding wasn't at all the type of work I'd envisioned! Was this to be my future? I had no special gift or taste for childcare. Besides, I had other priorities. As I explained to Joe and Avis, my overriding concern was to look for a job outside the home. To do so, I would need someone to look after Justine. I couldn't commit to the additional task of looking after someone else's child.

I don't think Avis ever forgave me. As a new immigrant without a job, I was at the bottom of the pile. She probably thought I'd be grateful for the opportunity she'd given me. Yet, there I was, behaving like an entitled English woman. She was right. I resented the place in American society to which she seemed to have assigned me and protested loudly to myself. Didn't she understand that I had been a senior lecturer at a respectable university in Ghana? That we hadn't arrived in the U.S. as mendicants? There was a deep gulf of misunderstanding between us.

A couple of months after we moved into the apartment there

was an unexpected power outage. A power cut in America? I was shocked. I thought we'd left such inconveniences behind in Ghana. It wasn't what I expected in a wealthy country like the United States, especially not on a cold winter's day. Toby and Isabelle were at school when the power failed. I bundled Justine up and went to pass the time at a store close by where we could stay warm. When I arrived home a couple of hours later, I had another surprise. Toby and Isabelle were waiting on the doorstep. They'd been sent home because of the power cut. Shocked again! Did the school check whether anyone would be home to receive them? Did they care? Was this how things worked in America? I had more to learn than I realized.

The outage persisted into the evening. The best we could do was open the door of the gas oven for what little heat would emerge. We had no idea when power would return; my calls to the electric company went unanswered. As the evening drew on, one of Clement's colleagues who lived close by kindly invited us to sleep over at their house. We gathered blankets and toiletries and were on the point of going out the door when the power finally returned. We've never forgotten Ron and Mary Leach's generous gesture on that cold November day and have often told them how much it meant to us.

I'd left behind the safe container of my youth and the familiarity of our life in Cape Coast. We'd dragged our three small children from one continent to another in pursuit of better long-term opportunities without pausing for long to reflect on the effects on their young lives. We didn't feel like the immigrants welcomed to Ellis Island, but we were—truth to tell—adrift in a foreign country. Much as we may have wished to "consider the future and the past with an equal mind," as T.S. Eliot advises in *Four Quartets*, it would be a long time before America began to feel like home. Amid so much uncertainty, the Leaches' kind gesture was a welcome moment of connection.

# Part IV

# A Rough Start

*I have wiped the slate clean,*
*No more reminders from the past.*
*Memories of what I have been,*
*Have vanished at long last.*
*I look forward to my future new,*
*Where all is territory strange.*

—*George Bernard Shaw, "A New Start"*

# Settling In—or Not

America is said to be a welcoming country. Having lived here many years, I realize how many groups and individuals work hard to make asylum seekers, refugees, and other immigrants feel welcome, but no groups reached out to us when we arrived. I've often thought that we would have been better understood and accepted if we'd arrived from Ghana poor and needy. We didn't fit that stereotype. We're grateful that we landed in Columbia where, as a biracial family, we were protected from the worst of the racism still prevalent in the U.S., but even in Columbia, we were outliers. We arrived straight from Africa and spoke with funny accents. We were better educated, more traveled than most of our neighbors. Moreover, we were not impecunious! We simply didn't fit into any recognizable box. Even now, we're something of an anomaly, our connections to the community not as tightly stitched as one might have expected after more than forty years.

## An Improbable Decision

Although Clement's contract was for just one year, we convinced ourselves we'd come to stay and set about buying a house. In retrospect the decision seems borderline irresponsible, but we aspired to middle-class normality even though our situation was far from normal. Clement's appointment was at a salary designed with hapless immigrants in mind; there was a possibility—but no certainty—of renewal. Our visa status was tenuous. I had no job and wasn't even sure I'd be allowed to work. We were both foreigners with no family close by. We had three small children. We had no idea what lay ahead. Looking back, it's hard to recreate exactly how our thinking went, yet I don't recall us hesitating once about the decision. We didn't even consider starting with a town house, which for many is the first step in home ownership. We needed a house, and that was that.

I wonder now whether we were suffering from a severe case of what in today's vernacular would be called White entitlement, expecting to be able to get whatever we asked of life. Maybe, except that White entitlement doesn't quite fit because Clement is Black. No matter, we acted in unison. Arriving in the U.S., Clement also carried with him a measure of entitlement, given his family background and the absence of pervasive racism in his childhood experience.

Although we worried about getting our green cards—a process that would take several years—we never seriously considered the possibility we might be deported. We'd never heard of redlining or the differential treatment of Blacks when it came to getting loans. Even the builder was surprised when the mortgage approval came through.

The house we purchased was part of a development under construction, and several optional extras were on offer. Our last-minute decision to include a basement may have been our one concession to the fact that a long-term stay was by no means assured. Americans liked basements, I told myself. Having a basement would add significantly to the house's value if, by chance, we had to sell.

The building site wasn't far from our apartment in Autumn Crest. We followed step-by-step as a deep hole was dug for the basement, the foundations were laid, and the four-bedroom colonial took shape above ground. We were familiar with solid-brick houses in England and concrete-block construction in Ghana, so we were amazed by what seemed to be the flimsy construction technique. The outside walls consisted of a simple wooden frame supporting fluffy insulation material sandwiched between a plywood sheet on the inside and a protective wrap on the outside. I called it disparagingly a "matchsticks and cotton wool" building, but soon realized that this was the standard method of construction in the U.S. It was just one example of the ways in which innovative techniques and mass production have enabled America to bring a middle-class consumer-driven lifestyle within reach of a large swathe of the population. We, too, were the beneficiaries.

The house was ready within six months. So, too, thanks to frequent visits to furniture warehouses and garage sales, was the bare-bones set of furniture we needed to augment what was already in our apartment. Our shipment from Ghana—with a few furniture items, household goods, books, and assorted documents—arrived shortly after we moved in.

We had achieved homeownership—a key component of the American Dream—more quickly than most immigrants. But that wasn't how we thought of it at the time. We loved owning our own house and the space it gave us, but we were by no means living a dream. We'd barely started on the long road to "belonging."

## *Fish out of Water*

Settling in involved figuring out some basic facts of American life. We were surprised that to arrange for telephone service, you have to go to a shopping outlet, not the telephone company's offices. When we first arrived in Tampa, we circled the telephone exchange building several times looking for the entrance before realizing that this wasn't the place to sign up for phone service.

We were surprised to learn that having a bank called First National doesn't mean there's a Second or—God forbid—a

Third National bank somewhere down the street. It was only later we realized that the term "first" is a common hyperbole of American marketing lingo and not a literal description.

We were surprised, too, at the extent to which mass marketing and the focus on profit conspire to limit customer choice. Good luck if you want to buy linens in a color that was so "in" last year but is passé this year and nowhere to be found. More seriously, good luck to those who live in low-income areas where market forces mean that fresh vegetables are simply unavailable.

We were surprised and angry when the insurance company in Maryland would only offer us a super-expensive policy reserved for indigents and miscreants. They deemed us outrageously irresponsible because of the policy we'd used in Florida, even though it was what the car dealer there had recommended. I still don't know whether there are real differences between Florida and Maryland where car insurance is concerned or whether the dealer in Florida sold us an inferior policy he considered appropriate for people who looked like us.

We were surprised again when Sears refused our credit card application just when we needed the convenience of a card to furnish our house. The reason they gave was not because of bad debts (we had none), nor because of what we owed (we had no debts of any sort), but because we had no credit history on record. Did it mean that if you have never borrowed in the past, you can't start borrowing now? The logic escaped me. It certainly didn't feel very welcoming.

I understand better now. We weren't yet on the treadmill of the American financial system. The system works well for us now that we're "on the inside" but makes little provision for outsiders or those who are on the wrong side of the socio-economic divide. We found that to be true of many aspects of American life. For all its focus on the rights of the individual, the American system has serious shortcomings when it comes to serving individuals who are not part of the mainstream.

In the end we managed to persuade Sears that, if they wanted us as customers for the long term, they should provide us with a credit card then, when we really needed it. Duking it out with Sears was the first in a long series of situations where I found myself doing battle with "the system." It became quite a habit. The children got to recognize signs that my indignation had been roused and I was about to lock horns with some unsuspecting third party. Their embarrassment at my entanglements has relaxed to good-humored amusement as the years have passed.

Bit by bit we learned to cope with the day-to-day practicalities of homeownership in America, but we were not in a hurry to integrate with the prevailing culture. Anchored in—or should I say "boxed" in—by our own traditions, we didn't feel obligated to adopt, or even try very hard to understand, American values and behavior patterns.

I wasn't at ease with the informality that led every last reception clerk to call me by my first name and was infuriated (still am) by young doctors who chose to introduce themselves by saying, "Good morning, Sarah. I am Dr Smith." If I responded, "And I'm Dr. Lutterodt," the appointment usually went downhill from there! Although I have learned to hold my tongue and swallow my pride, I still lean toward the principle gleaned from G.K. Chesterton's writings many moons ago: The name you call another person represents the relationship you have with them. First-name calling, with its implication of equality and familiarity, should be reserved for those with whom you have an established bond. Alas, time has passed me by as far as that maxim is concerned.

I was floored, too, by the lack of exposure to other countries and cultures. When we said we'd just arrived from Ghana, many asked, "Were you close to the massacres?"

"Uh?" I'd respond, wondering what on earth they were talking about.

"You know, the cult, the ones who committed suicide. Jonestown," they'd offer in explanation.

"No! No! That wasn't Ghana." I was shocked at their confusion. "You must be thinking of Guyana. Different country, different continent."

A deep ignorance of the world outside America seemed to underlie their question. "After all," they appeared to be saying, "both countries are far away, have similar sounding names, and likely are subject to the same types of excesses." Few were able to engage with the particularities of our recent experience. It was just too remote.

Complementing the lack of familiarity with other countries—and equally surprising to us as newcomers—was the flag-waving and extreme displays of patriotism on national holidays and days of remembrance. While I was happy for the children to participate in the neighborhood Fourth of July parade and enjoyed Columbia's lakefront fireworks display—visible from our front yard until the trees grew too tall—the holiday didn't have the same deep significance for us that it did for those in our community.

The closest the British get to such demonstrations of national pride are during times surrounding royal weddings or jubilees and the raucous—and oh-so-dated—rendering of "Rule, Britannia" on the last night of the Proms at the Royal Albert Hall. "Britannia rules the waves!" Really? How many English people take that seriously anymore? Certainly not me, not then. Having lived nearly half of my life outside England, extreme forms of British patriotism were as alien to me as the patriotism that seems so deeply rooted in the American psyche.

A professor who gave me some part-time research tasks while I was looking for a job asked me once, "Where is home for you now?" I hesitated before replying, "Ghana, I guess." No sooner had I said it than I thought, "Ghana is now part of my past. How can I call it home? We've no plans to return there." The truth of my status confronted me. I didn't really have a home country. We didn't have green cards, let alone U.S. nationality. I carried a British passport and was still a British national but hadn't lived there in years. National identity didn't seem very important to me, but we all need to belong somewhere.

Then—and now—I like to think of myself as a citizen of the world. Yet no matter how long I've lived outside England or how much my relationship to the U.S. has changed, I cannot escape my English persona. I wouldn't be surprised if casual acquaintances in the U.S. still refer to me as "the English woman" or "the woman with the English accent." Ever the outsider, my English roots are an inextricable part of my identity and will always set me apart.

Clement likes it that way. An anglophile at heart, he still gets upset when my language reflects American usage, even though my accent remains easily recognizable. But retaining my accent is only part of the story. Despite my transnational aspirations, I cannot escape the indelible imprint of my formative years, the safe container that shaped me and the principles imbibed from earliest childhood. I'm thinking, for example, of my attitude to material goods.

The values absorbed during the rationing of my post-war childhood and reinforced during the times of scarcity in Ghana were at odds with the consumer culture we encountered in America. I was puzzled by the close association between God and Mammon in the American worldview. Epitomized by the business acumen and financial success of religious groups as disparate as Quakers, Mormons, and Mennonites and finding its modern expression in the purveyors of a "prosperity Gospel," the close link between religion and worldly success seeps into American life in many ways—not least in the guise of an overly materialistic, throwaway mindset. Even though I have now been acculturated more than I like to admit, and live surrounded by far more "stuff" than I truly need, I still find the rush to consumer spending deeply troubling. I stay away from stores and shopping malls as much as possible.

When we first arrived in the U.S., I didn't even try to conform. Our income dictated the need to manage our expenses carefully. Our children didn't get new school outfits every year if what they already had was still serviceable. We didn't replace silverware or linens just because we fancied something new and different. And if a toaster or iron stops working, I still seek out someone to repair it rather than buy a new one, even when that is the less costly solution. Above all, food is never wasted.

During our first years in Columbia, I was appalled by the many occasions when the children's friends who had stopped over for a meal left half of the food on their plates without any appearance of compunction. Afterward I would remind our children of our experience in Ghana.

"Don't you ever waste food like John [or Jim or Ann or Mary] did," I would admonish them. "Only put on your plate what you can eat." They would nod dutifully as I continued my rant, "Don't you remember how difficult it was to find food in Ghana? Many people in the world go hungry every day. We should never let food go to waste."

More generally, neither Clement nor I were ready to adopt prevailing modes of child-rearing. I was shocked by the long summers when children seemed to drift idly between pool and home, with frequent stops at the ice cream truck in between. I enrolled our children in whatever summer schools were available. Their education was paramount. I was floored when a third-grade teacher told me she spent several weeks, if not months, at the beginning of each school year repeating the math the children had been taught in second grade, presuming they'd forgotten it all over the summer.

Nor did we share most American parents' passion for sports. While many immigrant parents try hard to fit in with American culture by immersing their children in sports and other after-school activities, this was not our way. Although I enrolled our children in music lessons and cub scouts, even soccer and basketball, they didn't have the same endless succession of after-school activities that other children did. For his part, Clement remained singularly focused on the children's academic education, giving notional support to other activities. He railed against the lack of discipline in American homes, to which he attributed the high levels of cigarette smoking, alcohol use, and worse among American teens. One high school principal referred to it as "middle-class neglect." We could relate to that.

## Outsiders By Choice or By Design?

After we'd moved to our new home, we were in the catchment of a different primary school, meaning yet another change in school for Toby and Isabelle. We decided instead to enroll them in a Catholic school in nearby Ellicott City. Columbia schools were open plan, and we thought the more traditional structure and discipline of Catholic school would be closer to what they had known in Ghana. Besides, they would be introduced to Catholic values, which were important to me. We were unprepared for what we would find and unsure how to respond.

As newcomers, we didn't understand how Catholic schools fit into the landscape of American education, nor did we understand how Ellicott City—just a few miles down the road—could differ so much from Columbia in its social mix and racial attitudes. There were few children of color in the school. I was too naïve to recognize what that meant and too unfamiliar with America's deep-seated racism to prepare our children for what they would experience.

At first, and for many months, Isabelle would come home

complaining, "They don't like me because I'm brown." I talked with the teachers, but we didn't understand each other. Later, a child called Isabelle the "N-word" in the playground. When she complained to the head teacher, the response was, "Never mind." Isabelle was then in fourth grade, and we had already decided to move her to a different school, so I didn't complain. I regret that now. If such a thing were to happen today, I would certainly speak out—and very loudly too!

At the first parent-teacher conference, Toby's fourth-grade teacher told me, unashamedly, she hadn't expected Toby's mother to look like me. I was confused. Had she never encountered a mixed-race family before? It didn't seem like she meant to be offensive, but how else was I to understand her comment? Was she oblivious to how her words would land with me?

From the start I'd drilled into the children how important it was for them to speak up in class in America, unlike in Ghana where such behavior might be frowned on. I reiterated the lesson after the parent-teacher conference, when Toby's teachers said he wasn't participating actively in class. One or two weeks later, the music teacher, Ms. Williams, called to say how pleased she was at the change in Toby's behavior.

"What did you say to him? He's like a different child," she said. "I just thought he wasn't very intelligent!"

"I'm happy to hear he's started speaking up," I responded politely.

What I was thinking was far from polite: Do you know who you are talking to? My children are among the brightest, most intelligent on the planet. If you haven't yet understood that, you really have a problem. The older me, more familiar with the stereotyping that is so widespread in American society, might have reacted more cautiously: You are up against a system that consistently fails to recognize that Black children can be high achievers. You are dealing with a centuries-old power structure and the biases that have helped perpetuate it. While continuing to advocate for the children, you need to prepare them for this reality.

Clement understood our children would need to perform twice as well as their White peers for their ability to be recognized. He told them so frequently. I wasn't so sure then; I know now that he was right. It's possible that if I had been more aware of the systemic racism we were facing, I would have succumbed more readily to its presumptions, less confident in championing my children's progress. It could be that my own naïveté was a blessing in disguise.

If Ms. Williams was guileless, Ms. Quist's intention seemed more sinister. When in second grade Isabelle wanted to bring her schoolbooks home one weekend so I could help with her reading, Ms. Quist told her not to. "Don't think you're ever going to get ahead!" Isabelle heard her say. From what deep well of White exceptionalism did that come? Didn't she realize the implication of her words or the damaging effect they would have on a sensitive seven-year-old? Microaggressions of this sort are common still today. All too often, the perpetrators are simply unaware of their deeply held assumptions and the damage their words can cause. This lack of awareness is a "privilege" White people still enjoy. The harmful effects of Ms. Quist's discriminatory attitude—conscious or otherwise—lingered with Isabelle well into her adult years.

My efforts to help the children develop friendships met with very mixed success. For Isabelle's seventh birthday, we invited all the girls in her class to her party. They came and seemed to enjoy themselves. I waited all year for Isabelle to get a return invitation. None came. I was deeply hurt.

Since the school was several miles away, most of her classmates lived at a distance, so I was happy when I learned that one of her classmates lived a couple of blocks away and took the same school bus each day. We invited the girl for a playdate, but the favor was never returned. The family's subsequent behavior sent a clear message that while token politeness was appropriate, any closer relationship between the two families wasn't welcome. There was an unspoken barrier. Thus far, but no further.

My response to such incidents was to join the school's PTA board, hoping my involvement might help soften attitudes as teachers and parents got to know me better. It didn't work out that way. My contributions were often sidelined; the school secretary, whose son was in class with Isabelle, made little effort to hide her dislike. I tried to blow past the sidelong glances and innuendos but may have been too thick-skinned to understand the extent of the animosity simmering below the surface. Later, Isabelle developed a genuine and lasting friendship with Adrienne, who joined the class in second grade. When they were adults, she confided to Isabelle that her mother often wondered why the other parents disliked me so much. The pervasive animosity hadn't been a figment of my imagination.

Toby, too, had his share of rejection. In sixth grade, he wanted to work with a classmate on a science fair project. The boy's parents nixed the idea on the grounds that we lived too far away for them to be able to work together. Nonsense, I thought to myself when Toby told me. Were Americans ever reluctant to drive a few miles? I resolved to teach the other parents a lesson! Toby's project would be unbeatable.

With the benefit of a little coaching, Toby won first prize in the science fair competition that year and went on to repeat the success in both seventh and eighth grade. Three years in a row! By the time he had completed middle school, even the most die-hard parents had to admit he was the best student in the class, and we started to notice subtle changes in their behavior toward us.

Sometimes the behaviors were not so subtle. At one birthday party toward the end of eighth grade, Toby was greeted by the boy's grandmother. She wanted to "stroke his skin" because he was "so intelligent." Should we have counted that as progress? Today, few serious commentators on race relations would fail to label such behavior as one of the more offensive forms of micro-aggression.

I thought I might find a welcoming community at church, but it was not to be. The local Catholic parish operated—and continues to operate—out of two interfaith centers. In each of them, different congregations—Catholic, Protestant, and Jewish—share common worship and office spaces. Here was a church community that was open-minded and progressive. I hoped they would extend a hand of welcome. None was offered. My deep disappointment lingered for many years. Even now, I get angry when I think about it.

After I submitted the parish registration form, offertory collection envelopes started arriving regularly, but the only personal response was a call from the parish secretary. She wanted to check on a detail concerning one of the children's baptisms. I almost shouted into the phone, "Is that all you're interested in? Don't you have a better way to welcome newly arrived families to the parish?"

My outburst was greeted with shocked silence. I was asking the secretary to step out of her habitual role, and she didn't know what to do. I doubt she passed on information about my angry "cri de coeur." In any case, there was no follow-up.

I attended Mass faithfully with the children each Sunday and learned to recognize other regulars, but no one thought to greet us. There was barely a smile or a simple "hello." My British sense of propriety prevented me from making the first move. Once, when the chair of the pastoral council was greeting people after Mass, I complained to him about the lack of welcome. He was surprised. "I thought we did a good job of welcoming people," he told me. He seemed to be listening, but nothing changed. We joined Amway—the multilevel marketing company—for a while soon after our arrival in Columbia and found them to provide a more responsive, welcoming community.

When I arranged for Toby to make his First Communion, the associate pastor came on a home visit to make sure he was suitably prepared. I looked forward to the opportunity to connect with a parish leader. Alas, Father Frank was in a hurry and singularly focused on the task at hand. After talking with Toby, he didn't pause to enquire about the family's well-being and refused my offer of a drink. I have no reason to think he was being deliberately exclusionary—just unthinking. I'd hate to count how often I have been similarly insensitive to another's need for a kind word or a moment of attention.

True, I could have been more proactive in trying to forge connections with the parish, but Clement wanted nothing to do with organized religion, and I found it difficult to make the first move. If the parish had reached out to us, it would have felt different. So why didn't I go in search of a more welcoming community? There were surely many religious congregations in Columbia who would've been happy to reach out to us. The answer is as clear to me now as it was then. The strictures of my Catholic childhood were too deeply embedded in my psyche. Apostasy was unthinkable. The Jesuits had been right! I wasn't ready to step beyond the religious boundaries erected so indelibly in my youth. That part of the container held me still.

Our neighborhood was mostly White, but there were one or two families of color. An African American couple with two boys similar in age to our children lived opposite. The father was active in local politics and well-known to everyone in the community. They were outgoing and friendly, always including us in their celebrations and family events. We also got to know another family living on the far side of the neighborhood who were attuned to racial complexity. The parents, both

White, had adopted four mixed-race children and were very open to our situation.

Our relationship with others was more tenuous. One time, I was among a group of mothers gathered in the street while our children were playing. One of them—a mother of three boys—commented that a new family with "two nice, fair boys" had just moved in. I don't think she meant to be offensive or unkind. Rather, she seemed completely unaware of the effect her comment might have on me, a mother whose children were certainly not fair. Could they nonetheless be "nice" in her estimation? I wondered.

Oftentimes it was difficult to know whether the challenges we experienced were simply behavior patterns that were unfamiliar to us—what any newcomers to the area might experience—or whether they carried a racial undertone. When there is a frequency and pattern to such events, however, it is difficult to avoid jumping to conclusions. On one occasion a member of the neighborhood babysitting group volunteered to look after Justine—still a baby—for a few hours. When the day came closer, however, she mumbled something to the effect that it was going to be very difficult for her and that Justine might have to sleep on the floor. Whatever was she thinking? Needless to say, I found another solution.

When it came to connecting with our neighbors, my own stiff upper lip may have been more of an impediment than any prejudices they harbored. At the end of a meeting with other mothers in the babysitting group one time, the conversation turned to their time in college. Finding no point of connection, I didn't join in. My college experience had been so different. I listened as they talked about the classes they had taken and their life in the dorms. I was amused by their delight in being alums of what I considered, with an unhealthy measure of British snobbery, to be "red brick" institutions (and therefore substandard in British eyes). They didn't think to include me in the conversation, and I took refuge in the nostrums of my British upbringing. Who knows what they were thinking or how they interpreted my silence? There was an invisible barrier. I didn't try to position myself within their frame of reference; I didn't even know how.

I had a similar experience when Isabelle was in middle school. Many is the time I sat by myself during Saturday morning basketball games while the other mothers chatted idly together, making little or no effort to include me. To be sure, I made no attempt to join them either. I observed their world, but simply didn't feel I belonged. I can't say for sure that race was an issue. Was it hubris on my part? Or simply that our interests and experiences diverged so widely?

In response to such events, Clement chided me for not sharing my own background. He thought that my story would surely have changed their attitude toward me and not doing so reinforced their stereotypes of a woman married to a Black man. If I was disrespected by people of lesser attainment, it diminished us both. True, they seemed to have put me in a box—and Clement too. True, too, the real box was probably not the one of their imaginings. Although telling my story might have shifted the way they viewed me, I thought that speaking up would simply reinforce the distance between us, replacing one set of barriers with another. I preferred to stay silent, even if it meant being alone. I simply didn't belong.

Thinking back, I wonder what I could have done differently. It was probably foolish to think the other mothers would be able to relate to my life experiences. Even my own family has trouble doing that. Maybe I should've made more effort to connect beneath the level of idle chatter. As parents, we could surely have found common ground. But I was never good at small talk, and that is where any conversation would've had to start. I had an outsider mindset. Even today I'm ill at ease when similar situations arise, as they often do.

## *Who Was I Now?*

The problems adjusting to our new life were compounded for me by the difficulty I had finding a job. Cut off from the satisfaction of a career—and thrust into a life without domestic help—I was presented with a personal challenge. Who am I? I asked myself. I no longer entertained any illusions I could "save the world;" I just needed a job. I would take what I could get. Given the feminist struggles of the time, staying home with the children just didn't seem to count in terms of being a productive member of society. I needed the stimulation of work outside the home. Moreover, we needed the additional income.

With Clement's help, I walked my résumé to numerous university departments in the area, but to no avail. I answered a ton of classified ads. Nothing. My work experience in Ghana simply didn't count. It was even difficult to have my university degrees recognized since, at that time, British universities didn't provide transcripts. When I sought a statement of educational equivalence from a respectable organization in order to get a teaching job, I was told I didn't have sufficient math credits to teach the subject. "How did they think I got a physics degree from Oxford without math?" I wondered.

When a neighboring school system offered me a job, it was at a salary that barely covered the cost of daycare! They gave me credit for having a Ph.D., but my years of experience counted for nothing. I was insulted. "I know it's hard" was the recruiter's unhelpful response when I complained. I declined the offer.

A vacancy as head of science came up at a high school closer to home. The salary was better, but the job would've been a stretch since I had no inside knowledge of the school system. As head of department, I would surely have floundered. Thankfully, a wise official on the school board stopped me short: "Would you want to be around American teenagers all day?" he asked.

"Well, when you put it that way, maybe not," I responded after a few moments' thought.

I will always be grateful for his question. It helped me recognize that school teaching wasn't for me. The line of work in which I eventually landed was far better suited to my temperament and abilities. I needed to focus what caring abilities I had on my own family. Besides, I was told that after teaching school, it would be difficult to move back into academia, and that was still my goal. As weeks stretched into months, however, I had no choice but to look for other possibilities.

I ended up doing a wide range of part-time jobs, whatever I could scrounge—odd-ball educational research tasks for a professor at a local university, development of a curriculum for first-line supervisors, teaching a lab class at a community college, writing scripts for training videos. It was while preparing material for the training videos that I came across training materials for power plant technicians developed by a company right in Columbia. I could do that, I thought, and sent in my résumé.

The call came on a snowy day when school was canceled and we were all home. I was on the floor playing games with the children.

"Would you like to come for interview?" the caller asked.

"You mean right now?" I had to do a mental U-turn to take in what was happening. After all my failed attempts to find a job, was I finally being asked to come for a serious interview?

"Sure. Come on over."

"OK. Give me an hour or so, and I'll be there."

I quickly changed my clothes, hid my disheveled hair under a woolen cap, and drove the few miles across town to the company's office.

It was as simple as that. A snowy day. On the floor with the children. A phone call. A brief conversation. An invitation to come for interview. In little more than an hour I was catapulted into an office where everyone was busy doing something important. Or so it seemed. Suddenly my life had taken a new direction.

The interview that snowy day was my entry point into the world of American business. General Physics was to be my home away from home for many years. It was a world with its own rules and boundaries and blindness, different from any I'd ever known. Survival in that world would require me to assume a new identity. I would have to put the past firmly behind me.

However much I welcomed the opportunity, settling into my new future wasn't easy.

# Thrown to the Wolves

The initial interview with General Physics (GP) led to others, each more promising than the last. After a few weeks I received a job offer. It was my first major break into the U.S. job market after nearly two years of searching. I was ecstatic! GP management, for their part, figured that with my qualifications in nuclear physics and curriculum development I was well positioned to help them address significant new training requirements in the nuclear power industry and were pleased to vaunt my credentials. Neither of us understood the extent or durability of the barriers I would face.

## An Alien World

Founded by Dr. Bob Deutsch, a former professor of nuclear engineering at Catholic University in Washington, DC, GP provided training and other services for the commercial nuclear industry. In 1982, when I was hired, the industry was subject to increased scrutiny following the catastrophic accident at the Three Mile Island (TMI) nuclear plant in Pennsylvania. Unlike the accident at Chernobyl in the USSR seven years later, TMI hadn't led directly to any deaths, nor had there been any leakage of radioactive material. Nonetheless, the horror of what might have happened sent shockwaves through the industry. The Institute for Nuclear Plant Operations (INPO) was established to initiate or tighten standards governing all aspects of plant operation, including training. My role would be to help the company comply with the new training standards.

GP was staffed largely by officers and enlisted men who had served on nuclear-powered submarines. To join the "nuclear navy," as it was called, they had been through a rigorous selection process and were justly proud of their technical prowess. To minimize any ill feelings carried over from their days in the service, the officers—mostly engineers educated at the elite U.S. Naval Academy—were separated organizationally from enlisted men. I was hired by the training division, which was staffed by the enlisted men. These "navy nukes" had spent many long tours of duty under the ocean on nuclear submarines; they were tough and resilient with a can-do attitude. They were successful as seat-of-the-pants trainers but, with little or no formal education beyond high school, were ill-equipped and disinclined to comply with the structured approach to training INPO now required. Along with many of their clients, they saw little value in the new standards and resented the implicit criticism of their customary teaching methods. It should have been no surprise that many projected their resentment onto me. I represented all they found objectionable in the standards; my expertise was definitely not welcome.

My years in academia and my British upbringing left me ill-prepared for the rough and tumble of the American workplace, still less one staffed largely by former military men—and they were all men. I was a complete novice. I had no knowledge of workplace training. I had never set foot in a nuclear power plant. I had no real-world experience outside the classroom. I was now immersed in an environment where educational credentials took second place to experience and where qualified women were few and far between. But I needed a job and eagerly accepted the offer of a part-time position. I realized it would take time to figure out how to apply my knowledge and skills in this new setting, but I didn't know how much I had to learn. Moreover, I lacked the interpersonal and political skills that might have helped lower barriers. To my coworkers, I must have seemed like an alien from another planet. They were probably just as nervous as I was. Even those who were well-intentioned didn't know how to help. In retrospect, I wonder what I could have done to allay their fears and calm my own apprehension.

## Baptism by Fire

On my first day at GP, I met my boss, Ed, and his boss, Ernie, who was vice president, at Baltimore/Washington International Airport for a flight to Sacramento, where we were to discuss INPO's training requirements with senior managers at the Rancho Seco Nuclear Power plant. We had agreed for me to start the job as soon as the children were back at school. I had no days in the office to get ready, but I'd read the INPO document backwards and forwards. I was excited. I'd even bought a new outfit. But I was nervous too. Maybe not nervous enough. I was being thrown like a lamb to the wolves.

Though coming from quite different backgrounds, Ernie and Ed worked well together. Ernie was the personification of elitism. A graduate of the Naval Academy and an expert in nuclear plant operations, he often conducted plant audits on behalf of the Nuclear Regulatory Commission. His office was always immaculate, the desk cleared except for a ledger in which he made occasional notes. Always suave and gracious, he seemed to regard me—the obvious outsider—with benign amusement. In contrast, Ed had come up through the ranks. He had risen to a position of leadership within GP, where his quiet competence was well regarded. Both treated me with respect during the three-day site visit. Having made the decision to hire me, they had a vested interest in my success. The managers at Rancho Seco knew Ernie and Ed well and valued their judgment. If they were skeptical about my role, they kept their misgivings to themselves.

Back in the office, my navy nuke colleagues were not so reserved.

Brad, the manager of Operator Training Services, who reported to Ed and would be responsible for ensuring GP's work product complied with the new standards, was my nemesis-in-chief.

A few weeks after the trip to Sacramento, Brad called three of us into his office: Rick Dobbs, Herb Jones, and me. Rick, a personable young man, always anxious to please, was a supervisor in Brad's organization. Herb served as a content expert. He had been a reactor operator at TMI at the time of the accident and assisted in the recovery. Both Rick and Herb reported to Brad. They were part of the "line" organization while I was in a "staff position." People in line positions made money for the company, while those in advisory or staff positions were treated as a cost. Making money was what counted. The way an employee's time was accounted for made a big difference to the company's bottom line. I learned that later. When I first joined the company, I was oblivious of its significance.

The rigid hierarchical structure at GP, and the autocratic or subservient attitudes that prevailed, surprised me. The hierarchy seemed at odds with the U.S.'s democratic traditions. I wondered whether it was a carryover from the military, where many employees started their careers. Whatever its origin, the pecking order was evident in the day-to-day workings of the company. VPs had corner offices; directors and managers got windows; worker bees were stacked in office cubes. My staff position earned me a window office, but the physical separation from my coworkers probably reinforced the cultural barriers between us.

Being in a staff position protected me to some extent from the worst predations of the profit motive, but even in a staff position you were expected to add monetary value to whatever projects you worked on. This reality was entirely new to me. In academia, you worked on a project or research paper until you got it right. In business, you had to work within the hours allocated in the project budget, which was driven by tight deadlines and what the client was willing to pay.

In time, I came to identify completely with client satisfaction and profitability as the drivers for company decision making. But when Brad called the meeting, I had no insight into this way of thinking. Brad saw no value in academic qualifications. As manager, he was looking for evidence that my advice added value—or quick proof that it didn't. Ed had probably told him to include me in the meeting, and he had no option but to go along.

Brad kicked things off, saying, "We need to get our ducks in a row. The Muddy Ridge Plant wants a course on reactor physics in line with this new stuff coming out of INPO." Then, grinning at me, he added, "Bunch of baloney if you ask me. But Sarah knows all about it—eh?" I smiled nervously in response.

After reading one or two sentences from the client's document, Brad threw it down on the table. "What do y'all think they're looking for? Beats me."

Rick and Herb shared a few jumbled ideas. Then, sensing their confusion, I held up a copy of a classic text that INPO had used in developing the standard and started to explain. I hadn't got far before Brad interrupted. "Doesn't make a lot of sense to me," he said, sounding irritated.

Herb intervened. "We should get Sarah's input. She's worked with this stuff before."

"Very well," Brad responded. Then, ignoring Herb's comment, he turned to Rick. "Rick, see if you can figure out how to handle that part."

He picked up the document again, saying, "Moving right along. Let's see what else they're asking for."

After reading a section describing how the client wanted tests constructed, he concluded mockingly, "Darned if I know what they're getting at. Some goddam Ph.D. guy has come up with all this fancy language."

As the three of them tried to tease out what the client was looking for, Brad wondered aloud, "What do you think NU.S. will do?" NU.S. was GP's main competitor. I had kept quiet, listening to their back and forth, but Brad's question gave me an idea that might give GP an edge over the competition. I decided to jump in.

"We could propose a test item bank," I ventured. "In other words—"

No sooner had I opened my mouth than Brad made a T with his rough, workman hands. I raised my eyebrows, not sure what he meant.

Herb interpreted. "He's saying time out. He wants to end the meeting."

And that was that. Brad wasn't ready to listen to me. None of them understood what INPO was asking for, but neither the client nor the competition knew any better. Anything I said would be just whistling in the wind.

With time, the industry changed. Client organizations hired personnel with knowledge of formal instructional methods; the old ways were no longer good enough. There were even clients who specifically sought out my expertise. But that was later. At the time, Brad could safely sideline me, ignoring my input as being too academic, outside his comfort zone, and ill-suited to the client world he knew and understood.

Only Herb tried to include me in the work of the department. He had been chastened by his experience at TMI and understood what I was up against as a professional woman. After we'd been discussing a work-related matter one day, the conversation turned to the upcoming company picnic. I planned to attend even though I didn't much enjoy such functions.

"I'd like you to meet my wife, Dorothy," Herb said. "She will be at the picnic."

"I'd love to meet her," I replied.

"You know, she's still working at TMI. She's the only woman engineer on the cleanup team." I sensed that Herb empathized with what I was going through at GP, knowing what his wife experienced at TMI as a professional woman. I was grateful for his thoughtfulness.

Others in the department were conflicted, unsure what to make of my advice. They were inclined to follow Brad's lead, but knew that Dr. Deutsch, the founder and president of the company, supported me. Maybe things would've been easier if they hadn't found me intimidating or if I'd found a way to soften my message. But we didn't find common ground. Although I was rapidly losing confidence in my ability to make a useful contribution, I'd fought too hard for the job to give up easily.

To his credit, Rick Dobbs looked for opportunities for me that didn't interfere with "business as usual." One such task was to package GP's courses so that students could receive university credits for completing them. Many former military personnel were looking for a way to earn a university degree quickly and at minimal cost. The opportunity to earn credits certified by the American Educational Association would be a good selling point for GP.

I worked hard to complete the required paperwork, assemble the training materials in the required format, and organize a visit by the team of evaluators. As department manager, Brad hosted the evaluation team's visit. He opened the meeting by introducing staff and instructors within his organization, happy to claim ownership of the course documents that were laid out for review. He didn't even mention my name. All my work in preparing for the visit was simply ignored. I was devastated. I crawled home that evening, pouring out my tale of hurt and anger on the family. At work, I lacked the confidence to voice my complaint.

It became more and more apparent that no matter my paper qualifications, I needed to show I could "turn a buck." This was how Ernie put it a few months after I'd started at GP. The edge to his words was carefully hidden beneath his usual polished manner. Even in a staff position, a high percentage of one's time should be billable. Better still, one should be winning profitable contracts. I was doing neither. Although no one said so directly, it was clear that the job opportunity I'd grasped so eagerly was slipping away from me. I was worried.

Ed was still my boss, and he supported me as best he could, but he, too, needed my time to be billable. The bottom line was what counted. He hinted gently several times that maybe I could teach a reactor physics course for a client. There was always a need for on-site instructors. The thought terrified me! It would put me in front of a class of navy nukes—or equivalent grunts (to use the language of the time)—who would be merciless in their critique. I was, after all, a woman who'd never worked at a plant. I'd never got my hands dirty adjusting valves or experienced the delicate maneuvers needed when inserting or removing fuel rods. While familiar with the basic principles of reactor physics, I would be teaching a subject whose detailed application to plant operation was new to me. Moreover, such an assignment would require extensive travel which would be incompatible with my family responsibilities. I ignored Ed's hints, hanging on as best I could. Fortunately, Ed didn't press the point, but my worries increased.

If it hadn't been for the patronage of Dr. Deutsch, my days at GP would almost certainly have been numbered. I sensed he was protecting me behind the scenes. Coming from an academic background himself, he knew I needed time. Many years later, when I had proved I could make money for the company, he commented with satisfaction that he'd been correct all along. For all my naïveté at the beginning, his decision to retain me paid off in the end.

After six months, Ed left GP to go into business for himself. When he did so, he gave me a parting gift: an excellent six-month review and a handsome pay raise. It was quite a surprise! With hindsight I realize this was his way of buttressing my tenuous hold on the job; he was sending a message to Brad and his cohorts to find ways to tap into the expertise I had to offer. Ed's gesture gave me hope there was light at the end of the tunnel, but I still had a long way to go.

## A Way Forward

Slowly, things started to improve. A GP project to train industry personnel how to apply the new standards gave me the opportunity I needed. Training instructors wouldn't be so different from teacher training, which had been my bailiwick at Cape Coast. I was confident I could do it well.

I was asked to develop a project plan and present it at a meeting of company directors. At the time, GP had no women directors, so I would be the only woman there. My boss was nervous and insisted on a trial run to help me avoid the inevitable traps.

"Dr. D [the president's nickname] will have your back, but watch out for Joe—he may try to trip you up," one colleague advised.

"Al's not going to like it if you say that trainers should be more professional; he thinks he's the best instructor ever," another warned.

"Avoid the 'whale words.' You'll be way over their heads!" was yet another piece of advice.

Gerry Cauley—with whom my career was to intersect later in significant ways—asked, "If the project is approved, who will manage the money?"

The message was clear. I might do a decent job of presenting the project plan. I could probably be trusted to develop the program. But I was presumed incapable of managing the money. It was a wake-up call. If I wanted to be treated seriously, I needed to master the company's financial processes.

Once the project was approved and the program had been developed, we used it to train both GP and client personnel, bringing in some money to the company along the way. "Turning a buck" was a definite plus! I was promoted to a line manager position and able to hire my own staff. My star was rising, but there were still bumps in the road.

It was the mid-1980s, and the number of professional women within the company could be counted on one hand. Only one other woman was in a managerial position. She had adopted the stance of being "one of the boys" and wasn't going to risk her own position by offering me—still an outlier—any advice or support. On one occasion, a large request for proposal was received from a government organization and she was flown in from Florida to take charge. I still wasn't trusted as a contributor to the business; I wondered where to turn for help.

I delved into the management literature and asked around for suggestions. What could I do to make my way in this largely male business environment? "If you don't toot your own horn, no one else will" was one piece of advice I received. Tooting my own horn was antithetical to my British upbringing, but I took the advice on board. Ironically, this was just the advice I had given the children concerning the way to behave in an American classroom. I needed to be more proactive in speaking up for myself and showing what I could do.

A pivotal incident is seared in my memory. Over a period of one or two years, INPO's standards had been extended to include the training of all nuclear plant personnel. Cynicism about the standards had evaporated; contract work was plentiful, but so was the competition. Instructor training didn't give me enough billable time, so I continued to support nuclear training projects, competing hard for my share of the work.

On the day in question, I was working after hours when a VP—my boss at the time—came to talk with someone in the next office. They were discussing who would represent the company at an upcoming pre-bid meeting. "Not Sarah

Lutterodt!" I heard; "Not Sarah Lutterodt!" Their frequent repetition of my name rang in my ears. I knew I had to do something.

The next day, I walked into the VP's office to confront him. "I was working late and overheard your conversation with Chris yesterday evening. I need to understand why you both thought I shouldn't go to the pre-bid meeting." I asked. "What should I be doing differently?"

The VP looked shocked and mumbled something in reply. I don't remember much that was said. Any advice the VP offered has been lost in time, but I heard the underlying message loud and clear: I still wasn't a good fit in the nuclear training world. Was it that I was still too academic or simply that I was a woman in a man's world? I will never know. What is clear in hindsight is that the incident was a turning point in revealing both my isolation from the mainstream culture of the organization and the need for me to take charge of my trajectory. What mattered was that I had stood up for myself. I had no option but to confront the way I'd been labeled and fight for what I deserved.

And so it was that I immersed myself in the world of business with its emphasis on winning and making money. I shed—as best I could—my demure British demeanor. I became hard-charging, outgoing, marketing myself within the company and the company within the industry. Marketing brings with it a lot of rejection, and I certainly had my share. I became increasingly thick-skinned. Within the company, I was nicknamed the Iron Lady. (It was the time of Margaret Thatcher and the Falklands War.) I had some successes, and my work was grudgingly acknowledged, but I still didn't really belong.

Then, quite unexpectedly, a new opportunity came along. Gerry Cauley—the very person who had questioned my ability to manage the financials for the instructor training project—opened the door. A request for proposal landed on his desk, and he handed it to me. I will always be grateful.

# Part V

# Level Ground

*In this world you have become clothed and rich,*
*but when you come out of this world, how will you be?*
*Learn a trade that will earn you forgiveness.*
*In the world beyond there's also traffic and trade.*
*Beside these earnings, this world is just play.*
*. . . this world is a game.*

—*Rumi, as quoted by Kabir Helminski*
*in* Living Presence

# Saved by Power Systems

I f anyone had said to me when I was growing up—or even as I emerged into adulthood—that I would spend more than half my life in America, I would've been astounded. Even when my interests and inclinations took me far from the container of my childhood, I remained tightly bound to my place of origin in my values and way of thinking. Even my escape to Africa might be considered an extension of that container, the connections held firmly in place by the bonds of empire and Commonwealth that were only slowly being eroded. America was a different matter altogether. A future life there had no place in my youthful imaginings.

If anyone had gone further to predict that I would become a well-respected training consultant to the people who oversee the real-time operation of the North American electric grid, I wouldn't have known what they were talking about. But that was, in fact, where I landed. It is a measure of the distance I have traveled—to a place and a purpose far from the cocooned world of my childhood and the safe haven of my years working in African universities, far from the ivory tower of academia and the idealism of my youth. Thrust into the unforgiving world of business, I gradually found myself adopting its goals and values as the imprint of my early years faded into the background.

When Gerry handed me a client request to evaluate a training program for electric power system operators I was excited because it offered at the possibility of working outside the world of nuclear training. While that world had enabled me to get a foot in the door at GP, and instructor training had provided a vehicle for advancement, power system operator training was to provide me with a pathway to success.

## Controlling Power from Underground Bunkers

Power system operators occupy a special place within the complex organizational structure of electric utilities. They control the flow of power on the high-voltage electric grid minute by minute. While enjoying a high degree of autonomy within their own companies, they operate in close communication with a nexus of control centers across North America, connected to each other by telecommunications and the network of transmission lines and generating units that constitute the nation's bulk-power electric system. Together, they are responsible for ensuring that electric power is available whenever it is needed—everywhere and at all times. Lapses can lead to power outages, serious accidents, even wide-area blackouts.

Unlike water or gas, electricity cannot be stored in a reservoir to be dispensed when required. It must be generated in real time to satisfy consumers' needs. (Battery storage capacity is still a marginal resource; it was almost nonexistent when I worked in the industry.) Whenever someone turns on a TV or starts up a dishwasher, a generator somewhere must feed more power into the grid, and it must do so without delay. Matching the supply and demand for electric power is a real-time balancing act for which power system operators are responsible. And they have to achieve this balance without overloading the transmission system. Theirs is a demanding and important job. Despite the availability of state-of-the-art computer systems, operators must be ready to intervene quickly in the event of an emergency or if their computer systems fail, as they have done from time to time with disastrous consequences.

I was fascinated by the high-tech look and feel of the grid control centers: flashing lights, audible alarms, computer screens updating every few seconds with data from distant plants and substations, and the ability to control the output of a generator or open a circuit breaker with the click of a mouse. I was intrigued by the tempo of the operators' jobs: sitting back in their chairs chatting casually one moment and the next engaged in a complicated maneuver to respond to an alarm. Confident, no-nonsense, and authoritative, they have the last word in all real-time decision making. Even senior management has to take a back seat during emergencies.

Over the years, I spent many hours talking with system operators about their jobs, often sitting beside them at their desks. I felt privileged to be admitted into their inner sanctums, to feel part of their world. The importance of their job rubbed off on me as I cataloged the tasks they performed, learned to interpret what they saw on their multiple computer screens, and tried to understand how they made and communicated real-time decisions with such quiet assurance.

Because security of the country's grid control centers is of paramount concern, many are located in underground bunkers in unmarked buildings. Despite their isolation, operators are always in touch with the life of the community. The ever-changing demand for electric power is what drives their jobs. Old-time operators in the U.S. loved to tell me about the sudden peak in demand at 11 pm on August 3rd, 1969, when Tiny Tim got married on *The Johnny Carson Show*. I learned that in England the load surges suddenly when the half-time whistle blows during popular soccer games and viewers rush to turn on their tea kettles; that in Spain there is a deep drop in demand during the month of August, when city dwellers leave for the beach; and that in Brazil electric usage spikes in the early evening when workers take a shower after getting home, using water heaters that turn on when water is drawn. Changes in electric usage due to school vacations, public holidays, and community events are planned for. And everywhere, at all times, weather is a major factor to be reckoned with. The Weather Channel runs continuously in most control rooms.

## The Innocence Game

I grew to know the system operator population well. They had an immense and justifiable pride in their craft and doubted an outsider could ever really understand what they did. It took me a while to earn their trust. My experience with navy nukes had taught me to play the "innocence game," and it served me well. Had I posed as an "expert," I would have been doomed from the outset. When I presented myself as an outsider willing to listen and learn, all was well. They were delighted to explain their responsibilities in excruciating detail. "Sarah, you ask the darndest questions," one operator remarked as he proceeded to explain for the umpteenth time the meaning of an n-1 contingency. I finally realized that what he was saying was no different from what I had understood all along, but when I played it back in my own words, he thought I'd got it wrong. Using their language, finding a way to enter their world, was critical.

The operators' attitude to me was, doubtless, partly gender based. When I started working in control centers, I was usually the only woman in sight, and what would a woman know? Playing a little dumb—or innocent—was a useful strategy that invariably elicited a warm, paternalistic response. Helping me understand the finer points of their jobs gave seasoned operators a lot of satisfaction, and confidence that the training materials I developed would serve their needs. Their expertise and my ignorance were mutually accepted guideposts that framed the conversation. I wasn't part of their world, but it was OK if I positioned myself as a curious outsider.

The client request that Gerry handed me in 1984 was my entry into the world of power system operations. The request came from the PJM Interconnection, a consortium of utilities that coordinates grid operations in the mid-Atlantic region. PJM stands for Pennsylvania-New Jersey-Maryland. In the 1980s, PJM included most of the utilities in those three states as well as PEPCO in Washington, DC. Its reach is now much larger.

In 1966, there was a major blackout in the whole mid-Atlantic region, and in 1977, New York City went black. To avert such incidents in the future, PJM had commissioned General Electric (GE), a giant in the industry, to provide a training program for all their operators. It hadn't gone well. GP was asked to help figure out why.

The problem was easy to spot. The GE engineers who delivered the training had an in-depth knowledge of power system theory but little idea of how it applied to operators' jobs. Moreover, they hadn't seen the need to ask. They didn't use language familiar to the operators and, importantly, didn't show operators the required respect. I heard stories of blackboards filled with equations, of hours of engineer-speak, and endless explanations of megawatt accounting, which was irrelevant to the operators. Engineers take time to study an issue. Operators often have only a few seconds in which to respond. The GE training program did not speak to their needs.

I quickly realized that the methodology mandated by INPO for training nuclear personnel would result in a far more effective program. I set this out in my report. PJM liked it. When they asked GP to design and implement a program per my recommendations, I became the project manager. My ability to "manage the money" was no longer in doubt. I embraced the opportunity gratefully, but it came with its own challenges.

Although designing the program was well within my competence, we needed subject matter experts to help us and no one in GP had experience of grid operations. Somehow, I cobbled together a team, and we learned as we went along. Gerry Cauley, no longer in a management position, was a key player. Additionally, Dr. Deutsch offered the services of a senior engineer, John Young, to serve as in-house "content expert."

John was well versed in plant operation but knew little about the job of system operator. Unfortunately, he didn't know what he didn't know. A few weeks before the six-week pilot class was to start, PJM asked me to remove him from the team of instructors. It was a difficult moment. How could we find anyone to replace him at such short notice? I felt I had no option but to step in and teach in his place. Although I didn't have any operating experience, I was confident I understood the topic, having spent long hours developing the training materials. Standing up in front of a class of system operators seemed less daunting than the thought of teaching reactor physics had been a few years earlier. My confidence was soon shaken!

Teaching the class required me to step outside my preferred role as the naïve outsider. In the classroom I was the authority; I could no longer play the innocence game. For the experienced operators who were auditing the pilot program, having a woman who understood their world—or thought she did—was quite a stretch. I was eaten alive. It wasn't that the trainees were overly aggressive. Rather, they smothered me with "friendly suggestions" about what they thought I didn't understand or why the class exercises just didn't cut it. At the end of a day's teaching, I felt like crawling into a hole and hiding. Gerry, who was teaching different topics, had a much easier time.

## *Winning Industry Recognition*

PJM's CEO had taken a risk in having GP develop their training program. He was an outlier in believing in our methodology and wanted to spread the word. As current chair of the North American Electric Reliability Council (NERC) Operating Committee—the body responsible for grid operations across the continent—he invited me to address their annual meeting in Charlotte in 1985. I was honored.

In my presentation I explained how our process enabled us to leverage the knowledge of the operators themselves, that our goal was to develop training that was performance oriented, not theory based. The audience, consisting of eighty senior managers—all men—listened politely.

Several of them congratulated me afterwards, but there was at least one participant—a senior manager within the PJM network—who was antagonistic from the start. If ever our paths crossed at industry meetings, Ron made a point of walking in the opposite direction. At the Operating Committee meeting in 1987 he gave a talk on the very same topic I had addressed in 1985. He made no reference whatever to my earlier presentation or to the program GP had developed for PJM using the methodology we both described. I was gobsmacked. As an influential member of the group, Ron knew he would be listened to. Did he assume that as an industry outsider—and a woman to boot—my contribution could simply be erased? His message seemed to be, "You're not part of our [all-male] club. Why don't you just get out of our way?"

Ron was exceptional in his overt hostility, but in his underlying attitude he was probably not alone. Gaining recognition in this exclusive men's club couldn't be taken for granted.

A very different client encounter a year or so later illustrated the barriers I faced. A company in the deepest reaches of Missouri approached GP for advice about operator training, and I was selected to do the work. When I arrived on site, the control center manager was quick to tell me he would never hire a woman to work shift because he couldn't be accountable to the men's wives for what might happen. It wasn't a good start!

The manager had just appointed Will, an operator close to retirement, to be the trainer. The situation wasn't untypical. Trainers don't work shifts, and the position was often treated as a reward for length of service. Will was a good ol' Southern boy if ever there was one. Charming and respectful, he had solid operational experience but showed little aptitude for training.

At the end of my visit, I tried to alert the manager to the problem as tactfully as possible. "It's important for trainers to be able to communicate their knowledge effectively," I said, going on to enumerate other skills trainers need. I didn't say explicitly that Will wasn't cut out for the job, but my meaning must have been clear.

The manager came right back at me, "You know, some people think having a smart accent is a sign of intelligence and that those of us who speak in the Southern way are just not very bright." He had to have been talking about me with my pronounced English accent. It was a sharp put-down. How dare he express himself so openly? In doing so, had he found cover for his gender bias, freeing himself to dismiss any recommendations I might make?

I was determined to confront his misogyny and did so over lunch at a nearby Chinese restaurant. After the meal, I pulled out my credit card to pay. He was visibly discomfited. This was Missouri in the mid-1980s, when it was probably unheard of for a woman to pick up the tab.

"Don't worry," I assured him. "As a manager, I get brownie points for taking clients out for meals."

He had nothing more to say. Needless to say, I wasn't invited back.

Fortunately, Ron's influence wasn't as widespread as I

feared, and the Missouri incident turned out to be a minor blip. After the PJM project, the small group I now led went on to win training projects for grid control centers across the country. News of our work spread quickly. Word of mouth in the close-knit world of grid operations proved to be a powerful marketing tool, and GP's reputation in the nuclear industry helped. Within a few years, GP became recognized as the provider of choice for developing system operator training programs. We'd arrived.

## The Staffing Challenge

As our workload grew, we needed more staff. My strategy of playing innocent could only take us so far. We needed people with content knowledge to complement the instructional expertise that was my own specialty. The problem had started with the PJM project when John, our supposed content expert, was rejected by the client. Gerry, who, like me, had learned as we went along, continued to make a valuable contribution, but we needed others, preferably people with control-center experience.

Unfortunately, my understanding of what was needed clashed with GP's can-do attitude and soon became a source of tension with company management. "If you can man a submarine or run a nuclear plant, you can do most anything. What's so special about operating a power system?" they seemed to be saying. "If you can't find someone in-house, you can hire from the outside."

I was caught in a three-way tussle between clients' conviction that their job was unique and their suspicion of anyone who didn't come from within their ranks, GP management's contention that we could easily find a nuke who could learn the job, and my own insistence on maintaining the quality of our work product. All this within a business environment in which employees' ability to complete project work on time and within budget was a sine qua non.

I found one or two GP employees to join our team, but it wasn't enough. Outside the company, it was difficult to find people with the required mix of technical aptitude and communication skills. Graduate engineers who could have mastered the technical material were generally not interested in training, and those with instructional skills had difficulty handling the technical content. Eventually we hired a few engineers with related expertise, and it was thanks to them that our work gradually won recognition within the industry. But our clients were still looking for our project teams to include people with firsthand operational experience. The search proved almost impossible. Even those who'd been successful trainers in their former companies seemed paralyzed when it came to delivering a written product in a timely manner. The very quality that made them good real-time decision makers seemed an impediment when it came to articulating basic concepts and principles for others to learn. It was hard for us and for them.

Henry's case was especially poignant. Henry had been a leader among trainers in the Western region when we hired him to teach a course that was very popular with our clients. Unfortunately, it didn't work out. Faced with a class of students, Henry was unable to articulate the knowledge he had drawn on instinctively as a real-time operator. When we tried to leverage his experience working on other projects, the result was the same. He was unable to deliver an acceptable product. I had no option but to let him go.

I chose a quiet moment in an airport café after an industry meeting to deliver the bad news.

"You know, Henry, this just isn't working," I began.

"It's been tough," he replied. He must have known what was coming.

After enumerating some of the opportunities we'd given

him, I continued, "I'm really sorry, Henry; we're going to have to let you go."

I was relieved to have delivered the bad news, but it was a hard moment for both of us. Henry had moved from Colorado to Maryland to take the job. He'd be returning home empty-handed. Henry was stoic, humbly accepting the inevitable without registering any obvious anger or resentment. I was grateful.

Henry's attitude toward me then and in our later encounters wasn't untypical of what I experienced working with grid operations folks over the years. Although many may have wondered about my presence in their world, few let their misogyny get the better of their basic human decency. We came from very different places, but our worlds were joined by a shared purpose and bonds of mutual respect.

## Never a Complete Insider

Despite the staffing challenges, the early 1990s was a good period for me professionally. I was finally "turning a buck," and this won me recognition within the company. Because GP operated in a very decentralized way, I was responsible for every aspect of the business, from marketing, through proposal writing and sales, to managing projects on time and within budget. I became well-attuned to the world of timesheets, monthly status reports, and the tyranny of the bottom line. I learned business skills that were to stand me in good stead when I launched my own business several years later. I will always be grateful for the opportunity GP provided, but I remained in many ways an outlier. Although my former career was worlds away, it had never left me entirely, leading me to insist on a level of work quality that many found burdensome.

Racial issues played relatively little part in my work life. When I was interviewed, I'd been quite open about my previous job as a university lecturer in Ghana, but I doubt I was heard correctly. Some years later, a senior VP asked me about my experience "in South Africa." It may have been the only African country he could name! West Africa, in general, and Ghana, in particular, meant nothing. I didn't burden him with more information than he could handle. Besides, I didn't want to throw doubt into what had become a cordial working relationship.

Once I'd achieved a degree of success within GP—but not until then—I felt comfortable having a photo of the family on my desk. My employees and immediate colleagues knew Clement was from Ghana and didn't seem to hold it against me, though who knows what was said behind my back. Clients had no reason to know. When they enquired about my unusual name, I would simply say that it was my husband's name and of German origin. There was no need to say more.

Gender was a different matter. The words said to me long ago at Oxford University's Appointments Board still resonated: "Industry is no place for a woman." Not only did I have to work hard to earn the trust of my utility clients, but within GP I still had to deal with male chauvinism, much of it quite subtle, some less so. The fact that I was known within the company alternately as the "Iron Lady" and "Mother" gives some indication of the ambiguity of my situation.

For the most part, the younger engineers working for me didn't have a problem working for a woman. On the contrary, their wives seemed to regard me as a role model. It was more difficult for the older wives. I was told that Gerry's wife, for example, never missed an opportunity to bad-mouth me. When I invited our small work group and their families to a backyard picnic, she was the only one who didn't come.

Among other company managers, my outlier status stood out more sharply. For most of my time at GP there were very few women in management positions. On one occasion, I was invited to attend a senior meeting in the president's office to discuss a promising opportunity with General Motors (GM). I was sitting next to the president. At one point, he turned and asked me to make copies of a document. For once, I had my wits about me and replied, "I'd be happy to ask the secretary to do it." Given GP's entrenched culture, he may not have got the message.

A few weeks later, the executive VP assembled a day-long meeting to plan the company's response to the GM opportunity. The evening before the meeting, my boss called me at home. He told me, essentially, to keep my mouth shut the next day. Wow! I wondered if I had heard correctly. He offered no good reason. Was I in the habit of running my mouth? Or was it that my opinion as a woman wasn't welcome? Or simply that the executive VP didn't like me? I will never know. I was cautious in what I said the following day but didn't stay silent. When work for GM started trickling in, however, I was sidelined. By that time, my work with grid operators was keeping me very busy, so I wasn't too concerned.

On another occasion, we were in the process of responding to a new opportunity at Con Edison of New York. A major steam explosion at Gramercy Park had caused asbestos to be sprayed all over some high-end apartment blocks. The cleanup was costing Con Edison millions of dollars and a ton of bad publicity. They needed a training program for workers on their steam system, and they needed it now. Our small group had developed many different training programs for Con Edison's electrical trades and were confident we could do the same for steam system workers.

One evening, I was working late on the proposal when a senior manager from another department stopped by my office. I'll call him Charlie. He got straight to the point. "I don't think your group should be handling this steam work for Con Ed."

"Why ever not, Charlie? We're just finalizing the proposal." I was amazed by his chutzpah.

"I'm from New York. I know how these people think."

"What are you trying to say? We've done many projects for Con Ed."

Charlie looked skeptical, so I went on. "We know their people. We have an excellent track record. They approached us for help."

"You don't know the whole story," Charlie responded. "Let me handle it." He shrugged his shoulders as if to say, "Take what's coming if you don't believe me." He hadn't provided any justification for his assertions. I wondered what I was missing.

Charlie's tone reminded me of the time our furniture shipment from Ghana got held up in New Jersey. I wanted to know why our valuable hardwood crates had been retained by the shippers. A mafia-like voice over the phone warned me darkly not to ask too many questions. I understood New Yorkers could be different; I realized there might be some backstory I was unaware of, but Charlie's threatening tone was unacceptable. I was confident we could handle the project. And by now I knew how to stand up for myself.

"Thanks for your input." I stood up to indicate the end of the conversation. "We'll come to you if we need help."

As soon as Charlie left, I slumped back in my chair, unnerved by the conversation. Whatever was he thinking? Was he simply trying to bully me? Did he really know something I didn't? If so, why didn't he tell me instead of issuing dark threats? The competition for work within GP was undoubtedly a factor, but it was hard to dismiss the idea that he was engaged in a male power play. And a rather crude one at that!

A lack of awareness of gender bias became evident when my then boss, Van, held a retreat for lead personnel within his organization. Van and I had a good working relationship, and he had been supportive of my work, but his career as a graduate of the Naval Academy and an officer in the nuclear navy had left its mark. At the retreat, about twenty of us were seated around a large table. There were only three women: a senior instructional expert who had no management role, a newly appointed first-line supervisor, and me. We'd been invited to submit questions in advance. My question related to women in leadership. "Could it be," I asked, "that GP values male qualities as those best suited to leadership?" I was genuinely seeking to understand.

Van looked skeptical as he read my question. He nonetheless went around the room, asking what people thought. No one showed any appreciation of the underlying issue.

"I've always been fairly treated," the instructional expert contributed in her usual, deliberative tone. "I can't say I experience male dominance at GP."

"I don't see this as an issue," the new supervisor commented, unwilling to stick her neck out, I supposed.

I was out on a limb. It was the late 1980s. Not a lot had yet been written about women in leadership, or differences in leadership style between men and women, or why recognition of feminine qualities was important. I was still groping for understanding myself. GP had treated me well in many ways. I never felt discriminated against when it came to salary or bonuses, but I sensed my disadvantage as a woman in leadership. I was never "one of the boys" and, as such, wasn't privy to a lot of company backchat. I was still trying to figure out how I fit—or didn't fit—into the landscape of company management.

## Managing Up

**P**eople management was always the hardest part of the job for me. I found managing employees who worked for me difficult enough, but it was "managing up" that, in the end, proved my undoing.

Despite the negative response to my question about leadership, the GP division headed by Van provided a relatively benign environment for our group. When Van heard we'd won our first large project after PJM, he greeted me with a big hug. He supported our efforts to hire qualified people from outside the company and respected my insistence on quality. But we were the only training group within the division and had no organic connection to other groups working there. It was no surprise therefore when, in yet another organizational reshuffle, we were moved to a division whose main work product was training. I found myself once again working for former navy nukes!

Relating to other managers within the group, and to my chain of command, was a constant struggle. Although our financial success had won recognition of our contribution and a degree of untouchability, the senior management team didn't share my concern for the unique needs of our customer base. Nor did they show much respect for the engineers we'd hired; they didn't fit much better than me within the prevailing culture at GP. Knowing the engineers were critical to our success, I felt I had to protect their sense of self-worth relative to the technicians who worked elsewhere in the organization. Many is the time I bent over backwards to appease them against the wishes of my bosses, who saw no reason to give them special treatment. It wasn't a recipe for success! To the contrary, my deference to the engineers' elitism must have been a great source of irritation to my bosses, most of whom lacked formal qualifications themselves.

Occasionally, senior management's frustration surfaced, and I glimpsed the anger normally hidden beneath a veneer of politeness. At a budget meeting, my projections for the year ahead were met with a series of vicious questions by the VP in charge. My immediate boss, with whom I was constantly at loggerheads, graciously stepped in to defend me. But the veil had parted. The dislike was palpable.

## *Time to Go*

**S**adly, the group of engineers and trainers that had enabled our success in the niche world of grid operator training didn't stay together for long. Gerry left first to take up an influential position at the Electric Power Research Institute (EPRI). From EPRI, he rose to national prominence as NERC's CEO—a position far beyond my interest or aspiration. Following Gerry's lead, others left over the next one or two years.

As the grid operations community began to recognize the need for better training programs, the demand for qualified trainers exploded. Both clients and competitors looked to GP to find them. Each resignation was painful, and the cumulative effect on the business was serious. My bosses didn't hesitate to question my leadership.

In retrospect, I see clearly that the decline was inevitable. Operating as a niche business within GP wasn't sustainable. The company offered no career path for our young engineers; as a group, we were increasingly isolated and at odds with senior management. When we started losing contracts that should have been ours for the taking, I removed myself from line management to focus on marketing. I hoped to leverage the national recognition I'd achieved to secure additional contract work, but the strategy wasn't successful. Our competitors outpaced us at every turn. It became abundantly clear that my days at GP were numbered. If I didn't go at a time of my choosing, I would be let go.

GP had been my only employer in the U.S. I'd been with the company for fifteen years. I was fifty-seven years old. What should I do? Where should I go? Over the years, many employees—equipped with the unique set of skills they had acquired for survival at GP—had split off to form their own companies. Many had flourished. Businesses that had been spun off from GP were scattered all over Columbia. Most people had left in groups of two or three, but there was no one I felt comfortable partnering with. Nor did I feel inclined to seek a position with one of our client companies or with a competitor. I saw no alternative but to go it alone. Like so many immigrants to the U.S., I would start my own company. I'd call it Quality Training Systems. I set the wheels in motion.

On the afternoon of July 7, 1997, I stood in my office looking out of its large picture window, breathing deeply. I rehearsed what I had to say. Then I walked next door to my boss's office to tell him I was leaving.

Don was the most recent in my long line of bosses. He had been a young supervisor in the operations department when I first joined the company. Now vice president, he'd proved himself to be a tolerant, respectful boss, albeit unable to help in responding to the problems we were experiencing.

"So, when's your last day?" is all I remember him saying. He didn't express any great surprise or disappointment at my decision. He probably knew it was coming.

My career at GP ended quietly, with no unpleasantness and no elaborate farewell. It was the end of an important chapter in my life, but by no means the end of my career. I had established a place for myself in one small segment of the utility training world. It was a niche where I could still make a contribution.

I have never regretted working for GP—or the decision to leave. At GP, I'd learned everything I knew about "turning a buck." I had also learned—too well—to function in a hard-driving bottom-line culture. I'd become acculturated to values that were alien to me in many ways. At Quality Training Systems, I'd be my own boss; I'd be able to soften the edges, reconfigure my boundaries.

# Home and Family

A friend of mine, a mother of four now in her eighties, once told me she often approaches young mothers in her neighborhood, advising them to treasure the years when their children are still young. Yes, indeed! The time passes all too quickly. The years when our children grew to adulthood coincided roughly with my time at GP. Justine wasn't yet three when I was hired as a part-time employee; she was a freshman at Yale the year I left, Isabelle had just graduated from college, and Toby had already embarked on his career at Boeing.

During these years, my life spanned two very different worlds: the fast-paced business world in which I struggled, first to survive and later to build a career, and the needs of a family trying to find its way in a world that often seemed alien and uncomprehending. The task of balancing work and family is never easy and was much less understood and appreciated in those days than it is today. It was complicated in my case by the two core realities that defined our family: our interracial identity—not Black, not White—and our immigrant status. We were in the U.S. but not really part of it. Our outsider status made the search for connection and belonging more necessary; it also meant that as a family we were often at odds with the cultural norms and mores of those around us.

Pragmatism—my default coping mechanism—prevailed. I didn't have an explicit strategy for responding to the challenges we faced, but managed as best I could, one day at a time. My life was absorbed by work and family. I didn't have the bandwidth for anything else. I didn't pursue personal friendships or spiritual concerns. Connecting with neighbor-hood or community was driven by the needs of the family. My interest in developing countries settled at the back of my awareness.

## An Ongoing Dilemma

I liked to think that in balancing work and family, I always put family first, trying as best I could to create a safe and secure environment for our children such as I'd enjoyed myself grow-ing up, albeit in a far different context. The children may have experienced it differently.

As my career at GP took off, so, too, did the need for work-related travel. One September, I committed to a full week's teaching assignment in Sacramento. I knew this would be a stretch, but the children were back in school, and I thought the family could manage without me. As it happened, there was a late-season heat wave, and without air conditioning, the schools told the children to stay home. It wasn't a scenario we'd envisioned.

"They're going to be home all week," Clement told me over the phone.

"I've committed to being here till Friday," I said, distraught about the situation but powerless to do much of anything to help. "I can call Connie [our babysitter at the time] to see if she could come in part of the time. Maybe you could take them with you to Howard on days when you're teaching." I didn't know what else to suggest.

They got through the week somehow, but I vowed never to accept a weeklong assignment out of town again. And I didn't, to the chagrin of my coworkers who sometimes had to pick up the slack. I had set a boundary between my responsibilities to work and family I wasn't prepared to cross.

On another occasion, I was invited to address a conference

in Boston. It was an opportunity I couldn't afford to refuse, but it happened to be the very day Isabelle and Justine were starting at a new school. I took them to school and made sure they were settled into their classes before heading to the airport. The school bus was to drop them off in our neighborhood in the afternoon. I thought the plan was watertight. From Boston, I called the house when I expected them to be home. No answer. I became frantic with guilty concern when one call after another went unanswered. Eventually I called the school and was told the buses had left late. Sure enough, after about thirty minutes, I was able to verify they were home safely. I breathed a deep sigh of relief. It was an unsettling experience.

The incident brought into sharp relief the dilemmas I faced so frequently: to travel or not to travel? To stay till the end of a meeting or leave early to pick up one of the children from an afterschool activity? To enroll one of them in a program that involved a substantial commitment of my time or not?

There was never a right answer. I was always mindful of the effects of my decisions on the children but realized that any concession to their well-being that compromised work-related responsibilities could easily threaten my job security. I could almost hear management saying, "She's a mother; what can you expect?" Much as I relished my role as wife and mother, I knew that succeeding—even surviving—at work meant grasping opportunities as they arose, knowing they mightn't come again. I couldn't allow my decisions to reinforce the prevailing gender stereotypes.

The traditional definition of gender roles wasn't restricted to the workplace. It carried over into the home. Issues concerning our respective roles that Clement and I had experienced in Birmingham resurfaced. The "un-ironed shirt" strategy I had tried when we were first married wasn't viable now that there were five of us. When Clement stepped in to help—as he often did—it was out of a sense of obligation to me and the children rather than from a sense of fully shared responsibility. Deeply buried in my psyche, that was probably my position too. We'd both grown up with traditional assumptions about gender roles in which family responsibilities fell heavily on the mother. It wasn't an untypical situation for couples of our generation, or even now.

One incident stands out. I'd accompanied my boss to South Carolina for a client meeting, a trip that involved a long, weary day of travel but not an overnight stay. I arrived home just after our usual dinnertime to find the family sitting around waiting for me. "What's for dinner?" they asked as soon as I walked in the door. There was no "Glad you're home safe" or "How was your day?" I was home, and they were hungry. I better get busy. Without missing a beat, I changed out of my business attire, donned an apron, and got to work in the kitchen. Today it might be called code-switching. It was what I did every day.

When I was away overnight, Clement managed valiantly. I planned all the meals ahead of time, leaving detailed instructions about the "what" and the "when." Covering piano lessons, soccer practice, and the like was never easy. Clement often had seminars or other activities in the late afternoon that prevented him from getting home in time to do the necessary chauffeuring. I never really questioned that it was my responsibility to ensure all needs on the home front were met while I was gone. Yet, despite the logistical difficulties and a certain angst at leaving the children, I have to admit that I found the short breaks from domestic chores refreshing. The time away gave me a chance to focus 100% on my professional responsibilities, and I usually returned home with renewed energy and appreciation for the family.

Even when I was not traveling, the need for babysitting support to cover afterschool hours, as well as teacher workdays and other nonroutine events, was an ongoing concern.

When wintry weather was forecast, we'd turn on the radio early, dreading the all-too-familiar announcement, "Howard County Schools are closed for the day." GP never closed, so it was especially difficult when the list of closings didn't include Howard University and Clement had to go to work. These were times when we experienced our isolation most keenly. We missed not having family close by or trusted friends with whom we could share childcare responsibilities.

The children may have experienced the tension between my roles at home and at work more acutely than I realized at the time. We were on a family vacation in California in 1986 when the PJM project—my first big opportunity at GP—was at a critical point. I felt the need to phone in to check on progress almost every day. I knew that people back in the office would be happy to override my authority when I wasn't there.

Back then, making a call meant finding a public phone, which was something of an inconvenience to the rest of the family. At one point during the vacation, Toby, aged thirteen, asked in an innocent voice but with devastating intent, "What's your most important project right now?"

"PJM," I answered without hesitation, focused intently as I was on the phone call I was about to make.

"Wrong," was his immediate retort. "The family should be." Ouch! His response really hit home.

"Of course, the family comes first," I remember saying. "But then the family's not just a project. It's much more than that."

I don't recall how or if the conversation continued, but Toby's question and implied corrective caught me off guard. He had moved around a lot as a small child; he was normally quite reserved in showing how much it had affected him. Was he fed up with the frequent phone calls? I wondered. Did he really feel I was insufficiently attentive to the family? Was he simply being a teenager trying to needle one of his parents or was his question a deeply felt *cri de coeur*? It was probably an unarticulated mixture of all of these.

During the remainder of the vacation, I was more cautious about letting the PJM project interfere with the family's enjoyment of the natural wonders of Yosemite and Sequoia National Park. I wasn't about to let work concerns spoil our time together as a family. But the conversation echoed in my mind then as it still does today. However much I tried to balance the needs of work and family there was no way to get it exactly right.

Given my personality—especially as it had evolved under the pressures of my work life—there is no doubt that I homed in more easily on the tasks in front of me, whether at work or in the home, than on the children's unspoken need for attention. I see that clearly now, but I'm not sure I would have known how to do things differently. Although Toby's question lingered, it didn't change my trajectory significantly. Even though in my own mind I always prioritized family needs, I realize that workplace challenges may have absorbed more attention than they deserved. But half measures at work wasn't a realistic option given the competitive environment at GP, and giving up my job altogether wasn't an alternative I was ready to entertain. Although Clement was moving steadily up the academic ladder, his salary still lagged that of his American peers and wouldn't have been sufficient to support the family in a middle-class lifestyle, let alone put funds aside for the children's college education. I told myself many times that I had no option but to commit to workplace success.

Truth to tell, I couldn't imagine myself as a full-time homemaker and parent. I had always worked, and my identity was bound up with my job. Who knows what type of mother I would have been if I'd been housebound or stuck in a routine type of job just to make ends meet? I would've had difficulty containing my frustration. I may regret not being more attentive to the children's inner worlds, but I have no real sense of guilt. I did what I could at the time. Just as the children inherited my DNA, for better or for worse, so were they the beneficiaries or otherwise of my personality as their mother. I am who I am. To have resolved the tension between work and family by becoming a stay-at-home mom would have been unbearable.

While I balanced the needs of work and family as best I could during the week, weekends were devoted almost exclusively to family. The days were packed tight with shopping and cooking and laundry, as well as the occasional soccer or basketball game or piano recital. Public holidays provided a welcome respite from routine, an all-too-rare space to just breathe and be together. They were days when we could sit around and play a game together or go to a movie.

"The extra time at home over the holiday made all the difference," I commented to a colleague after one long weekend. "It gave me time to reground myself with the family."

Vacations, too, were keenly awaited. Not the long vacations when I was working and had to find programs or childcare for the children. Those were times when I really missed my former life as a university teacher and the opportunity to take an extended break from my normal work routine. It was rather the short two weeks of vacation that my job at GP allowed—weeks when we could do something together as a family—that I looked forward to with outsize pleasure. In addition to visiting England every other year, we traveled widely in the U.S. and Canada: Niagara Falls, Monument Valley and the Grand Canyon, Vancouver Island, Cape Cod, and more. These trips were eagerly anticipated then and are fondly remembered now.

## Reaching for Family Near and Far

Our physical distance from family—both mine and Clement's—was always a concern. The children needed to know they belonged somewhere and were not totally adrift in a foreign land. I stayed connected to family as best I could.

My only relatives in the U.S. were Aunt Milly Stanley and her family. Aunt Milly was my mother's third cousin at several removes, but they shared the same maiden name. She had a great sense of family and remained close to her European relatives—including my mother—throughout her life. She'd first appeared in our lives like a fairy godmother shortly after the war, coming to Brewerstreet laden with undreamt-of goodies from America. When Mother told her we were now living in Maryland, she reached out to us generously, as she had to many immigrant relatives before us. Her husband had made a lot of money on Wall Street. When he died, she took up residence in a penthouse in the Ritz-Carlton in New York and traveled widely, including several times to Africa. She seemed intrigued by our situation. Her son, Ted, and his new wife, Jenny, had just moved from New York to Maryland's Eastern Shore—a one-and-a-half-hour drive from Columbia.

At Aunt Milly's prompting, they invited us for lunch on our first Easter Sunday. I was excited, albeit somewhat apprehensive. We were still living in the apartment in Columbia, and I was getting used to my position at the bottom of the pile socially. We were nobodies and were being invited to lunch with an established, wealthy family. How would we fit in? How should we dress? How would they relate to Clement? They knew I had married a Ghanaian, but we'd no idea how they'd respond in practice to a mixed-race family. I hadn't seen Aunt Milly since childhood and had never met Ted, let alone Jenny. Fortunately, I needn't have worried. "Sally, how good to meet you!" Jenny greeted me when we arrived. It felt odd to be called by my childhood name, but it was a sure indication that we'd be treated as family. And we were! That first visit opened the way to a long and valued relationship with the only relative I had on this side of the pond.

Among her many activities in the local community, Jenny

ran the Oxford Kids Camp each summer for local children as well as other strays and hangers-on. She and Ted kindly hosted our two girls many years in a row while they attended the camp. We came to rely on it as a highlight of the program I stitched together for the children each summer. Strapping their bikes on the car and joining the weekend traffic crossing the Chesapeake Bay Bridge became part of our summer ritual.

We always got a great welcome. Jenny regaled us with her wonderful cooking while Ted recalled his occasional visits to Brewerstreet.

"I got to meet The Honorable Hubert," he told us many times, emphasizing my father's honorific title. "He was quite the country farmer!"

While staying with Ted and Jenny, the children got to enjoy their lovely garden and swimming pool, plus an occasional ride in Ted's sailing dinghy. Jenny was a gifted educator and awakened the children to the natural beauty of Chesapeake Bay. It was during those brief summer visits, too, thanks to Jenny, that Isabelle developed her lifelong love of reading.

Our way of saying thank you for their generous hospitality was to invite Ted and Jenny for a festive meal at Christmastime. Many years it was our only family occasion during the holiday season and it became a cherished routine: an occasion to bring out our best china and silverware. This was one of the few ways in which I was able to create family traditions that I hoped would live on in the children's memories.

I did my best to ensure that the children also got to know my family in England. We saved up to visit every two years throughout the 1980s, planning carefully to pack as much as possible into the short two-week vacation my job allowed. We stayed mostly with Mother at Stychfield. She always went out of her way to make sure we had a good time, fitting two years of grandparenting into our short visits. She treated the children to their favorite English foods, such as fish fingers and treacle tart, and made sure that toys and games were always available to fill idle moments. As a dutiful grandmother, she arranged for Isabelle to play her most recent piano piece on a friend's piano and listened admiringly to Justine's first steps on the violin.

"Maybe they've inherited the Lambi's musical talent," she'd say hopefully, recalling the musical gifts of her own mother's family.

During our stays at Stychfield, we made almost daily visits to Brewerstreet where Christopher and Sacha were now living. It was just a short walk away. Mother would call Sacha in the morning to check in.

"Can the children come over for a swim? Looks as though it's going to be fine."

The answer was nearly always yes. In addition to swimming in the pool, the children enjoyed visiting the farm and playing with the domestic animals. Justine always made a bee-line for the cat, Snuffles, smothering the poor animal with attention that wasn't always welcomed. She would dearly have liked a cat of her own, but I wasn't ready to assume responsibility for a pet on top of everything else.

We took advantage of our trips to England to visit Gresham and Miguel, Clement's brothers, living in England and Denmark, respectively. When they were old enough, our children visited on their own and our relatives generously hosted them. We were happy to return the favor on the few occasions when family members came to visit us in the U.S. One year, we shared a week's vacation in France with Miguel and Ingrid's family. Their children were of similar ages to ours, and we wanted them to get to know each other.

Mother visited us in Maryland only once. It was in 1981, the year after we arrived. Clement had returned to Ghana to deal with some unfinished business, and I was on my own with the children and not yet working. It was a great sadness to me that she never came back. It would've been an opportunity for her to get to know her "other grandchildren," as she often referred to our three. Besides, her presence at home for a short period during the long summer vacations would've been a tremendous help once I had a full-time job. "I'm too old to make the long trip" was the excuse she gave, even though she continued to lead a very active life for another ten or fifteen years. Despite her generosity to us during our many visits to England, it seemed she had drawn a line in the sand when it came to visiting us in the U.S. More than once, I wondered whether she would've responded differently if I had told her, "Clement will be away for two weeks in August; please come," but I chose not to shine a light on the lingering difficulties in their relationship.

Thankfully, the family bonds that we strived to develop and sustain across the ocean have endured. Our children's relationships with their cousins may not be close on a day-to-day basis, but they follow each other on Facebook and are glad to see each other again at the occasional family celebration.

I like to think of our short visits to England as *kairos*[2] moments, times of heightened intensity full of new experiences and the chance to savor family connections. As such, they stood apart from the measured *chronos* of our day-to-day lives in the U.S., with their regular rhythms of seasons and semesters, workdays and weekends.

In the U.S., we sought opportunities to spend time with Clement's family members as much as possible. Clement's older brother, Papaa, lived in Poughkeepsie, New York, and we drove the five hours to see the family there many times. Grandma lived with them for more than a year, so a trip to Poughkeepsie was also an opportunity to visit with her. One

---

[2.] The two words for time in ancient Greek, *kairos* and *chronos*, help differentiate qualitative moments of awareness or opportunity from the quantitative march of time as measured by clocks and calendars when we are caught up in the routines of everyday living.

summer, she came to spend two weeks with us, but given our work routines and the fact that her sight was failing, I didn't think it possible to have her stay with us for longer periods. Should I have made more of an effort? I wonder now. Did I allow work to outweigh concern for family? The children would certainly have benefited from her presence, which would have helped connect them with their Ghanaian roots. I see it now as a sadly missed opportunity.

Gerhard Lutterodt, a distant cousin of Clement's, was the relative we saw most often. He was a welcome visitor, but the window into Ghanaian culture he provided was very different from what Grandma would have offered. We'd known Gerhard since he was a young boy at boarding school in the UK. Later, when he was at secondary school in Cape Coast, he'd walk to our house on campus a few miles away, ready for a good meal and some family time. "Where are the trains?" he'd ask Toby as soon as he arrived. Though many years older, Gerhard would happily play trains with Toby on the floor for hours at a time.

A few years after we moved to the U.S., Gerhard came to college in Pennsylvania and again became a frequent visitor. His father, who had many children scattered widely over the globe, was relatively old when Gerhard was born and died when he was quite young. His mother and brother were far away in Ghana, and Clement became a father figure to him; he came to rely on us for advice and a place to stay when needed.

Soon after he got married, we invited Gerhard and his wife, Vera, for Christmas lunch—a formal holiday meal that Gerhard had shared with us many times. He was often late, so it was no surprise that they didn't show up on time. When the doorbell eventually rang, we were taken aback to find a party of six on our doorstep; they had brought their friends along with them, people we'd never met. After the initial shock, we regrouped quickly, reset the dinner table, and enjoyed the meal together. Fortunately, we had enough turkey and plum pudding to go round.

Afterward, we chided Gerhard privately, "Why didn't you ask if you could bring your friends? Or at least let us know they were coming?"

"Vera wanted them to come with us. She wouldn't have come otherwise," he explained.

"But you should've let us know in advance. It was just lucky we had enough food for everyone."

He mumbled an apology but seemed unaware that arriving with unannounced friends for a formal holiday meal wasn't customary behavior in America. Such was Gerhard's naïveté.

## Cultural Crosscurrents

Gerhard's Christmas surprise was the most extreme unplanned event we experienced, but I became accustomed to the flexible planning needed when Ghanaian visitors were expected. They were coming, then they weren't. It would be tomorrow, or maybe next week. They would stay for lunch, or they wouldn't. If they told Clement they would arrive in time for lunch, I was prepared for them to show up two or three hours later. I learned never to make up a bed or serve up a meal until the putative visitor crossed our threshold. But I maintained a state of readiness with multiple contingency scenarios bouncing around in my head, prepared for any eventuality. If they don't arrive in time for lunch, should I save the meal for dinner and give the children something else to eat now? What if they have already eaten when they come or call to say they're delayed and will come tomorrow? The fluidity of the arrangements kept me connected to a world with a rhythm quite unlike that of the hard-driving, tightly scheduled one in which I functioned every day at the office. Different, too, from that of my English family.

Staying with family in England required us to navigate other cultural norms, ones that are quite strict when it comes to planning and punctuality. Although we did our best to fit into their regimen during our visits to England, we joked privately about what often felt like excesses.

During one of our visits, we were invited to Sunday lunch by my sister, Jane, who lives in Camberley—a forty-five-minute drive from Bletchingley in normal traffic; it is family custom to allow an extra fifteen minutes in case of heavy traffic on the M25 motorway. Sunday lunch is always at 1 pm sharp, with about twenty minutes allowed for before-lunch drinks. When it was getting close to noon, Mother hustled us out the door, saying, "You're going to be late for Jane."

We thought we had plenty of time and stopped briefly at Christopher's place to deliver a message. Seeing our car coming down the driveway, he came to the door to greet us.

"I thought you were going to Jane's for lunch. You're going to be late." He was quite agitated.

"It's not yet twelve o'clock. We have time," I reassured him.

"I'll call her and tell her you'll be late," he continued. "You never know what you'll find on the M25 on a Sunday."

In the event, traffic was light, and we arrived on time, not too perturbed by the family's anxious concern. After all, what's a few minutes here or there on a Sunday afternoon? Even in America, we were used to a more relaxed approach to mealtimes.

Unfortunately, we'd gained a reputation in my family for not having our act together when it came to planning and punctuality. It dated back to the time when we were returning to Ghana shortly after Isabelle was born. We arrived at Heathrow to find Ghana Airways was closing the check-in counter. They had overbooked the flight and there were no seats left.

I have a clear memory of arriving before the stated deadline, but the family remembers it differently. Christopher had taken us to the airport but had to get home for another engagement later in the day. Gresham had come to see us off and kindly stayed until we'd figured things out. Getting booked on the KLM flight from Amsterdam to Accra the following day was easy, but we waited all day to get a flight from London to Amsterdam. With a newborn and two-year-old in tow, it was quite a hassle!

Two years later, our arrangements were derailed again when we were leaving Accra for vacation in England. Things were tense politically in Ghana, and medical doctors weren't being allowed to leave the country. Because Clement's passport identified him as "Dr. Lutterodt," he was arrested by the military as we went through the final boarding formalities. No amount of explanation could convince the authorities they were making a mistake. British Caledonian delayed the flight as long as they could but, in the end, had to depart without us. I couldn't leave the country not knowing Clement's fate but had no way of alerting my family that we wouldn't be arriving as planned.

We returned to Grandma's house, uncertain what to do or where to turn. To our great relief, Clement walked in, unharmed, at about 12 am. The military had figured out their mistake, but the damage had been done as far as my family was concerned. The British Caledonian crew failed to contact them as promised, and they had waited in vain at the airport, not knowing what could have happened. I understood their anxiety.

Although Americans are generally more laid back than the British, punctuality is still an issue to be navigated with care. If we're visiting Clement's friends or relatives, I am not too worried. They will tolerate a little lateness. (One colleague, knowing our tendency to turn up late if we're invited for a meal, now gives us a time thirty minutes ahead of when he would like us to arrive. That works!) When we're visiting my family or friends, however, I am always concerned that a late arrival will reinforce an unfortunate stereotype. In Ghana, it's different. There, the stated time for nonwork activities is almost always quite fluid. I can relax.

Our children inevitably found themselves caught in the cultural crosscurrents. They were pig-in-the-middle between what we saw as a laidback approach to child-raising in the U.S. and the much stricter standards of discipline to which Clement adhered. For Clement, adaptation was out of the question. He blamed many of society's ills on the lack of discipline in American homes and schools. I tried to steer a middle course. Although I made some effort to adapt to the ambient culture, I often defaulted to British norms.

When Justine wanted a new pair of shoes in the fashionable style that other children in her class were wearing, I refused on the grounds that her existing ones were still usable. Why spend money on shoes that are not really needed? I wouldn't be drawn into the consumer peer pressure that seemed to be at play. When she needed a new pair the following year, I was happy to get the type she had yearned for. Unfortunately—horror of horrors—the fashion had changed, and Justine was teased for being out of style once again.

Toby got luckier. When I bought him some very respectable boy's shoes in England, he was teased mercilessly in the U.S. for wearing what his classmates thought looked like girls' shoes. I gave in and got him footwear that American children considered appropriate for boys. I acceded to other pressures, too. When Isabelle absolutely had to have a Cabbage Patch doll, I joined the Toys "R" Us lines before Christmas to be sure she got one.

## Growing Up Mixed Race

Just as I was positioned imperfectly at the interface between work and family during the years when the children were growing up, so they, too, lived at the intersection between different worlds: not completely English, or Ghanaian, or American;

neither Black nor White. Their mixed-race status set them apart.

We knew few other biracial families, and few students of color attended the private schools—whether Catholic or Quaker—that the children attended. In the public schools, few of the Black students were in the honors classes. High-achieving Black students were referred to disparagingly as "Oreo cookies" by their peers: Black outside, White inside. In some twisted way their combination of achievement and ambition was thought to be a betrayal of their community. How had society come to stigmatize academic achievement as White folk's business? I wondered. As a result, the children's friends at school were mostly White, with the notable exception of Justine's closest friend, Gina, an African American whose achievements matched her own. Gina gave Justine valuable insights into the African American experience, but we weren't socialized into that community; our experience was different.

I didn't realize at the time how a lack of a community with shared experiences would affect our children's social connectedness. I may not even have acknowledged to myself that our children were different. To me, they were standout kids in every way; I hadn't internalized the reality that others might judge them on skin color alone. In middle school, Justine was teased mercilessly by both Black and White students for her mixed-race appearance, combined, incongruously in the view of her tormenters, with her high achievement in math and other subjects. Black students were not supposed to be good at math.

The one-drop rule used in America to determine racial identity perplexed us. Culturally our children weren't really "Black," certainly not "African American Black." Even though they were always very aware of their Ghanaian identity, the norms at home were largely British and White. And yet in America, there was no doubt about it: They were Black. Justine called me one day from school to say she had to fill in a form that asked her to check a box for her ethnicity. The form had one box for White and one for Black. "It doesn't let me check both," she complained. "What shall I do?" I talked it through with her, concluding, "Well, if you have to choose just one, pick which you prefer?" After she hung up, one of the teachers called her aside and explained to her that, by American criteria, there was no ambiguity. "Because your father is Black, you're Black. That's the box you have to check." She wasn't happy having to renounce one half of who she was.

Some of the issues the children faced are only now emerging, many years later. Isabelle recalls not wanting to tell her classmates she was going on vacation to England, because of the jealousy it might provoke. "How could a Black girl have experiences that my family can't afford?" was the reaction she anticipated. Being friendly with a Black classmate was one thing. It was quite another thing for White students to accept that their Black classmate might be more privileged than they were. It seemed like a replay of what greeted us when we first arrived in Columbia: "If you come from Africa, we expect you to be poor."

Influenced partly by my lingering idealism and certainly by the values that pervaded the Quaker secondary school she attended, Isabelle has always articulated her concern for social justice loud and clear. When she was fifteen, she composed a beautiful dialogue between Archbishop (now Saint) Oscar Romero of El Salvador and a young girl in his diocese. She enacted the dialogue in the form of a dance at an end-of-year performance. I was deeply moved. As an adult, though rejecting the church Romero represented, she made a pilgrimage to the site of his murder.

As an undergraduate, Isabelle shared her outspoken views about local events on the college radio station. It was a Quaker College in North Carolina. Even though the college was in the South, we'd hoped and expected it would embrace the same

Quaker values she had been exposed to at secondary school. We were disappointed. One morning, she woke to find the tires on her car had been slashed. It was an Easter weekend. Clement and I were both at home and immediately drove the six hours to Greensboro to find out what had happened. Neither the college authorities nor the local police would admit to any racial animus or any link to her broadcasts.

"We have these types of events all the time," the police told us.

Yes, sure! I thought.

"Unfortunate, but these things happen," the dorm mother tried to assure us.

"Could she have been targeted for some reason?" I queried, not wanting to use the R-word explicitly.

"Certainly not!" was the dorm mother's response. She was either too naïve to understand or too aware of the potential ramifications to admit that racism might have been at play. We were not surprised to learn a few years later that an incident on campus led the college to undertake a major evaluation of its racial policies.

Toby, though more inclined to dismiss any suggestions of racial discrimination, has also had his share of negative experiences. In his junior year at high school, he inexplicably started getting C's in English. He was normally a straight-A student, with occasional B's. We wondered what was going on.

"The class he's taking is for the top students. He would do better taking English composition," the teacher told me when I questioned his results.

"How could this be?" I asked. "He was placed with this group in his freshman year and has done fine so far. If he's in the wrong group, why didn't the school find it out sooner? He's always been an excellent student." To prove my point, I showed the teacher an outstanding evaluation he had received after participating in a challenging program the previous summer. Is this the same student you're talking about? I wondered.

Normally, I was the one to interact with teachers, but on this occasion, Clement was furious and insisted on a conference with the principal. It emerged that Toby was being teased by other students and had become withdrawn in class. This affected the teacher's evaluation of his ability, leading to a downward cycle in his performance. Since Toby was the only student of color in the group, there may well have been racial undertones. I would have agreed for Toby to take a different English class as the teacher recommended, but Clement would have none of it.

"Toby stays where he is. He can do better," he said with unusual assertiveness. And Toby did just that. The teacher took control of the class dynamics, and his grades improved. At the end of the year, the teacher complimented him on the way he had turned his performance around. She was among his strongest supporters when it came time to write recommendations for college admissions.

At Princeton, Toby undoubtedly experienced the racial pressures that persisted even in the '90s. Planes were always his passion and remain so today: from the time when he drew planes endlessly as a very young child, to the time he spent transfixed by the planes he could see landing at the airport from our apartment window in Tampa, to the many side trips he makes to plane spot, even now as an adult. His ambition as a child was to be a night pilot, but when his shortsightedness made that impossible, he shifted to "route and fleet planning" as his career goal. Not a long shot from the work he does now at Boeing.

During the long vacation of his sophomore year, Toby worked as an engineering intern for Boeing. When the CEO was to pay a visit to the university, Toby was actively involved in the preparations and was confused that he was not invited to the reception. Since no explanation was provided, it's likely race was a factor. For sure, there may have been other reasons, but when such incidents occur again and again, it is hard to ignore the common thread. The embrace of diversity in Princeton's admissions process didn't appear to extend to the way students were treated once they'd been admitted. Like many organizations, Princeton didn't seem to be "walking the talk."

As adults, all three of our children are immersed in racially diverse communities and, in their different ways, contribute to the work of dismantling racial barriers that persist today. Our two daughters have drawn on the lessons learned in their own lives to move the needle of racial understanding and acceptance forward. Isabelle, as director of an art gallery in Los Angeles, has promoted the work of artists from ethnic minorities and those who are disadvantaged in some way, while Justine, as a leadership consultant in London, supports previously excluded groups as they rise within the ranks of senior business leadership. As a senior executive at Boeing, Toby models a career path for people of color in the company. His wife, Miryam, is Spanish and spent many years studying in the U.S. In marrying her, he introduced another international dimension to our family. Having started her career as an engineer at Boeing, Miryam is now an executive coach; in this role she, too, reaches out to those from different ethnic backgrounds to support them in their leadership journey.

The children grew up in the shadow of my struggles at GP and of the fragile balance of work and family I tried hard to maintain. The freedom I acquired in starting my own business was a product of those struggles: freedom to work from home, freedom to set my own working hours and vacations, freedom to forge stronger links to the community. It is a sad irony that these freedoms came too late for the children to benefit.

# Reclaiming Myself

As a child I loved playing games. And I have to say, I was quite good at them. Not physical sports: I don't have an athletic bone in my body. But card games and dominoes and board games. Games that involved a bit of strategy and some cunning, laced with luck. For me, business in America was a high-stakes version of the games I had enjoyed as a child. As with any game, you first had to learn the rules. Then, with a bit of luck, you could outsmart the competition and win. There would be some painful losing along the way, of course, but on balance and in the end, it was important to win. In business, the stakes are higher, because your livelihood depends on winning much of the time.

After a rough beginning, I had learned to play the game at GP and succeeded—for a while. I found a way to operate within the business environment and according to its rules. In doing so, I was able to set aside my youthful idealism without too much discomfort. I had to earn a living, after all. I could've taken solace in Rumi's words, "In the world beyond, there's also traffic and trade," had I known them at the time. "Traffic and trade" was the name of the game I played every day, but there was also a world beyond.

At GP, I had adopted a hard-nosed business persona. I learned to make decisions without asking permission; to fight for my share of the work; to forge alliances and, if need be, push aside those who got in the way; to speak out and, sometimes, to shade the truth. I developed a thick skin to absorb the inevitable criticism and rejection. I built fences around myself, lived with stress as with a friend. I couldn't admit to vulnerability. For sure, I dealt with daily challenges and solved problems when needed, but it was all within a defined framework.

These adaptations suited my temperament—for a while. I do not "do deep" well, so escape was an easy option. I sidestepped issues that were uncomfortable or I didn't understand. Managing people with their complex emotional landscapes has never been my forte and was always my most difficult challenge at GP. As a Catholic, I hadn't been taught how to live with ambiguity. Despite the church's rich rituals and mystical traditions, which at their best plumb the deepest reaches of the human spirit, too much of its life and practice is rigidly rule-based.

For a while at GP, I had the benefit of a friend who ran interference for me when interpersonal issues raised their ugly heads. When she left the company, I had to figure out how to handle such issues myself as best I could. Although I achieved a good measure of success in the niche I had carved out, I remained an outlier in many ways. It is clear to me now that my tenure there couldn't last. I am glad I was the one to end it.

Despite the superficial derring-do of my life's journey, I am at core quite risk averse. But at a few well-defined moments I have had to make life-changing decisions and step into the unknown. Uprooting the family from Cape Coast and moving to the U.S. was one such moment. Another was leaving GP when the business within a business I had built began to unravel. I would be giving up a secure salary for an uncertain future when we still had one child to put through college. But it was time to go. It was a risk I had to take. I hoped some of the contracts I was working on would follow me out the door, but there was no certainty. For Clement—without inside knowledge of the situation at GP—the decision seemed even riskier.

At GP, I had learned what I needed to know—and paid the

price. With many strokes of good luck along the way, Quality Training Systems—the company I started—succeeded beyond expectations. But success was by no means assured.

## *Taking Off*

**I** had prepared a small room in our basement and purchased basic office equipment. I had registered the company. Letterheads and business cards had been printed. I had initiated arrangements with an accountant, an insurance agent, a graphic designer, and other service providers. My last day at GP came and went. The next day was my first as an employee of my own business. After breakfast, I went down to the basement to work. How strange if felt!

One of my first tasks was to send an email to contacts in the industry to inform them of my change in employment and explain my choice of Quality Training Systems (QTS) as the company name. Quality—which would never be compromised; Training—because that would always be the primary focus; and Systems—because as a system, training must interact synergistically with all the other systems at work in an organization. I never wavered from these principles.

An immediate priority was to chase down contract opportunities. Picking up the remainder of a project I'd been working on for Landsvirkjun, the electric utility in Iceland, was easy. I had laid the groundwork before leaving GP, and the manager quickly transferred the project to QTS. Other work soon materialized.

In the late 1990s, in accordance with the pervading zeitgeist, electric utilities and their regulators were convinced that the price of electricity should be market driven, not cost based as it had been historically. One of my former employees was now co-owner of a small company helping utilities work through the changes. His resignation had been a major disappointment for me and so, partly to make up for jumping ship, he engaged my services on a procedure-writing project in New England. I welcomed the revenue. Moreover, the work gave me insight into how market pricing affected the system operator's job. I knew this information would have to be factored into any training programs I worked on in the future.

Then there was "Switching Safety." After Gerry Cauley left GP to work for EPRI, he sponsored a landmark study on the causes and effects of errors when high-voltage electric circuits are switched in and out. Switching errors can lead to power outages, severe injuries, even death. Just one error is one too many. The study was conducted by GP's human factors group with Arthur Beare as lead researcher.

Gerry's introduction to the report, published in 1996, indicated the need for follow-up. I saw an opportunity. If EPRI would allow us to use their good name, we could put on a conference to publicize the findings. I reckoned the conference would pay for itself so we wouldn't need external funding. It worked out well. The conference took place shortly before I left GP and generated considerable interest.

When the EPRI manager responsible for switching safety received the email about my start-up company, he reached out to me, offering to sponsor some small-scale research and a second conference. That was good news indeed! With Arthur and others, I got to work. Over the next few years we completed several research projects on ways to mitigate switching errors and the conference became an annual fixture. Gradually we developed a community of utility personnel committed to promoting safe, reliable practices. I am proud to say that the tradition continues to this day: The 27th Annual Conference was held in New Orleans in September 2023.

Another lucky break opened the door to a long and fruitful relationship with a major electric utility in California. A few days into my new job, I was sitting quietly in my basement office when I got a surprise call.

"Hello, this is Bill Ellis." Bill was responsible for the purchase of a large training simulator for the substation training school. I'd met him at conferences on training simulators but didn't know him well.

"Hello, Bill. Good to hear from you. How did you track me down?"

"I called your office," he replied. "There was a message to call this number." No one had erased the message I'd recorded on my office phone! It was a real stroke of luck.

"As a matter of fact, I'm no longer at GP," I said. "I just started up on my own."

"I wondered what was going on," Bill replied. "I thought I'd give this number a shot anyway."

"Really good to hear from you. How's the simulator project coming along? Anything I can do to help?"

There was. A few weeks later I traveled to California to meet Bill, who introduced me to Tom, the manager of the Substation Training School. Tom had only just taken up the position; he was eager for new ideas and fresh expertise. We hit it off immediately. With Mary, a well-seasoned operator and one of the few women in the department, it was a different matter. She had been designated as the simulator trainer, so we needed to get along, but I saw right away she was suspicious. She could scarcely look me in the eye. I almost heard her thinking, "What can this person possibly know of the operator's job? A woman of a certain age, who speaks with a la-di-da accent?" It was a familiar theme.

Fortunately, the initial project worked out well, and more contracts followed. Gradually Mary's attitude changed, and over time we developed an excellent working relationship. She came to trust my instructional insights, while I was always careful to respect her technical knowledge and operating experience.

After the simulator project, Tom hired QTS to design training programs for every craft that came through the school, and more. I got an insider's view of tasks as diverse as climbing poles, managing outages, swinging in baskets to reach otherwise unreachable high-voltage transmission lines, and entering vaults to work on underground transformers. We worked with technicians designing lighting systems, planning transmission projects, maintaining transformers, and implementing the complex relay schemes needed to protect electric circuits when faults occur. I relished every opportunity.

The people whose jobs we documented lived in a different world. Or I should say different worlds—plural—because each craft was like a world unto itself with its own expertise and sense of self-worth. Almost without exception, the employees we worked with were serious, committed to their trade, and keen for us to recognize their unique expertise. They had difficulty believing that anyone on the outside could understand what they did, still less a woman—and several of those who worked with me as subcontractors to QTS were women. The "innocence game" proved its value yet again. By positioning ourselves as naïve questioners, inviting job incumbents to tell us about their work, and listening well, we were able to win the confidence of the most ornery characters and develop relationships of mutual respect.

Tom personified the restless Californian appetite for change and innovation. He was a fund of new ideas. On each visit he had a fresh project he wanted me to work on, another book he thought I should read. It was stimulating to work with him as he tried new ways to move the organization forward. For a consultant, it was a perfect relationship and provided a steady flow of project work for many years.

The transition to working on my own had been easier and more seamless than I ever expected. There was scarcely a gap in my income stream. When the first checks arrived in mid-September, Clement and I cracked open the champagne!

## *A Welcome Change of Pace*

As my workload increased, I needed administrative help, and it soon became clear that I needed a larger office than we could configure in our existing home. We were fortunate to find a house close by that perfectly matched my needs. It had a large finished basement with its own bathroom and external entrance. We moved there in 1999.

The new house bordered the pathways that thread Columbia, and Clement and I developed the healthy habit of taking a brisk walk each morning. The streams we crossed rose and fell according to the rainfall. It was a good prelude to my working day. Going down to the basement to work became my norm. I wouldn't have had it otherwise. I didn't miss the rough and tumble of office life or the water-cooler conversations. The morning coffee I depended on was always available. I loved the freedom. I loved not having to manage employees. I wasn't troubled by the need to please the boss or worry about the bottom line beyond the need to contribute my share of family expenses.

From my desk, I looked out across a grassy space that sloped gradually down to a stream—it was too rough to be called a lawn in the British sense. There were many trees on which to rest my gaze. Beneath the trees, there were daffodils in the spring and flowers in the summer if I got around to planting them in time. From time to time, a deer—sometimes two or more—could be seen feeding in the distance. Occasionally a fox would wander through. One winter evening, two owls with large, solemn eyes huddled by the window. It was a rare sight. Once, an employee nearly tripped over a snapping turtle as she came down the path to the office entrance.

Often Justine's cat, Annabelle, lay curled up on my desk, enjoying the warm glow of the reading lamp. Things got a little edgy the year that Isabelle was doing her master's degree in England and her cat, Elektra, lived with us too. The two cats didn't get along and, at first, competed for the same spot under the lamp. Fortunately, the basement had enough space for them to live their separate lives, and they soon achieved a modus vivendi.

Much of the time, I was in the office on my own, but others came quite regularly for meetings. Carolyn Zimmerman, a former colleague at GP, was part of the QTS team on almost every project. I couldn't have managed without her. Arthur came to help with the switching safety projects. Temporary admin helpers came and went. Later, Debbie Marcin joined me for four hours each day. She had been my secretary at GP and was a tremendous asset. We knew each other well, and our customers came to rely on her. She stayed for ten years.

At first, I hued closely to the business rules and model I had internalized at GP. No doubt those practices enabled my success. But as time went on, I was able to relax and pick up threads of my earlier life; the boundaries became less rigid. It was an opportunity to shed elements of the business persona I had assumed and reconnect with my center. Debbie noticed the change.

## A Small Investment . . . and a Lot of Luck

In the early 2000s, the stock market was in decline, but Quality Training Systems was doing well. I wondered how best to invest for retirement. The pundits suggested putting money in companies one knew and understood. Why not invest in QTS? I asked myself.

During the January lull—when last year's projects have been completed and clients haven't yet finalized their budgets for the coming year—I had an idea. One of the projects we'd done for EPRI involved a generic task analysis of the job responsibilities and training needs of switching personnel. A colleague had taken the initiative of storing the data in

Microsoft's database program, MS Access. Why not extend the database to include all the tasks performed by system operators? A database with generic data could be used as a starting point for the company-specific training programs clients were asking for. I thought it was worth a shot. Besides, sorting and organizing the data would be a fun thing to do during the dull days of January.

I asked the colleague if she'd like to work with me on the project since the database had been her idea. I wasn't sorry when she declined. I could do it my own way and would have sole ownership of the result. It was another stroke of luck; there would be many more. I never imagined that the product I dreamed up one grey January day would succeed as well as it did. When I sold QTS some fifteen years later, more than a hundred electric utilities across the U.S. and Canada were using what I'd called, quite simply, Quality Training Database (QTD). By then, its capabilities had been vastly expanded to become a repository for all grid operators' training records. But it didn't happen all at once.

As I worked on the prototype, I sought advice and feedback from many friends in the industry and ran demonstrations at industry meetings. Some thought the idea had real potential; others thought it was premature—or way too complicated. The family wondered who would ever pay for such a tool. Despite the mixed messages, I persisted. It wasn't costing much to develop the content and I was able to hire a small software company to improve the programming for a relatively small initial investment.

Fast forward to the afternoon of August 14th, 2003. I was on vacation, riding the London underground, and glanced at the headlines in the *Evening Standard*: "Blackout in the Northeast of the United States! New York and other major cities in the dark!" Could it be? This was the rare event that system operators train for, only half hoping it will never happen. Like the proverbial ambulance chaser, I realized at once that what was bad news for electric utilities and their customers meant good news for training.

Returning to the States, I found the industry abuzz. The trainer from Con Edison in New York City had been on vacation in South Carolina when the blackout hit and had driven home immediately to assist with the restoration. Thanks to their intensive training, the operators at Con Edison and across the region restored power as efficiently as possible, but black-start restoration is necessarily a slow, methodical process, and it was a day or more before restoration was complete. The damage was considerable, and consumers were upset.

The final report of the Investigation Committee identified three major culprits: Tools, Trees, and Training. Training! It was clear that training standards would soon become mandatory. The 2003 blackout was a big wake-up call for grid operations, just as the accident at Three Mile Island (TMI) had been for the nuclear industry. For training consultants, it was a huge opportunity.

I realized that QTD could become a valuable tool in monitoring compliance with whatever standards emerged in the future, but I was uncertain whether companies would put up money for it when its usefulness wasn't yet assured. In December 2003, I demonstrated the database's still embryonic capabilities at an industry meeting, having made a promise to myself: if four or five companies committed to purchasing QTD, I would continue to invest in it. But I wasn't sure what the price tag should be.

I was in luck again: A young go-ahead manager from a government entity in the Midwest was interested; his spending limit was $2,500. I had my answer: I would charge $2,490. Three other companies were prepared to buy for that price. And so, for initial sales of just under $10,000, I committed myself to QTD's future. I knew I would have to make a big push to sell the product more widely.

A break came when Henry—the GP employee I had fired several years ago who was now, once again, influential in the training community—invited me to demonstrate QTD to utilities in the Western part of the U.S. It was a generous gesture after his humbling experience at GP; I will always be grateful for the opportunity he gave me. The demo bore good fruit. After a couple of years, most of the electric utilities west of the Rockies had become QTD users.

Progress in the Midwest was slower. I had come to know Midwesterners as savvy albeit somewhat conservative: slow to spend money on anything that is not tried and true. They may let you believe they're naïve, but don't be deceived! They just take time to make decisions. Most of the trainers in the region gathered for a seminar each year at Iowa State University. I knew many of them. They were almost exclusively men. They drove pickups and ran businesses on the side. Many of them had grown up as farm boys but gained solid technical skills in the military. They knew their stuff. And they enjoyed their food—particularly if it was free. I decided to hold a Happy Hour during the annual seminar. I'd provide finger food and drink while demonstrating QTD. Hopefully I'd drum up some interest and make a few sales.

The attendees turned up in their numbers and listened attentively as I went through the demo. So far, so good. Alas, I hadn't realized another vendor was offering a complimentary dinner the very same evening. My Happy Hour was at 6:30 pm, and the dinner at 7:00 pm. I had barely finished my presentation when, like Cinderella on the stroke of midnight, they got up and left. All of them. I sank into a chair like a deflated balloon. The hotel server tried to console me as she cleared away the food and drink.

At GP, I'd learned you need thick skin to survive the rejections that accompany any marketing activity. Sure enough. Eventually I made several sales within the Midwest region, but I'd paid a price.

## Growing the Product

In its first incarnation, QTD was simply a repository for task-analysis data, but it had the potential to be much more. Listening to trainers gave me ideas for features that would be key to its widespread adoption. When NERC introduced an operator certification requirement, one trainer asked, "Can we use QTD to store certification results?"

"Great idea," I thought and quickly set to work with our programmer to figure out how to do it.

"It'd help if we could link tasks to on-the-job training records," one person commented. I seized on the idea.

"We should be able to upload operators' records to the NERC database," others advised.

"We'll do that for sure!" I promised, even though I had no idea how.

Each year, we added features requested by users or ones that were logical extensions of QTD's core capabilities. I was lucky with the timing. QTD was taking off just as training standards resulting from the blackout were being formalized. I followed each twist and turn.

Our programmer exploited every capability of MS Access to build a robust and reliable tool, but our clients wanted a more professional platform. I wasn't sure where to begin. I barely knew how to spell SQL Server, which seemed to be the platform of choice. I searched online and spoke to friends, neighbors, and acquaintances. Some, seeking a business opportunity and sensing my ignorance, offered to reprogram QTD at their expense, after which they would take ownership. I didn't much like that idea. Other companies quoted exorbitant prices once they had figured out the number and complexity of the business rules to be accommodated.

Eventually I settled on a small company in Arizona that used teams of programmers in India. They proposed to complete the transition for a reasonable price and had credible references. Unfortunately, it didn't go well. During a demo early on, I protested that what they were showing us did not include functionality I had specified. The project lead responded patronizingly, "What we're showing you is better." It wasn't an encouraging sign. After many delays and minimal progress, I asked an experienced programmer I knew to look at the code. His verdict was unambiguous: "This is the worst programming I've ever seen." I had no option but to cancel the project.

I returned, humbled and cap in hand, to our original programmers. It was like a homecoming! They bore us no resentment. Their SQL programmer, Bill, was skilled, courteous, and always a good listener. He remained our primary programmer for many years. When, at my retirement party, I chose to quote from *Four Quartets*, Bill told me it was one of his favorite poems. I wasn't surprised. Bill had that quality about him. It was a moment of connection I remember fondly.

To help manage the transition to the new platform, we hired an industrial engineer, Lakshmi Gopalaiah. She soon became a treasured employee. I came to rely on her unreservedly in responding to the many technical challenges we encountered during the changeover and in subsequent developments.

As the industry's training requirements evolved, we kept adding new features to enhance QTD's usefulness to our customers. Managing the new releases soon became a nightmare. It was our daughter Justine, working for QTS between jobs, who came up with the idea of a licensing arrangement. In return for an annual fee, customers would automatically receive new versions as they were released. For our customers, the annual fee became a routine budget item; for us, it provided an assured revenue stream. It was a win-win solution and one that many prominent software sellers have now adopted.

## *What of the Future?*

As the number of QTD users grew, my thoughts turned to the future. Who would take over QTS when I retired? I was in my mid-sixties and was already looking for more flexibility in my working life. Besides, I was beginning to tire of "playing the game." Had I been working only as a consultant, I could have simply closed shop, but with QTD it was a different matter. I didn't want to walk away from the twenty-five or more utilities now using the database as the repository for their training records.

One consultant I approached visited me in my basement office and quickly jumped to a conclusion.

"Let the users have the code. Then they can maintain it themselves," he advised. "I'd be glad to help in any communication with the clients."

"Hmm! I guess that's an option." I replied hesitantly.

"Your programmer could teach them the code," he went on.

"That might be difficult," I said. "The programmer doesn't speak good English. He's Ukrainian." It was before we transitioned to SQL when Bill took over the programming.

"All the more reason to get out now," he pronounced, confident he had the solution.

I could almost see his mind ticking over: woman—home office—rinky-dink software—MS Access—foreign programmer—hopeless situation! He made no effort to understand QTD's market potential and showed little respect for the time and effort I had invested in it. I found him arrogant and glib.

"Thank you. I'll think about it," I said as I showed him to the door. Male hubris, alive and well, is what I was thinking.

I considered selling the company but soon learned it wasn't a simple matter. QTS was not like a dental practice or dry-cleaning company. There were no comparable businesses. Moreover, it served a niche market. It would be difficult to settle on a price and locate a buyer. I talked to several people who specialized in business valuations. Each time I circled around the question I came back to the same conclusion: It wasn't going to be easy. GP was the only company that showed any serious interest. Although their operations personnel favored the acquisition, the deal fell through because the financial folks wanted to know how much capital had been invested in developing QTD. Oh well! Keeping track of capital investment wasn't part of the business game I was familiar with.

It was time to approach the future in a different way. Whether or not I sold the business, I needed someone who could work alongside me and eventually take over day-to-day responsibility. Besides, QTS would be more saleable if our flagship product was supported by staff who knew it well. One of my contacts in California put me in touch with Stefanie Pressl, who had previously worked as a training manager for Tom, my client in California. She and her husband had moved to Chicago to help her parents with their business. It hadn't worked out, and she was in the process of deciding her next steps. The timing was perfect; it was another stroke of luck!

Stefanie agreed to give it a try on the understanding she would gradually move into a position of responsibility. Over the next couple of years, she helped QTS evolve from an eclectic group of subcontractors working out of my basement to a small company with regular employees. It was Stefanie who helped hire Lakshmi, who then joined Debbie each day in the office. Stefanie herself was based in Chicago but visited regularly. Carolyn and Arthur were also frequent visitors. Joyce Engmann, an old friend from Cape Coast days, was there quite often, too. I roped her in to work on many of our projects, and she enjoyed the work, even if it meant traveling all the way from England. The office hummed with activity, and I loved it.

Stefanie was instrumental in putting processes in place that were needed for the company to grow. With her penchant for order and precision, she was always several steps ahead of me in wanting to proceduralize operations. I dragged my feet, concerned that too much bureaucracy would bog us down. I saw it as a healthy tension, allowing us to edge forward gradually. With hindsight, I realize that Stefanie may have experienced it differently.

## A Kinder, Gentler Me?

With Stefanie on board, QTS changed; its future seemed more assured. While I was interested in winding down, she was interested in growth. I got used to the idea of having employees once again, but I wanted to do things differently. I wanted to model healthier work rhythms and relationships than I had experienced at GP. My early idealism was beginning to resurface.

Being free of the constraints of corporate life gave me time to reconnect with my spiritual center. As I delved into the teachings of Thomas Merton, Gerald May, and others, I pondered my situation. It was one thing to embody spiritual values in occupations such as teaching or nursing or eldercare, quite another to transpose them into the business world. How does the imperative for love and compassion square with the demands of competition and efficiency? In a piece I wrote at the time, I expressed it this way:

*Contrary to life in the spirit, life in the free-market economy is loud, self-congratulatory, impersonal, addicted to partial truth-telling . . . free markets may be the best we've got for now but we can and should manage free markets in a way that promotes and does not undermine morality . . . we live with the paradox of a system that depends on competitive self-seeking but is enhanced by cooperation. How should we live with this ambiguity?*

Although I concluded that living with ambiguity is a challenge in all our relationships, this period of reflection certainly led to a shift in the way I hoped to relate to people I encountered in doing business: customers, competitors, and employees. Whenever possible I wanted to shift from "It-it" to "I-thou" interactions, to use the words of the early twentieth-century philosopher Martin Buber or, stated differently, to move from transactional encounters to relationships. As leader of my own business, I could take distance from the rigid imperatives I had known at GP and reevaluate some of the boxed-in thinking I had taken on board. It didn't hurt that we were making good money and could afford to take a more relaxed attitude to the bottom line.

I found the ambiguity easiest to resolve in our dealings with customers. We had a stake in their success, so the relationship was inherently win-win. Moving from "us and them" to "we" was not too much of a leap. We could develop personal relationships with prospects—who might otherwise exist simply as names in a marketing spreadsheet—as we helped them work through internal battles to get approval to purchase QTD. These relationships were strengthened if we could anticipate problems they might experience in using the product and if they—for their part—were prepared to accept the difficulties we might face in meeting their needs in a timely manner.

I like to think we were largely successful in building a community of QTD users with whom we could relate in a way that wasn't purely transactional. There was Carolyn—the manager of training for a very large multi-site utility—who always referred to me endearingly as "Dr. Sarah." On a visit to their head office, I was waiting with her in the conference room when she called a key participant to remind him of the upcoming meeting. Not realizing he was on speaker phone, he asked, "Has what's-her-face arrived?" After a moment of embarrassment, we both burst out laughing and teased the manager about his choice of words when he eventually showed up.

Then there was Eddie, who struggled with learning how to use QTD. When he finally understood how to perform a particular task, he thanked us, apologizing sadly for his slowness, "I'm just a worn-out old operator." It was a moment of human connection.

Although I believe that the principle of putting the customer first filtered through to all those who worked for me, I don't want to imply there wasn't sometimes a tension between what a customer wanted and what we could offer. Or that there were not customers who, for whatever reason, seemed impossible to please. On one occasion, Lakshmi was at her wits' end trying to explain what could and couldn't be done to solve a problem faced by a customer in New York. He wasn't the end-user of QTD but someone in the IT department checking for compliance with the company's internal standards. Let's call him Zach. Zach was unwilling to listen to Lakshmi's explanation and was coming back at her in a tone that was as direct and demanding as New Yorkers can be. Lakshmi was almost in tears. Our desks were just across from each other in the open-plan basement office, so I heard what was going on and decided to step in.

"Lakshmi is doing her best to help you," I told Zach. Then—in a rare moment of scolding a client—I went on, "I would appreciate it if you could talk to her in a more respectful tone." He calmed down a bit, then said, "I'd like to speak to your supervisor."

"That would be difficult," I replied.

It was very unusual for a customer to try bullying one of our employees. Mostly they were grateful when we went the extra mile to help them. And we almost always did.

Relating to competitors is an entirely different matter. The relationship is almost always zero-sum and therefore tends to be adversarial. You win, I lose. Or you lose, I win. Even when you adopt the attitude "let the best person win" or "win one, lose one," there is almost always an underlying tension. While I tried to establish relationships of mutual respect with our competitors, it didn't always work out that way.

On one occasion, we lost a competitive bid that should have been ours for the taking. The loss stung, so I was glad when the customer agreed to debrief me on his decision. When the customer told me the name of the winning bidder—Manny R.—I was shocked. I had known Manny at GP many years earlier. We had had a very difficult relationship. I thought I had long forgotten our past struggles, but at the mention of his name, I shouted into the phone: "That scumbag!" The words came out before I had time to think. This was hardly the newer, gentler me I had hoped to become!

Within the company, I tried to create an atmosphere where employees enjoyed coming to work each day and where each employee's contribution was valued. I knew of too many work environments where employees felt undervalued and hated their jobs. Alas, my efforts faltered as the company grew.

Our staff and contractors worked at several different locations. To promote teamwork, we held annual off-site meetings, including both fun and business-related activities. Following these gatherings, working relationships between employees at different locations were usually better for a while, but it was difficult to maintain the momentum throughout the year. In particular, an "us versus them" atmosphere emerged between those working in our Columbia and Chicago offices. The tensions arose out of typical workplace issues: an employee who was not pulling his or her weight was let go, what was intended as a generous gesture to one employee was interpreted as discriminatory by another, and so on. Dealing with human relationships has never been my strength. Try as I did, I wasn't able to respond effectively to these tensions and create as employee friendly a work environment as I hoped for.

## Stepping Back

Bit by bit, Stefanie picked up more of the day-to-day responsibilities of running the company, but I still didn't have an exit strategy. I continued to explore an outright sale, but the more I looked and the more people I consulted, the more impossible it seemed. Stefanie was interested in taking over, but she couldn't afford to buy me out. I went to the internet in search of a way forward.

Once again, I was lucky. The search led me to someone who specialized in the transition of small family-owned businesses: Ronen Shefer. Ronen was exactly who I needed. After studying the nuts and bolts of the business, he saw the opportunities that existed within our niche market. Importantly, he saw a path by which Stefanie could eventually purchase the company with relatively little starting capital. At first, it seemed like financial jujitsu. I wondered whether it could really work.

I vacillated for a while, hesitating over the details. I was concerned that Stefanie was not quite ready to take over, but maybe I was simply not prepared to cut loose from a company in which I had invested so much of myself. Eventually, with Ronen's help, we settled on a two-step process: Stefanie would first become a junior partner in the business, then proceed gradually to full ownership. As we worked out the financial arrangements, Ronen helped Stefanie develop a more strategic vision of the role she'd have to play as business owner, gradually alleviating any concerns I had on that account.

The process worked. I retired from active involvement at the end of 2014, and the sale was finalized in August 2016. Ronen provided a steady hand to help Stefanie and me through the financial aspects of the transition. Redefining our roles and working relationships proved more difficult. The underlying issues were never fully resolved, to my lasting regret. Happily, however, QTS continues to flourish under Stefanie's leadership. The company I founded lives on.

The decision to leave GP had served me well. As my own boss at QTS, I had started to dismantle the hard-nosed persona I'd found necessary for survival at GP. I was able to soften the fenced-in thinking that seemed an inevitable part of the "traffic and trade" of business. Now I was cutting loose from QTS, the company that had absorbed almost twenty years of my life. When I concluded the sale, after a year and a half of retirement, I had started to reach beyond the narrow confines of American business and reengage with strands in my life that had long been sidelined, including issues of global economic development that had absorbed me in my youth.

I was grateful for what I'd been able to achieve during my more than thirty-year career in the U.S., for the many strokes of luck that had enabled me to start a company and build a widely used training tool. Several people told me they didn't think I'd be able to let go, but when the final break came it was a relief. I was ready.

# Life Outside of Work

B eyond the poles of work and family around which my life revolved when the children were growing up was the wider community. In my work, I operated on my own as a White person; in his work as a professor at Howard University, Clement's identity as a Black person went largely unnoticed. Outside of work, it was different. There, we were together as a couple, and issues of race, for better or worse, were never far from our awareness. We navigated the situations we encountered with varying degrees of success. Belonging was elusive. Within the patchwork of our lives, the pieces were imperfectly stitched together.

## The Burden of Blackness

As immigrants, our experience of racial dynamics in the U.S. differs from that of African Americans, who have inherited the weight of America's history. In doing so, they have built individual and communal defenses of which we were quite ignorant. Per the "one-drop rule," our children were Black. Yet they—or I should say we—didn't have a Black community to prepare us for what we experienced or to fall back on when needed. Although we haven't suffered dramatic incidents of racial hostility, our lives in the U.S. have been permeated by micro-aggressions, misperceptions, and subtle or not-so-subtle forms of discrimination.

When we were on family road trips and arrived at our

destination for the night, I always went in to register and get the room key before the family appeared. It is all too common for Blacks to be assigned to less desirable rooms. It happened when we went to Mexico on vacation; we arrived at the hotel on the tour operator's bus and were shown to sub-standard rooms. It happened when Clement went to give a seminar at a university near Spokane. The university had arranged for him to have a room overlooking the mountains, but he was ushered into a basement room. "Did you enjoy the view?" his hosts asked him the next day. "Well, not exactly," he responded, not sure what they meant. When the truth spilled out, his hosts were shocked. Clement tells the story often. African Americans might have dismissed the incident as par for the course: "What do you expect? It happens all the time." It is what they have grown up with.

In the early years, our response to such slights was to adopt the critical posture of entitled outsiders: "Who do they think they are?" or "How foolish of them to carry on like that!" or "I can't be bothered with people who behave that way!" By harboring such thoughts—and conveying them subliminally—we probably deepened our own feelings of isolation and reinforced the hurtful behaviors we experienced. Later, my response alternated between angry dismissal and a desire to meet people halfway. Clement's response was to withdraw.

Because of the bias he so often detects beneath the surface, Clement always wants me to be the front person in dealing with "third parties," be they plumbers or bankers or even doctors. "You do it; they will listen to you" is his frequent refrain. All too often, his typically unhurried approach in getting to the point of a conversation—a form of politeness that serves him well in Ghana—is seen as ineptness by Americans who have little time or patience for his circumlocutions. His indirect approach is interpreted as inability to comprehend.

An extreme example that has become part of family lore occurred when we were crossing the border back to the U.S.

after a vacation in Vancouver, Canada. The customs agent asked Clement, who was driving, where we lived in the U.S. Hesitating, he turned to me for the answer. Justine—so like her father—helps me understand Clement's tendency to disengage from commonplace reality. She explains it as a consequence of his abstract mathematical mind and disengagement from practicalities, traits she recognizes in herself.

Too often, Clement's reluctance to engage leads to a downward spiral of disrespect; the White people involved, unaware of their own deeply rooted dispositions, prefer to address me, sidelining him. It happened on a recent doctor's visit. Clement was the patient, but I could sense the young White doctor wanted to direct his comments to me. I refused to engage, shifting my gaze between Clement's face and the foot being treated. This time, Clement didn't flinch. He kept his eyes firmly on the doctor. But the doctor's eyes kept wandering back to me. The dance continued throughout the consultation.

Over the years, Clement has been worn down by the negative stereotyping he has encountered and the need for pre-emptive behavior, such as wearing a tie if he wants to be taken seriously when checking in at an airport or buying a car or meeting the bank manager. He is quick to notice a cracked plate, a lesser portion of food, or being passed over in line and label it as discrimination. Within the family, we jokingly talk of his penchant for conspiracy theories, but I am surprised how often African Americans concur with his interpretation of events. For them, the constant slights are all too common, not imagined at all.

Whatever the truth of the matter, and however much Clement's interpretation of events may be colored by a lack of trust traceable to his childhood, it is indisputable that the cumulative experience of his years living in America has taken a heavy toll. What became of the young man who, at Cape

Coast University, was one of the few Ghanaians to mix freely with his expatriate colleagues, seemingly unfazed by differences in culture or skin color?

## An African Mathematician?

Clement's profession as a mathematician challenges stereotypes, often exposing an underlying need of White people to assert their dominance. When asked what he does—or did before retirement—he braces himself for the predictable response. A typical conversation goes something like this:

"What do you do?"

"I teach at Howard University."

"What do you teach?"

"Mathematics."

Clement offers the information with some hesitation in anticipation of what's to follow. Sometimes the person responds:

"Goodness, you must be so clever. I never could do math at school." The surprise evident in the person's voice seems to have a subtext: "What is an African doing teaching mathematics?" or "You don't look as though you are more intelligent than me," or simply, "I can't get my head around this."

Other times, the response is more enthusiastic, "How wonderful! I always loved math. What branch do you specialize in?" Clement's answer, "Complex analysis in several variables," usually leaves questioners entirely at a loss. It's as though they were expecting him to say "algebra" or "trigonometry"—subjects they might have studied in high school.

Thankfully, at Howard, Clement was not an anomaly. He was surrounded by Black mathematicians from all over the world. Howard provided a safe environment for his mathematical career to flourish. Thankfully, too, his initial one-year appointment was renewed and led, in due course, to tenure and the rank of full professor. With the help of the university, we were able to shed our temporary-worker status, get our green cards in 1983, and become citizens in 1995. Howard had enabled our integration into U.S. society.

As a pioneer among Historically Black Colleges and Universities (HBCUs), Howard is an institution with a proud history, but the faculty were not immune to the politicking endemic in most academic institutions. Ethnic tensions existed—with clear fault lines between African American faculty members, Whites, and immigrants of African or Caribbean descent. However, these divisions, deeply rooted as they were in America's racial past, didn't carry with them the crushing burden of perceived inferiority so often associated with Blackness. Clement's competence wasn't questioned a priori, as it almost certainly would have been in a predominantly White institution. But faculty debate swirled around what to expect of the students, most of whom were Black.

A recurring issue was whether to relax academic standards, given the disadvantaged educational backgrounds of many of the students. This very same issue had been a bone of contention at Cape Coast, pitting Ghanaian faculty, who for the most part wanted to maintain universally recognized standards, against expatriates. At Howard, the White faculty typically advocated for a "lighter" curriculum, while Clement and many—but not all—of the Black faculty argued against. Clement insisted that students whose undergraduate instruction in mathematics had been insufficiently rigorous should be helped to catch up; they should graduate with a Ph.D. that was second to none. Lowering standards, he maintained, would imply that Black students weren't capable of becoming qualified mathematicians. In the long term this would devalue Howard credentials and adversely affect all graduates of the program. It was another version of the question, "What's an African doing studying mathematics?" Ultimately it was a racist position, albeit not acknowledged as such.

## Outliers

Over the years, our efforts to build connections with others in the community have met with varying degrees of success. We have usually been outliers in the different neighborhoods where we've lived. Not easily assimilated. Even though we participated in block parties and included many neighbors in our own holiday parties or family celebrations, the invitations were not often returned. In hindsight, I realize the barriers were probably rooted in a lack of sensitivity to our situation or simply a lack of ease around us. Typically, Caucasians simply don't know what to make of a well-spoken African mathematician married to a well-educated English woman. But we have experienced a few situations of more overt rejection.

At one point, a nuclear chemist recently hired by GP moved into the house next door. Given Bill's particular skill set, his work consisted mostly of on-site assignments requiring long periods of time away from home. His wife seemed to resent my more privileged role as a manager. Although I traveled frequently, the trips were never more than a few days long; it was the line in the sand I had drawn for myself early in my career at GP. When the couple took a stroll in the neighborhood during one of Bill's home visits, they chose to cross the street rather than pass directly in front of our house. A simple case of human jealousy? Maybe, but it is hard to believe there wasn't a racial twist!

A rift with another of our neighbors arose when Mai—the Vietnamese wife of a former CIA officer—was taking care of the children after school. Mai was an expansive character, energetic and unpredictable. Although she had by this time lived many years in America, she was still not attuned to the culture. One afternoon, when the children next door had come to play, the older girl misbehaved in some way and Mai slapped her. Oops! The children greeted me with the story as soon as I got home. Sensing trouble, I immediately went to offer an apology to the child's mother.

"It shouldn't have happened. I'm really, really sorry. I told Mai she should never slap a child," I said, reiterating numerous times how sorry I was and concluding, "It's probably better if the children don't come over unless I'm home."

The mother listened politely. I thought she had accepted my apology, but I must have misread her. When the family had a party to celebrate the First Communion of one of their children, we were the only neighbors not to be invited. An invisible wall now separated their house from ours. Maybe the barrier had been there all along. It just took the incident with Mai to end the pretense of politeness.

There have, of course, been exceptions—individuals and families who have gone out of their way to be accepting. There was the family in our first neighborhood who had adopted several children of different races in addition to having one child of their own. They were among the first to extend a hand of friendship. Then there was the family of one of Justine's classmates in Montessori school—also biracial; they are still our friends. There was also the family of Isabelle's best friend in middle school who made a point of welcoming her for many sleepovers and extended their friendship to us as a family. When Clement had to rush to Ghana following the death of his mother just before Christmas in 1988, they included the children and me in their Christmas dinner. It was a gesture of friendship I'll always remember. A less probable friend was our right-wing neighbor of many years' standing. He and Clement often chatted in a mutually respectful way while doing yard work, teasing each other about their radically different political views.

Although Columbia remains a very mixed community—with its population rapidly approaching majority-minority and a lot of interracial mixing among the millennial generation—

as an older mixed-race couple, we are something of a rarity. The longevity of our marriage challenges stereotypes. When Clement had an extended stay in hospital in 2005, I spent long hours at his bedside. Seeing me there, many hospital workers asked, "And who are you?" I doubt they would have asked the question if we'd both been the same race. In a similar vein, we're often asked, "How long have you two been married?" Finding the question impertinent, I've always been happy to silence the questioner with my answer of thirty, forty, or—now—fifty years!

The dissonance that our family situation causes many well-meaning White people was evident at a parish event when a Ghanaian speaker we knew came to make an appeal on behalf of Catholic Relief Services (CRS). Clement came with me. One of the deacons, who had met the speaker when he visited Ghana as part of a CRS delegation, was there with his wife. When I introduced Clement, the deacon's wife, after looking first at me, then at Clement, then back again, said to me in amazement, "But I see you in church all the time!" And so? I thought. True, I was often at church on my own. True, too, I had a Ghanaian husband who was Black. She seemed to have difficulty putting the two together. I was mixing things up for her, and she was confused. I imagined the narrative playing out in her mind: "Africa is out there—other—poor people who need our help. I thought you were one of us." Her inability to reconcile the two realities and willingness to voice this out loud was almost comical.

## Finding Community

While the sense that we were outsiders persisted, the family gradually accommodated itself to life in the U.S., and we came to see Columbia as home. We were fully immersed in the systems—educational, medical, financial—that support a middle-class lifestyle in America. In fact, there was a time when I felt so settled in the rhythms of life, school, and work that I didn't envision a life elsewhere for ourselves or our children. When Justine was in her early teens, we were faced with a decision. British laws governing nationality had changed. Given that she has a British mother, she could claim UK nationality, provided she did so before she turned eighteen. I wondered whether we should bother. Fortunately, Justine was clear: "Yes, please apply." The decision was vindicated when she chose to make her home in England.

Bonds of loyalty and genuine affection connect me still to some of my former employees at QTS, but I've retained few friends from my long years at GP. Finding points of connection to the ex-military folks was just too difficult. My years at GP served me well, but it was never my true home. Friendships with Clement's colleagues have proved more enduring. They are an eclectic group from all over the world, bonded by their love of mathematics and many years together as faculty colleagues. I have developed a level of trust with many of his Black colleagues, even though it took time to achieve. And Clement is at ease with several former White colleagues whose racial attitudes reflect their long immersion in a mostly Black university. Knowing Clement in the work setting provided a pathway for connection and acceptance, undercutting the barriers that so often exist between the races. Yet, as I reflect on these relationships, the very need to describe them so cautiously speaks to the difficulty in forming deep interracial friendships in divided America.

If I have found community in Columbia, it has been mostly within the local Catholic parish, even though it took many years in coming. Our welcome by the parish had been nonexistent when we first arrived, but being a Catholic has always been a part of my identity, and it was important to me that our children be brought up Catholic.

When it came time for Toby to be confirmed, we didn't know anyone we could ask to be his sponsor. We were fortunate that Mark Wong volunteered. Mark is Chinese, his wife is Caucasian. In addition to having one child of their own, they adopted Afro-Korean twin daughters; here was a family who understood issues of cross-cultural identity. Several years later, when the Diversity Committee was forming in the parish, Mark invited me to join.

It was through participation in this committee that, after nearly twenty years of attendance at services, I eventually found a place in the parish where I felt I belonged. The group included parishioners from Haiti and China, Mexico and Nigeria, as well as Americans, both Black and White. We pushed our well-meaning but uncomprehending pastor to allow "other voices" to be heard in the parish, to hire non-Caucasian staff members, and to celebrate the music and traditions of other cultures. I was happy to be part of a group that was open to difference. Unfortunately, my involvement with the Diversity Committee came too late for our children to benefit from this internationally-oriented group of friends.

Later, I became involved with the social justice work of the parish, particularly as it related to issues of global poverty. There, too, I have found community with people whose interests and concerns align with my own. When the children had left home and I was my own boss, it was easier to find time for such activities.

While the parish has become community for me, it has not been so for Clement—or not to the same extent. My friends in the parish know Clement but, despite their genuine desire to be open-minded, have difficulty connecting with him. His rejection of formal religion, exacerbated by the hypocrisy he had witnessed in the Anglican Church in Ghana, hasn't helped. Though well-intentioned, they stumble when Clement offers his own idiosyncratic ideas about religion. Even in discussing secular topics, they find him difficult to understand if his point of view is out of step with their closely held assumptions. There was a time when, contrary to popular opinion, Germany was the world's largest exporter. Clement studied the stats in *The Economist* every week. He knew his stuff. But if he presented such information in casual conversation, his views—though rarely challenged directly—were silently dismissed. It was evident in their faces as they nodded in feigned agreement.

To mitigate conflict, my response has been to steer the conversation to safer ground, such as political positions on which I knew they'd agree, rather than expose assumptions about America's place in the world that often lie deep beneath the surface. It's possible that my desire to avoid conflict may have had the unintended effect of glossing over differences, such that true understanding and acceptance remain elusive.

I find common ground with other parishioners through our shared concern for social justice, but Clement, much as he abhors injustice and discrimination in any form, regards our efforts as doomed to failure. While I protest that we have to advocate for the poor and marginalized in whatever ways are available to us, he insists that "it won't change anything."

After more than forty years living in Columbia we are well settled here, but there's still a sense in which we don't really belong. Our close friends have been those rare families or individuals not totally immersed in the apple-pie rituals of American middle-class living, who remain open to a world in which an African mathematician married to an Englishwoman has a place. If we have remained outliers, it's partly our own doing. Without conscious effort, I have retained my English accent, which is always noticed and sets me apart from those around me. And Clement has been unwilling to sacrifice his sense of who he is—his Ghanaian identity, if you will—to win acceptance. (He would never play the role that those with a stereotypical view of Africa expect of him.) We have different modes of connecting and belonging.

When the children had left home and our retirement approached, Clement's attention turned increasingly to his roots in Ghana. I, too, was glad to reengage with the country that had meant so much to me earlier in my life. In Ghana, Clement's concern for his country's advancement is joined to my long-standing concern for justice and equality in the global community. Returning to Ghana—albeit as a visitor—opened a new chapter in my search for connection.

# Part VI

# Rediscovering Ghana

*If the house of the world is dark,*
*love will find a way to make windows.*
*For those who love with their heart and soul*
*there is no such thing as separation.*

—*Rumi, as quoted by Kabir Helminski*
*in* Living Presence

# *Another Time and Place*

For most White people, Africa—especially sub-Saharan Africa—is simply "other." The dark continent, unknown and mysterious. A large expanse on the map of the world. At worst, Africa is viewed with contempt—a continent of "s—h—countries," to use the words of the 45th U.S. president—beset by internal conflict, run by corrupt politicians who make a lot of noise at the UN. Somewhat better, but hardly less offensive, is the popular image of Africa as a place to be pitied and aided. A place where children are malnourished and families lack electricity and running water. For many, it is the wildlife, not the people, that defines the continent; the people are simply a backdrop to Westerners' extravagant safaris. For some, the elegant women in the tourist brochures, carrying buckets of water on their heads and babies on their backs, are objects of beauty to be admired. For activists, these same women are the victims of economic exploitation. For many African Americans, Africa represents the motherland, revered (and often idealized) source of their own vibrant culture.

There may be some truth in these images, but none captures the Africa that I know. Why focus on the poor or the exotic when there is solid, mainstream achievement to be found if you would only look? Why focus on difference when we have so much in common? The small corner of Africa I know well is a place where ordinary people lead ordinary lives, albeit ones imbued with a particular culture and set of values. As in any society anywhere, there are people of every sort. A few are wealthy, some get by, many struggle to make ends meet and feed their children. We know many who live comfortable lives—just like us—but many others live at the margin; poverty is not far away. However familiar I am with their life circumstances, however much I try to empathize with their struggles, it's not easy to bridge the distance between us in expectations and opportunities, nor the barrier that White privilege and the colonial past represent.

In Cape Coast in the 1970s, my identity in Ghana was as part of the expatriate faculty, notwithstanding my marriage to a Ghanaian. Now, in Accra, my identity is defined by my marriage to a Ghanaian. I am "the wife." Culture, skin color, and— above all—language are barriers to acceptance and belonging. It's not always easy to accept the role in which I'm now cast.

## Twenty Years On

We had left Ghana in 1980. I returned for the first time in 1994. We went for Christmas with the family. Clement's brother Miguel came, too, with Ingrid and their three children. I looked forward to the opportunity to reconnect with our past, for the children to get to know their father's homeland, and for us to spend time with our Danish relatives.

So much had changed, and yet so little. Under IMF supervision, Ghana's economy had reversed its decline, and goods were freely available. Hotels and restaurants had emerged from the economic devastation we'd experienced in the late 1970s. For those with dollars to spend, life was good, but for most residents the daily struggle continued. "It's better now," we were told, "but salaries have not kept up. People are suffering."

At Cape Coast University, a former student was now dean of education. The same departmental secretary was still there; she greeted me warmly. The vice chancellor, a former colleague in the physics department, had recently returned from

Nigeria. "We're trying our best," he told us, "but it's a struggle. We need money." Although we found several new structures on the university's new site, including a library and large administrative block, it would be another decade before the Ghana Education Trust Fund led to significant development of educational institutions across the country.

As I visited familiar places and felt embraced again by the humid ocean air, the realities of the 1990s merged seamlessly with my memories of the 1970s. It seemed for a moment as though my life in America was just an interruption. I was ready to pick up and continue where I left off, step back into the life I had so enjoyed in the past. But that couldn't be. I had changed, and so had Ghana. My life was now centered in the U.S. I had embarked on a different career. And Ghanaians were now fully in charge of their institutions. The university was no longer dependent on foreign faculty; I mightn't be welcome. It was time to begin a new relationship with the country, one in which my role was that of foreign spouse not expatriate faculty member, one centered in Accra not Cape Coast. I needed to reach for a different type of connection to the country, shedding definitively the neocolonial mindset whose vestiges still lurked in the recesses of my mind.

## At Home in Osu

After we'd moved to the U.S., Clement returned to Ghana from time to time, staying close to colleagues and mathematical institutions. He was often invited to participate in seminars and conferences during summer vacations and spent the 2004/05 academic year teaching at the University of Ghana. Following our 1994 visit, I went back quite often, albeit for much shorter periods. Clement's oldest brother, Nii, was still living in the family house in Osu, and it was there that we stayed much of the time.

Nii was the gentlest of souls, simple and undemanding. His life centered around the few sheep he kept on the compound. He tended them with biblical care, shutting them up in a makeshift shed at night and allowing them to scavenge in the compound during the day. It was a major event when he lost a sheep to theft or disease or a passing car. I don't remember him ever selling a sheep for monetary gain. I don't think he could have brought himself to part with one of them voluntarily.

When we stayed at the house, he kept himself very much to himself, rarely sharing a meal with us, but if we took him out for his birthday or other occasion, he always enjoyed the treat. In many ways life had passed him by, but he didn't complain. In the tribute I read at his funeral I said, "Nii led a simple life, but he wasn't a simpleton; a humble life, but he wasn't a fool. He asked little of life yet was grateful for what he had. He showed no bitterness or anger for life's missed opportunities. He had a warm and winning smile. He cared about family." During all the years when we were far away in the U.S., he never forgot to send a card for my birthday.

Nii's days followed the rhythm of the sun, and so did ours when we stayed at Osu. In the tropics there is little variation in daylight year-round. Twelve hours on, twelve hours off. In the late afternoons, as the light started to dwindle, we would gather on the porch, watching the sheep feed on whatever grasses or leftovers Nii had found for them. Outside the compound, radios blared. There was the clatter of pots and pans and the thud-thud of *fufu* being pounded. Looking protectively at his sheep, Nii would quietly tell us about each one: which ewe was about to give birth, what happened when one escaped.

"That one got into the road. The neighbor over there," he said, pointing in the general direction of a nearby house, "he helped me get it back."

"What have you given them to eat this evening?" I asked

one evening as the sheep chewed contentedly on some scraps strewn around the compound.

"Cassava peels," he replied. "I got them from the chop bar down the street."

When Nii told of a neighbor who had been swindled by a con artist going house to house, Clement—the youngest of the brothers but now his oldest brother's protector—instructed Nii about the importance of keeping the gate locked and not listening to anyone who came to the door asking for money. "Don't believe a word they tell you," he cautioned. Nii listened in silence. It was difficult for me to know what he was thinking. He always found it hard to resist a winning smile and a kindly word.

Although Clement's life and experience differed radically from Nii's, the family bonds remained strong. Often the brothers would share news of their siblings overseas or of relatives close at hand. "Did you know that Frank had a stroke? He's at the Ridge Hospital." Or "Auntie Lizzy will be buried in two weeks. Her children have come from London." Or "Jenny just got back. She stopped by this morning to say hello."

In deference to me, their conversation was almost always in English. During these quiet and intimate moments, I felt like family. I, too, belonged.

## Oxford Street

Osu was once on the fringes of Accra but is now an integral part of the city. Oxford Street, named after the eponymous street in London, is a vibrant hub of commercial activity at its center. The family house is just a few blocks away.

Like much of Accra, Osu is an eclectic mix of old and new. Houses of families who have lived there for generations survive side by side with the growing crush of modern glass and steel. Osu also has its share of modest dwellings, some little more than shacks, where small retailers and tradespeople live. I enjoyed being close to the life of the city. I had only to walk the short distance from the family compound to the local supermarket to observe traditional ways of life alongside pulsing modern rhythms.

I was amused by the way domesticity spilled into the street: young boys brushing their teeth, girls braiding each other's hair, coal pots with beans or stew ready to sell by the portion to passersby. On the way to the shops, I passed several stalls, little more than lean-tos, some selling cold beer or sodas, some fronted by wooden tables piled with avocados, tomatoes, and okra. The young people manning the stalls were probably out-of-school relatives who had migrated to the city hoping to earn a pittance and eat a full meal at the end of the day. They would often greet me with a cheery "good morning," not too concerned whether I stopped to buy anything.

One household close by sold bric-a-brac: combs, trinkets, razors, and the like. Each day, young boys carefully mounted the goods on stands set up in wheelbarrows, then fanned out to neighboring streets to sell their goods.

"Me, I go to Labadi. He go to Lokko road," one told me.

How much do you sell in a day? I wondered. It can't be worth more than a few dollars. What a hard way to earn a living.

Clement couldn't understand why I liked walking to the store, observing local life along the way. "How can you enjoy seeing such things?" he complained. "The children selling stuff by the roadside should be in school." To him, the presence of city dwellers still mired in poverty was a sign of backwardness; it felt like a stain on his country. Children out of school meant wasted possibility; a lack of hygiene, born of poverty, led to disease. How could such things be a source of amusement, even delight?

I was still wearing my tourist hat; I understand that better now. My attitude confirmed me as an outsider, a role I've found difficult to shed completely. I am chagrined to realize that when introducing visitors to Ghana even now, I am tempted to focus on the charm and color of the environment—surface features that differentiate it from the life they know. Too often, I've been complicit in the visitor's tendency to treat people they see by the roadside as museum pieces. Too often, I've failed to attend to the people I encounter, persons whose grief or greed, angst or anger may be skillfully disguised by a graceful stride, a winning smile, or an indifferent shrug of the shoulder.

Oxford Street is where most of the action is. There is a wide diversity of retail activity, ranging from well-constructed stores carrying brand-name British electronics and Korean home appliances for the well-heeled to street traders with little of anything to sell.

Hole-in-the-wall stores owned by traders from many countries—Lebanon, Syria, India, and more—exist side by side with the high-end establishments. They carry an assortment of goods crammed into a very small space. If they don't have exactly what you're looking for, they'll hunt it down.

"Let me go check," one store owner told me when I was searching for a particular type of electronic connector. "Won't be a minute."

After what seemed like an age, he returned triumphant with the required article, unapologetic for the delay. He had probably scoured his competitors' establishments in the effort to find just what I needed. My impatience at the long wait marked me as an outsider.

The wooden stalls lining Oxford Street, the province of Ghanaian street traders, represent yet another type of retail activity. They focus on made-for-tourist goods: T-shirts with the names and jersey numbers of Ghanaian soccer players famous in the European leagues, pieces of kente cloth, leather thong sandals, handbags, luggage, jewelry, and more. They cry out to passersby with enticements used by handcraft sellers the world over: "Come, see what I have!" "Mama! You look good in my necklace." They never seem to lose hope of making a sale.

Finally, at the bottom of the retail chain are the hawkers selling sachets of cold water, paniers of fish, garish oil paintings, even toilet rolls. They balance the goods precariously on their head as they weave their way among the traffic, vying for the attention of drivers.

The vibrant miscellany of the scene is a delight to the visitor but an aggravation to drivers pushing through the riot of activity to get to their destination. Indeed, Oxford Street is a parking lot much of the time, dense with a jumble of cars, trucks, and taxis making their way from here to there and back again. Drivers hoot loudly at other cars trying to force their way ahead, but invariably stop and wave graciously if they see an older person like me trying to cross the street. Taxi drivers look expectantly in my direction, tooting lightly on their horns, hoping to give me a ride, but move on good-naturedly if it's clear I'm not interested. Many overseas visitors find their way to Osu, so White people aren't too out of place. Most of them are young, in Ghana for a semester abroad or a research project, or simply for tourism. As an older *oborɔnyi*, I am something of a rarity.

Where sidewalks exist, they often straddle open gutters carrying the debris of urban living to the ocean a few miles away. Unlike their French counterparts, British colonials thought that open drains were appropriate for tropical living. Contrary to what hygiene and good sense suggest, their colonial subjects internalized the belief and continue the practice today. Clement is dismayed by the backwardness the open gutters represent. For me, they are simply part of the local scene. As I pick my way carefully over the rough concrete slabs and gaping drains, working my way toward a store where I know I can find cloth for a dress or ink for a printer, I feel quite at home. It is all so familiar. I'm just out shopping, doing what people do everywhere as part of their daily life. For a moment, I'm oblivious to the fact that I may seem like an anachronism to those around me.

Also something of an anachronism and standing apart— both literally and metaphorically—from the swirl of activity in Oxford Street is the jewelry store of Ms. Hakim. It is a frequent stop for us when we're in Osu and somewhere we like to take overseas visitors. Ms. Hakim came to Ghana as an eighteen-year-old bride; she has remained for more than sixty-five years. Since the death of her husband, she has run the business on her own. A diminutive figure, she sits behind a large countertop on which jewelry and ornaments with intricate filigree designs—a horse, a village hut, a spoon—are displayed. On the wall are pictures of herself and her husband with famous visitors, including Bill Clinton when he came to Ghana in 1998. All the items on display are silver. Gold items are locked away and brought out on request. If we would like something a little different, it can be made to order.

Ms. Hakim always welcomes us like old friends, offering us water or strong Lebanese coffee. She seems to relish our visits. Like me, she's at home in Ghana but doesn't fully belong. I will be sad when her establishment finally closes. She is a point of connection.

While I enjoyed staying at Osu, Clement couldn't wait to get away from the noise and bustle, the honking of traffic, the neighborhood clatter, and the loud sound of church singing at weekends. The distractions hindered his work as a mathematician; he wanted us to have a place of our own.

With the help of a lawyer cousin, we settled on an estate being developed a few miles from the city center. After what seemed like endless delays, the house was ready, just in time for us to welcome the family there for Christmas in 2007. Although I was glad to have our own home where we could stay for extended periods without troubling Nii, I missed the life of the city within easy reach. Residents on the estate keep themselves to themselves, protected by locked gates and walls topped with razor wire. It is a very different experience of living in Ghana.

## The Best of Both Worlds

When I visited Ghana during Clement's sabbatical in 2004/05, I was able to stay in touch with colleagues and clients, thanks to improvements in digital communications. It meant spending long hours at one of the burgeoning internet cafés because the internet wasn't yet accessible at home or by smartphone. On one occasion, I risked conducting a demo of our database product, QTD, over a landline, sitting at the dining room table at Osu. I talked through the software's capabilities as the prospective clients followed along on a prototype copy.

"Go to the drop-down menu in the top left corner of your screen," I directed. "Click on it and select Learning Objectives."

"Got it; got it," they responded reassuringly.

"Tell me what you see?"

As I led them step-by-step through QTD's key features, I held my breath, hoping the phone connection would hold and the clients wouldn't tune in to Nii's sheep bleating in the background.

Sitting there at the dining table in Osu, on the phone to business clients in the U.S., it felt as though my two worlds were joined. Yet neither Nii nor his companion, Joseph, could have imagined the work setting of the people I was talking with in America, nor the purpose of the tool I was demonstrating. Likewise, even if I had given the clients a detailed description of the scene around me—the mango tree, the sheep, the walled compound—they couldn't have envisioned it in any meaningful way. Moreover, it would have been difficult for them to understand what took me there. "You are where?" I could hear them asking.

Not for the first time, I wished I could have found a way to link the two worlds, both deeply embedded in my own experience. Yet they were just too far apart; finding points of connection seemed an almost impossible goal.

For many years, I hoped to find work opportunities for myself in Ghana. That would have been one way to bring my two worlds together. Ever the do-gooder, I was ready to provide services on a pro bono basis. I could help young Ghanaian professionals learn training techniques and business skills, I thought at the time, believing—perhaps naïvely—that what I had learned so painstakingly in the U.S. would transfer easily to the Ghanaian context. I put out many feelers but without success.

Developing a nexus of business relationships takes time and effort in any environment; it was particularly difficult for me in Ghana, where I was decidedly a foreigner. One of Clement's cousins put me in touch with a local marketing professional, and we agreed to work together. He would arrange meetings with local businesses and take a commission on any work we got. At one point, we had a promising lead with the local electric utility and submitted a detailed proposal. It went nowhere. The company used the advisory services of a major Canadian utility and saw no reason to engage a consultant with no track record in the country. "I couldn't persuade them to give us a try," my partner reported back to me.

Later, another cousin involved in the local business world thought he saw an opportunity for QTD. "It's a great tool. There are companies here that could make good use of it," was his initial reaction. After making enquiries, however, he came back empty-handed. "The government likes to use Deloitte for that type of thing," he reported.

My failure to insert myself into Ghanaian business life was—and remains—a disappointment. The fact that my visits were only two to three weeks long didn't help. I didn't have time to develop a network or get to understand the business mindset. My approach, honed in the U.S. marketplace, wasn't geared to needs that local companies had articulated. Moreover, from the perspective of Ghana's youthful population, my age was a definite handicap, increasingly so as time went on.

One of my last attempts was in 2017. I was introduced to someone helping the government build skill capacity for the oil and gas industry so that Ghanaians could replace the many foreigners still employed there. I arranged to meet the person at a local hotel. Clement and I arrived early, settling ourselves at the back of the lounge to wait. Exactly on time, a woman in business attire walked down the steps from the lobby. She took out her phone.

"I'm here; I don't see you."

"We're in the lounge—at the back."

"I'm coming down the stairs now; where are you?"

"Over here." I waved to be sure she spotted us, but my heart sank. As an elderly couple we were effectively invisible, not at all who she had expected to meet.

After the initial confusion, we had a good conversation about the training challenge to be addressed and followed up with an exchange of emails. I even sent her some PowerPoint slides outlining a possible approach. It soon became abundantly clear, however, that my efforts were going nowhere. "The government isn't ready to move forward," she kept telling me.

She was probably looking for excuses. Was it my age, or skin color, or simply that she didn't want interference from a potential competitor? Even if I worked pro bono, I might be taking work away from Ghanaians. Whatever the reason, nothing came of it.

## *White*

For most visitors to Ghana, the country is warm and welcoming. From the *akwaaba* signs of welcome at the airport to the smiles that greet foreigners almost everywhere they go, the country exudes friendliness and hospitality. But look a little further, dig a little deeper, and different voices emerge. Belonging is elusive, even for someone who has known the country as long as I have. I cannot escape the fact that I am White.

It's hardly surprising that White people in Ghana today don't enjoy the privileged status that was still common when I worked in Cape Coast—a holdover from the colonial era. Now, we carry the burden of our heritage as former colonial rulers and the huge legacy of distrust left in its wake. When waiting to greet people arriving from overseas at the airport, Clement has overheard others in the crowd ask themselves in Twi, the most widely spoken local language, "Why are so many White people coming to Ghana? Why can't they leave us alone?" The liberal Western goal of diversity and inclusion is simply not on the agenda.

As an older White person, I am treated with respect, provided I don't try to assert myself. But if I do, people have a way of indirectly, but decisively, ignoring me. Clement, on the other hand, is invariably well received, particularly if he pulls out his business card indicating that he's a professor emeritus of Howard University. When it comes to locating a service provider or negotiating with a contractor, it's best for me to keep my mouth shut. "You talk to them," I say, and Clement agrees. It is an exact reversal of the practice we have adopted over the years in the U.S.—and even of the situation I experienced in Ghana in the 1970s. I'm happy for him to be the center of attention. He has been sidelined way too often during our lives in America.

If Clement feels he isn't being treated correctly, he'll happily scold the offending party and instruct them professorially in correct behavior. It's what he wants and expects of his countrymen, and they rarely complain. Woe betide me if I do the same. Once, when we'd ordered sandwiches at a coffee shop frequented by foreigners, I noticed the person preparing the sandwiches wasn't wearing gloves as protocol required. "Please, could you wear gloves?" I asked him as respectfully as I could.

We noticed him getting flustered and angry. Clement handled the situation perfectly. He simply repeated what I had said—but in Ga. The person apologized, put on the gloves, and quickly regained his equanimity. It was a good outcome, reinforcing—quite succinctly—a lesson about my place in postcolonial Ghana that I still had difficulty accepting.

I should've learned the lesson several years earlier when I tried to help Ignatius, the son of a Liberian woman I knew in the U.S. who was living in Accra as a refugee. The English-speaking countries in West Africa have a common school-leaving exam administered by the West African Examinations Council. I thought I might be able to help Ignatius retrieve his certificate from their headquarters in Accra.

"This young man is a refugee from Liberia. He's looking for his exam records," I explained to the woman at the office. "Is that something you could help with?"

The woman refused to engage with me, and Ignatius was left to fend for himself. I don't know whether he ever got the certificate.

If we wish to help a young person advance their education or work opportunities, it works best if Clement takes the lead while I stay out of sight. When the daughter of our security guard—a northerner—wanted to gain admission to the local technical college, Clement went with her to the admissions office. I stayed in the car.

"They're going to take care of her," Clement assured me when they got back, a broad smile on his face. "The admissions officer was from the north and was happy to know I was supporting one of her own."

Sometimes, more explicit colonial attitudes to White people endure. In Ghana, as in other parts of Africa, White people are often accosted by children in the street, loudly and with no apology. In the Congo, the Lingala word for White person is *mundele*. "*Mundele, mundele,*" the children shouted after me if I ever set foot in the market. When we lived in Cape Coast and went shopping in town, the local children would flock around our car shouting, "*Oborɔnyi, oborɔnyi,*" pointing at our children who, though Black to Americans, looked White to them.

Nowadays in Accra, children are less inclined to trouble us in this way, so I was surprised by what occurred in the local grocery store one evening. Many people were shopping there—all Black except for me. It was such a common situation I hadn't even realized I was the only White person in the store. A man approached me, holding a child about twenty months old.

"Say 'Hello, *oborɔnyi,*'" he told the child. I was taken aback. I didn't like being singled out in this way, but I surprised myself with my reaction.

"Don't call me that," I complained. "Don't call me *oborɔnyi.*" I carried on a bit, repeating myself several times to be sure he understood. "How would you like to be called 'Black man' if you were the only Black person in a store in the UK?" No doubt, I was giving vent to a frustration I'd hardly acknowledged to myself.

The man fell silent. Indeed, the whole store seemed to stand still, uncomprehending. "Why is she making such a fuss?" they may have been thinking. After all, my skin color marked me clearly as a person from overseas and, almost certainly, the man meant no harm. I'd tried to push back nicely, but I'd been very firm. Clement observed from a short distance, recognizing me in one of my more strident moods but still somewhat bemused by my outburst.

We talked it over afterward. Years ago, after visiting with one of Clement's old school friends, we'd had a similar conversation. As the children played together, I heard the friend's wife refer to our children as *blafono*, the Ga equivalent of *oborɔnyi*. "Why did she refer to our children as *blafono*?" I complained. "Are we always to be marked as outsiders?"

I felt the mother was typecasting our children by referring to them by their skin color rather than using their names. Clement's interpretation was different. To him, use of the terms *oborɔnyi* and *blafono* is a benign, even respectful, way of pointing out a difference. It's certainly different from what he experiences in the United States, where Blackness invariably carries with it a negative connotation, but I still don't like it.

I should be careful not to overemphasize experiences that cast me as an outsider. If I present myself as an older White woman, content to remain on the sidelines, I am invariably treated with respect and addressed as "Mama" or "Auntie"— affectionate forms of address typically used for older women. Especially if I am needy in some way. An incident that occurred around 2015 stands out.

We'd been living in our own house for several years. I rarely drove because of local drivers' aggressive behavior, but I thought I'd be OK driving to my dressmaker's place a few miles away. Alas, when turning left at a traffic light, an ambulance in the lane to my right tried to cut in front of me, giving my vehicle a nasty scrape. We ended up at the local police station.

When questioned by the police, the driver admitted he didn't have a license. Moreover, the ambulance, which belonged to a small hospital across the street from the police station, was uninsured. The doctor who owned the hospital was out of town; his wife hurried across the street to speak with the police commander behind closed doors. Meanwhile, the driver was spinning a tale about my driving. The commander would have none of it. "I know that junction. The drivers there—I know what they do," he sighed. The driver's behavior was all too familiar; he'd been looking for a way to push ahead. He was clearly at fault.

Both the commander and the inspector who'd taken down my account of the incident behaved impeccably toward me, insisting the hospital pay for our vehicle to be repaired. As a conciliatory gesture, the commander decided not to press charges. "After all, we never know when we may need their [the hospital's] services."

A sequel to the accident highlighted for us the gaping inequality that separates the haves—by no means all foreigners—and the have-nots in this rapidly evolving society. I'd returned to the States, and Clement was finalizing the arrangements to have our vehicle repaired. The police inspector looked shocked when Clement showed her the estimate. "How can it cost so much?" she must have been thinking. "It takes me many months to earn that amount."

Aware of the financial struggles of many of those who perform essential, middle-level jobs as teachers, nurses, and—yes—police, Clement offered the inspector a small reward when everything was settled. With such small gestures of appreciation—a little cash or a bar of chocolate—Clement has established warm relationships with many service providers we deal with in Accra. They would find it more difficult to accept such gifts from me.

## Set Apart by Language and Culture

I can't do much about my color but knowing the language would help. However, the complexity of the linguistic landscape and my own tone deafness conspire against me. When I first went to Cape Coast, I learned a little Fante, but Clement's language, Ga—the original language of Accra—is quite different. Moreover, a third language, Twi, is the lingua franca spoken by many people in Accra who have migrated from elsewhere in the country. I took Ga lessons for a while but didn't persevere. I had difficulty distinguishing the two pronunciations of the English vowel "e" (different symbols are used when Ga is written), and my attempts at pronouncing the common phonemes transcribed as "gb" or "kp" merely evoke Clement's laughter. Moreover, Ga is a language full of idiomatic subtlety that I doubted I would ever master.

Maybe I should have tried harder; when we're in Accra Clement relishes the opportunity to re-immerse himself in the language and his family prefers to talk in Ga even though most speak English fluently. Their conversation is invariably peppered with English words and phrases, enabling me to follow the general gist of what is said, but my inability to converse sets me apart. For a long time, I suffered in silence.

During one family gathering around 2006, following the memorial service for Clement's nephew who had died tragically in the U.S., I was at a table where family stories were being shared. Nicho, a first cousin who was adopted by Clement's father as a teenager and remained close to the family, was on a roll. Her speech was animated. The occasional English word, together with her facial expression and gestures, gave me a rough sense of what she was saying. Those around her added comments here or there in more subdued tones, but Nicho held the floor; she was in her element. Knowing the turmoil of her early life, I marveled at her fluency and exuberance. Her delight in storytelling seemed to be both companion and foil to the astuteness with which she had survived the adversity of her childhood.

I realized Nicho's stories only carried their full meaning when told in the vernacular, but I thought someone around the table could have translated some of what she was saying for me to be able to follow along. No one even tried. Neither Nicho, nor Clement, nor anyone else seemed to notice that I was totally excluded from the conversation. As the afternoon wore on, I grew impatient and angry at their insensitivity. From time to time, I got up and walked around, interacting briefly with those at other tables before returning to my seat. No one took the hint.

When we got home, I let out my frustration on Clement.

"Do you realize you carried on for three hours and no one made the slightest effort to translate?" I complained. "You could have brought me into the conversation once or twice. I felt completely isolated."

He agreed to be more careful in future. For my part, I determined it was my responsibility not to play the victim. If this happened again, I would intervene—politely—and ask someone to translate. There was no reason to stay silent.

Several years later—during an extended series of funeral rites for a Lutterodt family elder—we were en route from a traditional ceremony at the Lutterodt family house in old Accra to the funeral home where we were to view the body. We'd offered a ride to three other mourners. The conversation in the car was in Ga. From the few scattered English words, I understood they were talking about the life of the deceased, including details about a relationship he had in his younger days. The traffic was bad, and the ride was long. At some point, my patience wore thin.

"Time out!" I complained. "You all speak English. You can at least let me know what you're talking about."

"Sorry, sorry." Though a little stunned by the interruption, they were apologetic and switched quickly to English, giving

285

me a filtered summary of what had been said. Clement filled me in on the juicier details later. When a story is translated for my benefit, I'm only told what the translator deems appropriate for me—a foreigner—to hear. Even as a long-time member of the family I remain, in some sense, an outsider.

It's not uncommon for family relationships that Westerners might call "irregular" to be known and accepted in Ghana with no shame or judgment attached. There are many cousins on both sides of Clement's family who are the result of his two grandfathers' extramarital liaisons. All are accepted into the family without question. I thought I understood the landscape quite well but was nevertheless surprised by the situation that Joyce, Clement's cousin on her mother's side, described. I knew she had half-siblings on her father's side, but I hadn't realized how many.

Joyce had come for Sunday lunch, and we were enjoying conversation—in English—after the meal. Well into her eighties, she is functionally blind but always elegantly dressed. She was wearing a light-orange two-piece with a lacy white blouse. She is fluent in Western culture, having spent several years in London in the 1960s and worked for the U.S. Information Service in Accra in the 1970s. In Ghana, she moves seamlessly between the Akan traditions of her father's family in Akropong—about an hour's drive out of the city—and those of her mother's Accra-based family.

"Whenever I go to Akropong, I am treated as a royal," she said, referring to a recent visit there. "My father was the paramount chief of Akuapim. It was a very important position."

"I knew you had family in Akropong. Do you have a lot of relatives still there?" I asked.

"Oh, yes! My father had a lot of children. He was a very handsome man. When he came back from abroad as a lawyer, everyone admired him."

"How many siblings do you have?" I asked innocently.

"We were fifty-five children. Only ten are left."

"Your father had fifty-five children!" I couldn't hide my amazement.

"That's right," Joyce was unfazed. "My father was a lawyer, you know. Everyone respected him." She paused. "My brother Paul tells the story of how my father met his mother. He was being carried to a durbar on his palanquin and spotted this young woman in the crowd. She was very fair, very beautiful. After the ceremony, he asked his aides to locate her and bring her to him. They found her and . . . well . . . Paul was the result."

"Hmm!" I tried to absorb the information, then asked, "Did you know all of your siblings?"

"Certainly. My father wanted all his children to be united. We all knew each other and got along." Laughing, she continued, "The women—that was a different matter!"

As the conversation elsewhere in the room drifted into Ga, I mulled over Joyce's father's "chiefly" behavior. I thought I was familiar with the complexities of Ghanaian families, but learning Joyce had so many siblings was quite a surprise. She sensed my puzzlement.

"Oh, Sarah. You're still troubling yourself about that. It was quite usual in those days, you know. Ofori Attah, grandfather of the president [at the time the conversation took place], had over eighty children. It was common."

I marveled at the untroubled way in which Joyce and others of her generation bridge the deep divide between the proud traditional culture that formed them and Western-style modernity that frames much of life in Ghana today. I feel close to Joyce, yet what she described of her family background was worlds away from the family in which I had grown up.

When I returned to Ghana in my sixties, I reentered the once-familiar country from a very different place. I no longer had an expatriate community to fall back on. I was an insider by family connections, long familiarity with the country, and genuine identification with its aspirations for a better future. But I came in most respects as a foreigner—by skin color, deeply ingrained attitudes, and—above all—language. I like to think that my interactions with the people I encounter have developed a more natural quality over time, less defined by race or color or unequal circumstances. There have indeed been many moments of human connection that I treasure.

# Intersecting Lives

Some expatriates, far from the societal restraints of their home environment, feel free to behave in ways that would be unthinkable back home. The freedom can be exhilarating, albeit risky, but there is a more significant value to being on the outside. Immersed in a familiar culture, one can easily be blind to the graces and subtleties of everyday moments. As the Buddhist nun Pema Chodron says, "The world is always displaying itself, always waving and winking, but we're so self-involved that we miss it." Most of us recognize moments of "waving and winking" more easily when we experience them as outsiders. Outsider status confers greater sensitivity to the ordinary details of life. Events that back home would merge, largely unnoticed, with the bland realities of day-to-day living, become moments for wonder and appreciation, and connection too: opportunities to bond with people we interact with every day.

Beyond our circle of family and friends are many Ghanaians whose lives intersect with our own. With some, the connection is fleeting. With others, it has endured over many years. Often, there is a significant level of inequality. The people I am speaking of could easily go unremarked. Yet, at one moment or another, I have paused in awe at their response to a particular sorrow or circumstance to wonder at the deep well of resilience or perseverance or unwavering faith on which they draw. In telling their stories, I hope to elicit empathy and respect. And so, bit by bit, dismantle the walls of pity or condescension that too often set us apart from people whose lives are much less privileged than our own.

## Joseph

Joseph has been with the family a very long time. First, he worked as houseboy for Clement's cousin Nicho. Then he moved to Osu to help Clement's mother, staying on after she died. Quiet and unassuming, he was an invaluable companion and support to Nii in his later years. Clement helped Joseph go to trade school and become an electrician—and a very good one too. "I will never forget what Uncle Clement has done for me," he once told me.

Since Nii's death in 2010, Joseph has remained at Osu as caretaker, and he continues to help the family in many ways. During our long absences in the U.S., he pays the bills and oversees the upkeep of our house at Nmai Dzorn. He maintains records of expenditures with meticulous care. Many are the woeful tales of Ghanaians of the diaspora who have entrusted friends or relatives back home with their property, only to be cheated in ways big and small. Not so with Joseph. He is eminently trustworthy, a true friend of the family. When we're at home in Accra, he regularly takes the long *trotro*[3] ride to help us out, whether to fix problems or simply make sure we're OK. If an electrical fault plunges the house into darkness, Joseph—our go-to electrician—is only a phone call away.

Our relationship with Joseph is one of reciprocity and mutual respect. While he looks after our property, we have supported the education of his three children. For most of their lives, Joseph has been a single parent. His wife left him when they were very young. They were cared for at first by his mother and sister. His son, Okai, came to live with him at Osu when he was about nine years old and needed a stronger guiding presence in his life. The two girls, Priscilla and Josephine, joined him a few years later after both their older

---

[3.] *Trotro* is the term used for the local minivans that are the most common form of transportation in Accra. The term derives from the English "thruppence" (three pennies), which was the fare charged for a ride on the rough trucks that predated today's minivans.

relatives died within a few months of each other. From then on, Joseph has been responsible for their every need. As young adults now, they are a credit to the care and singleness of purpose with which he has raised them. Okai has graduated from university, and Priscilla and Josephine are undergraduates at the University of Ghana.

One day when they had come to clean the house, I commented on the dress that Josephine, then in her late teens, was wearing.

"What a pretty dress! Where did you get it?" I asked.

"My father bought it for me," she replied without hesitation.

Josephine's reply conjured images in my mind of Joseph riffling through piles of girls' dresses at a market stall, looking for one the right size he thought Josephine would like; of him returning home and asking her to try it on; of Josephine twirling to show it off; of Joseph smiling contentedly.

There can be no doubt about Joseph's parental care. He has been both father and mother to his children. A true caretaker.

## Adongo

Adongo, too, is a single parent. His wife died shortly after his fourth child was born. A few months later he came to work for us as a night watchman; he has been with us ever since.

Over the years, Adongo and his family have become close to us. As close as one could expect, given the gulf in experience and expectations that separates us. While we have benefited from many years of education, Adongo is illiterate, but he understands money and speaks at least three languages. While our lives have been paved with opportunity, Adongo has struggled to get by and ensure a better future for his children.

When we moved into our house in 2007 and needed a night watchman, we asked John, a security guard on the housing estate, whether he knew someone. John, a large man with a wise face and genial smile, walked the streets of the estate, truncheon in hand. We felt we could trust him. He brought Adongo to meet us.

"Dis be my brudder Adongo," he said quietly. "We dey from same village." John and Adongo are both Frafra people from the north of Ghana. Shorter than John, Adongo has a slight, wiry frame and a keen expression.

Clement explained the job. "You should be at our place from dusk to dawn. Make sure it's safe . . . no intruders."

"Yessah! Make I do it," he agreed.

As night watchman, Adongo came each evening, bicycling one hour from his home in Nungua and leaving at dawn. He was as dependable as the sun. A few years later, we needed someone to live on the property and asked Adongo whether he would move in. The staff quarters behind our house—a two-room unit, complete with kitchen and shower—is very desirable accommodation by local standards. If Adongo moved in, he would live there rent free, wouldn't have to pay for electricity and water, and would receive a salary, to boot. We were surprised when he hesitated.

"My pickins," he said, seemingly thinking aloud. "They be a' school in Nungua."

"There's a school just up the street from here," I reassured him. "We can help the children get settled in there." Adongo didn't say what other concerns were running through his mind.

After some back and forth, John convinced Adongo to accept the offer. He moved in two weeks later with Esther, aged twelve, and Jacob, just five years old. Raymond remained at school in Nungua. The eldest son, Joseph, was already working.

We enrolled Esther in the local junior secondary school and Jacob in kindergarten. Jacob was small and thin, slightly bow-legged. He clung to his father. We helped him with his first steps in reading and arithmetic and spoke quite frequently with his teachers, but he didn't learn easily. As he moved into the primary grades, he had difficulty staying on task. Did he suffer from ADHD? I wondered. A condition that would surely go undiagnosed in Ghana except in the most exclusive schools. His mother's sister had taken care of him after his mother died. I wondered whether a lack of proper nourishment as an infant explained his difficulty in learning.

Completing homework was a persistent problem. With no formal education himself, Adongo was unable to provide the structure and support Jacob so badly needed once Esther had left for senior secondary school. We had placed Jacob in a private school, but he wasn't performing well and was becoming increasingly mischievous at home. "As for Jacob . . . hmm!" Adongo's exasperation was palpable. "My other pickins—Ray, Esther—they no gimme trouble. Not like Jacob."

Any child-rearing advice we offered fell on deaf ears. Our approach was just too remote. We asked Joseph to talk with Adongo. Joseph, too, had raised his children as a single father and had a softer touch.

After one particularly egregious incident when Jacob was about eleven, it was Joseph who got him to 'fess up. Jacob had "borrowed" Clement's iPad and hidden it in the study. As Jacob repeated his confession to us, Ray—then on vacation from university—had his arm protectively around his brother's shoulders.

I chided Jacob gently, "We've sent you to a good school so you can get a good education. Don't you want to grow up to be a fine young man like your brother Ray?" Jacob's tears flowed freely as he admitted what he had done. Ray, too, teared up; we were moved by his concern for his younger brother.

When Adongo learned what had happened, he was furious. He was done with Jacob's mischief. He would send him to his home village in the north. Jacob would learn the hard way. Adongo was determined—until Ray stepped in. Ray knew all too well what life in the north would mean for Jacob's future. He wanted Jacob to have the same opportunities as himself.

Adongo listened; Jacob stayed.

A single father, unschooled himself and overwhelmed by his young son's mischievous behavior; an older son better able to understand and respond. The incident epitomizes the distance between Adongo and the children he has worked so hard to educate. We often remind the children that they owe their education to their father's loyal service, but I wonder about the price Adongo has had to pay.

Adongo is central to the rhythm of our days when we are in Ghana. He trims the hedges, pumps the water, and makes sure the gate is secure. We joke about his ability to predict whether or not it will rain. He has a great sense of humor. We missed him when he fractured his leg and spent several weeks in hospital.

John often stops by at our gate to visit with Adongo. Sometimes I chat with him briefly. We're about the same age and we commiserate about the aches and pains of our advancing years.

"Adongo did good to come here," he remarked quietly one day, several years after Adongo had moved in.

"It certainly worked out for us," I agreed.

"I tell 'm. His children got education. It b'n good for him."

I wondered whether he and Adongo had revisited the decision frequently. Was John trying to reassure himself he had done the right thing in persuading Adongo to move? It hadn't been easy rearing the children as a single parent without the support of the Frafra community in Nungua. I understand that better now.

We admire Adongo's unwavering determination in pursuit of a better life for his children. But as I reflect on the intersection of our very different lives, I realize how much of his life lies beyond our reach. We know little of his struggles as a single father and the need to reconcile his traditional worldview with that of his better-educated children.

## Sophia

**A** crush of people pressed against the barrier surrounding the arrivals door at Accra's Kotoka Airport. The daily British Airways and KLM flights arrive at about the same time, and they are always full. There was a festive, expectant air as residents awaited the arrival of friends, family, or business associates from overseas. We were there to greet Isabelle, who was coming to visit for a couple of weeks.

As we waited, a man approached us, and Clement cautiously engaged him in conversation. It was Albert, who we'd known as a child twenty-five years ago in Cape Coast! Albert was one of several schoolboys from a farming village close to the university who helped us in the garden. They wore ragged shorts and minimalist shoes. We paid them a few pennies for their help. Clement lectured them to be serious about their schooling.

We could never have guessed how far Albert would go. Now chief accountant at Guinness-Ghana, he was at the airport to meet his daughter returning from vacation in the UK. We were astounded. As we reminisced, we asked whether he knew where Sophia was. Sophia had been nursemaid to our children for several years. We'd grown very fond of her and stayed in touch for a while after leaving Cape Coast. We knew she had married and gone to Burkina Faso, but there the trail ended. Albert thought she was working for the Ghana Education Service (GES) in Cape Coast.

Isabelle planned to do some photography in Cape Coast during her visit and determined to seek Sophia out. She had been very close to Sophia as a young child and remembered her fondly. In Cape Coast, she had no difficulty in finding the GES office and went in to enquire. "Yes, she works here," someone told her. "She's gone for lunch." Isabelle waited. When Sophia returned and was told an African American woman was waiting to see her, she was puzzled. Who could it be? What did they want? Noticing Isabelle waiting, she remained apprehensive. When we left, Isabelle wasn't yet five years old. Now she was a grown woman, six feet tall. There was no way Sophia could have recognized her. Sophia, too, had changed. She was now a buxom woman, smartly dressed in traditional attire.

When Isabelle said her name, Sophia's hand flew to her mouth. She was speechless. She never imagined a day when she'd reconnect with our family. She and Isabelle hugged with joy at finding each other again.

On our next visit to Cape Coast, we also sought Sophia out. She still had the same welcoming face, the same forthright manner. She walked with the same spring in her step. We were thrilled to see her again after so many years. Bit by bit, she filled us in on the details of her life.

Sophia's mother had died in childbirth. She and her siblings were raised by their paternal grandmother—a *gari*[4] seller in town. She grew up poor. "It's hard to learn in school when you're hungry," she told us. She came to work for us immediately after middle school. Her grandmother couldn't afford to send her to secondary school. When we went to Tampa, we enrolled her in a vocational school where she learned basic secretarial skills. After we left in 1980, a lawyer we knew hired her, but the job didn't last. Ghana's economy had hit rock bottom and she had no one to fall back on. When the offer of marriage came from a man with a settled job, she felt she had no option but to accept.

With her husband she had moved first to Burkina, then Nigeria and Cote D'Ivoire. They had three children, a boy and two girls. She nearly died after the youngest was born but treated herself with local remedies learned from her grandmother. Sophia told the story without drama or apparent emotion. She knew how to take care of herself; she had been

---

4. *Gari* is a food staple made from cassava that has been dried and fermented.

doing so all her life. When we reconnected, her husband was working in the UK. He called the children from time to time and occasionally sent gifts, but as far as we could tell the marriage was dead. She was effectively a single parent.

When we visited her at home, we were happy to find Sophia living in a very pleasant three-bedroom house, albeit reachable down an unpaved road traversed by deep gullies. We congratulated her on how nicely her house was arranged. "I learned how you did things," she told us. "I copied what I saw."

As we chatted, she complained about the poor English spoken by the university students.

"How is it that you speak English so well?" we asked.

"I read a lot," she told us. Sensing our curiosity, she went on. "I saw how you encouraged Toby to read. I used to borrow books from your shelves. I put them back so you wouldn't know." We laughed.

Sophia's children have benefited from their mother's love of books and commitment to their education. At the university school, they were often at the top of their class, competing favorably with the children of university faculty. Her son is now a teacher; her older daughter, with a degree in mathematics, works for a bank. The last born is a doctor.

Starting at the GES as a simple typist, Sophia had worked her way to the top of the secretarial hierarchy. For the final promotion, she had to take an exam that included economics and English. I wondered how she'd managed.

"What classes did you take to prepare?" I asked.

"Why would I take classes?" she replied indignantly, "I can study the books by myself!"

I was amazed. Sophia probably doesn't even know the American expression "pull yourself up by your bootstraps," but that is what she has done all her life.

We have remained in contact with Sophia, following the twists and turns of her life, which has continued to present challenges big and small. Through it all, she has remained strong, resilient, hopeful. Whenever we take overseas visitors to Cape Coast, we make a point of introducing them to Sophia. No one forgets meeting her. Her spunk and determination shine through.

## Bernard

**B**ernard is sturdy and reliable in an unvarnished sort of way. If you met him, you might think he was a boxer or a soccer player. You would be wrong. He had no opportunity growing up to indulge in sports or other childhood pursuits. When he was just ten years old, he was adopted by Clement's cousin Nicho. Bernard came from a poor family; his mother could barely afford to feed him. Nicho, a teacher, was happy to have a child to help in the house. For Bernard, living with Nicho provided a path to education, but it came at a price.

From the beginning, Nicho treated Bernard like a servant, working him hard. She sent him to primary school but couldn't support his education beyond that. Clement paid for him to go to secondary school, then university, but he continued to live with Nicho, taking on more and more household duties, subject always to her overbearing discipline. When we visited Nicho, she always had a tirade of complaints about him. Once, when he was about sixteen, she forced him to kneel before Clement in apology for an alleged offense. "Look at what you do. And when Uncle Clement is paying for you to go to secondary school," she admonished him.

As Nicho aged and required more and more personal care, the abuse grew shriller. No female assistant stayed more than a few months. Bernard looked after her every need but got little thanks in return. Once he had earned his degree, he wanted desperately to leave. "I can't stay there anymore," he told me, shaking his head. "Auntie Nicho . . . she's too trouble-some." But it wasn't easy to achieve financial independence.

298

Even after Nicho died, he remained living in the house with her son. It was the only home he knew.

Bernard's degree program included a year in neighboring Benin, enabling him to become fluent in French. For his mandatory year of National Service—a year of low-paid "service" required of all university graduates—he worked as a French instructor for the Border Guard. Because Ghana is surrounded by Francophone countries, it is important for Border Guard personnel to know the language. By all accounts, Bernard did well. He helped upgrade the French language program and was instrumental in procuring a grant from the French Embassy.

After completing his National Service, Bernard hoped for a permanent job, but no offer came. He lobbied those he knew in senior positions, hanging around their offices hoping to meet someone in authority, but to no avail. Meanwhile, he was earning a meagre living teaching part time in two private schools. He kept hoping.

When we were in Ghana Bernard visited regularly, taking the long *trotro* ride across town. Each time it was the same sad story.

"I had an appointment with the service chief. I waited for two hours, but he didn't show."

"I spoke to the head of training; she'd really like to hire me, but it's not up to her."

"They just had an intake, but the positions all went to friends and relatives of government officials. They told me, 'Maybe next time.' "

We suggested he pursue different opportunities. A job with a UN agency in need of French speakers? A certificate that might lead to a career in computing? A teaching position in the GES? While paying lip service to our advice, Bernard remained fixated on a future with the Border Guard. He kept angling for meetings with authorities that went nowhere. It seemed like a hopeless situation. We doubted he'd ever access the career that he craved so badly. He was aging out of the possibility of joining the service. Clement tried reaching out to Border Guard higher-ups on his behalf but to no avail. We didn't know how else to help him.

Then, quite suddenly, everything changed. We were in the U.S. when a cousin called to tell us that Bernard had been accepted into the Border Guard's training program. We could hardly believe the good news.

Once admitted, Bernard grasped the opportunity with everything he had, powering his way through boot camp with much younger recruits. After graduation, he was appointed instructor at the training school, the position he had coveted for so many years. His single-minded persistence had paid off. We were thrilled for him. With a steady job, he could afford to get married. He named his first-born son Clement.

## Ayitey

Daniel Ayitey—who we know as Ayitey, and Clement sometimes calls "Mr. Ayitey" in a teasing sort of way—has been around the family for a very long time. He lives in a one-room dwelling on the family compound at Osu. He stays there with his niece; he doesn't have a family of his own. Not tall but very muscular, Ayitey is definitely not someone you'd want to get in a fight with on a lonely road. He has a winning smile but doesn't say much—at least not when I'm around.

Ayitey trained as a mechanic and ran his own small business out of a rented workshop for several years. But things didn't work out. First, the landlord reclaimed the plot of land. Then his tools were stolen. It's not an unusual story for those who struggle at the bottom of the economic ladder, even those with skills and hands-on experience. Lacking the resources to rebuild his business, he had to find another way to earn a living. He now works as a driver serving visitors to the upscale hotels in Accra. Sometimes he's hired for multiday trips. If there's no work, he stays home.

When we see him in Accra, I often ask, "How's business, Ayitey?" His response, with typical Ghanaian economy of words, is always, "By the Grace," meaning "By the Grace of God, I'm doing OK." He'd never admit to anything less, but we know his life is often hard.

When we return to Ghana after months away, Ayitey helps us get our vehicles back on the road, fix minor problems, procure road-worthiness certificates, and the like. He is always ready to help—for a fee. The fee is often a matter for hot discussion.

"You can't expect me to pay you that much!" Clement complains, half seriously.

"But, Prof, I've been here all day," Ayitey remonstrates.

There is an underlying quid pro quo: his time, our money. But the relationship isn't purely transactional. I hadn't understood Ayitey's deep attachment to Clement until the day of the "blessing."

Ayitey isn't our regular driver, but we're glad of his services when we need a large vehicle for a trip out of town, as on one occasion when Lutteroth relatives from Germany were visiting. They'd come to Accra for a big family get-together. Gresham and Natasha were also in town. After the gathering, we planned a trip to Elmina and Cape Coast for the visitors to see the famed castles.

Ayitey arrived early. He was dressed impeccably in suit and tie with winkle-picker shoes. He always dresses this way on long road trips, no matter the heat of the tropical sun. The formality is important to him. It is a mark of respect: his respect for us and the respect he expects us to show him in return.

Clement wasn't feeling too well that morning. He rallied when Ayitey arrived, and we set off for Elmina, but by evening he was having severe abdominal cramps. He has had several similar episodes following a botched hernia operation.

Sometimes they pass quickly. This time it was bad; I've rarely seen him in so much pain. A friend in Elmina put us in touch with a well-respected local doctor who dispatched an assistant with pain medication to get him through the night. The next morning, we saw the doctor at his clinic.

"You should go back to Accra," he advised. "We don't have the right facilities here. In Accra, they'll be able to treat you properly."

So, leaving the rest of the party in Elmina, we headed back to Accra where Clement was immediately admitted to hospital. Ayitey drove me home. The next morning, he arrived early with a friend who would drive me around when he returned to Elmina. Before leaving, he asked if he could step into the house.

"OK?" I was puzzled.

Once inside, he asked, "Do you have a white handkerchief?"

"Um . . . Yes." I wondered where this was heading.

"Please bring it. I want to pray for Uncle Clement."

Fortunately, I had a white handkerchief, given to me at a recent Mother's Day service. I fetched it from upstairs. He asked me to hold one end while he held the other.

"Dear God, you are all-powerful. Please help Prof to get better," he prayed with great intensity. "You know how to make people better. You are all-powerful. If we men can fix parts of a car when they get broken, then you can fix a human body when it's hurting. If we humans can make new cars, you can surely make Prof's body well again."

Ayitey's prayer was long and passionate, direct, unselfconscious. It was an expression of his deep love and concern for Clement, his patron and his friend. He prayed with touching faith in the God he worships at church each Sunday. He was confident he'd be heard.

When he'd finished, he asked me to take the handkerchief, place it on Clement's body, and repeat the prayer over him. My ideas about God's agency in human affairs may be different from Ayitey's, but the spiritual intensity of his prayer was undeniable. I was deeply moved. Though less receptive than me to the power Ayitey had vested in the white handkerchief, Clement, too, was touched. No matter the gulf that separates Clement's life and beliefs from those of Ayitey, there can be no denying the deep human bond that connects them. "By the Grace!"

## John

**A**buri Gardens, beautifully situated on the hills overlooking Accra, was established by the colonialists in 1890. It still show-cases many species of trees and plants brought from all over the British empire; it's a place we like to take visitors. One time when we were visiting the gardens with Sophia, the guide introduced us to John, scion of a family of woodcarvers. We were fascinated to hear his story.

When a large tree had to be cut down, John envisioned a new role for the three-foot-high stump and asked that it be left standing. He has been carving a tree of life on it for more than five years and is not yet finished. The carving consists of a rich assortment of people and animals: a cornucopia of figurines reminiscent of the carvings in a medieval cathedral.

"These are the chiefs," he told us, pointing to a group at the top and the many people climbing up to reach them.

"And these here," he said, pointing to a side branch, "these are the military." At the top of that branch, we could clearly distinguish a figure in the uniform of the top brass. With a chuckle, he pointed to a short branch taking off near the base.

"These people have lost their way in life. They wasted their time when they were young. They're not going anywhere."

Sophia was intrigued; she looked closely at the carvings, as did our driver who was also following the tour. They noticed that some of the figures climbing upward were lending a help-ing hand or shoulder to those behind them, while others were dragging down those who had got ahead.

"It's like the difference between the Ashantis and the Fantis,"

Sophia commented, referring to two of Ghana's larger ethnic groups. "Ashantis like to help each other get ahead. But Fantis, they try to hold others back." Sophia is Fanti, likewise the driver. They both laughed at the failings of their own people.

But there was a sting in the tail. Sophia continued, "The Ashantis, when they've helped someone, they let you know. They like to tell everyone what they've done."

We all laughed. Then, looking again at the carving and the stories he had rendered in such painstaking detail, I asked John how he had come up with the idea for his masterpiece.

"I'm a carver by trade," he told us. "My family are all carvers."

"But this tree of life? Where did you get the idea?"

"It came to me from God."

We were in awe.

Each of the people whose lives have intersected with my own has invented or reinvented their lives with courage, perseverance, and imagination. I feel privileged to know them. But there is much I don't know. I'm not privy to the resources they have drawn on in their struggles. Have they shared with friends? Or sought the wisdom of their elders? Or prayed to a God they trust? Or did each of them simply, bravely take one step at a time, facing each challenge in the moment as it presented itself? I will never know. Nor can I know how they regard us, who are so privileged and wealthy by comparison. The bonds are strong, the affection genuine, but there are boundaries we can never cross. Our life journeys are too different. When we fly back to America, they remain.

# An Archbishop, an Accident, and a New Adventure

When my attempts to offer professional services in Ghana ran into one brick wall after another, I looked for other ways to help. Friends whose connections to poor countries were far more tenuous were engaged in substantive development activities in India and elsewhere. What was I doing? People who knew I spent a lot of time in Ghana assumed I must be engaged in teaching, or nursing, or missionary activity. I wasn't, and it bruised my ego. Even as I rejected the assumption that spending time in "poor, needy" Africa implied being there in some "do-gooder" capacity—"Why else would anyone go to Africa?" they seemed to be asking—I wasn't sure what I could do.

The answer came in an unexpected way: by way of a visit to the north of Ghana, a meeting with an archbishop, and an accident.

## Tamale

Toby visited us in Ghana in 2005, and together we went on a brief trip to Tamale, the main city in the Northern Region. Driving around, we were struck by the poverty of the life around us. The northern towns and villages lacked the color and vibrancy of the south. Life seemed dusty, slow, and arduous. There were a good number of bicycles, just a few cars;

most people walked. Many children were out of school, business activity seemed sluggish. Along with the ubiquitous mosques, NGOs were the most visible signs of movement and activity. Their pickups and SUVs radiated outward to remote villages, the latest tentacles of neocolonial outreach.

In Larabanga, the iconic mosque dating to 1421 was crumbling before our eyes, but the imam sitting under a tree nearby studying the Koran revealed the deep roots of Islamic culture in this part of West Africa. I paused in admiration at the calm attention he was giving to the text before him. He seemed unperturbed by visiting tourists and the potentially disruptive effect that Western-style schooling would soon bring to his community.

Although Clement had visited the north long ago, it seemed to him like a foreign land. Few of his relatives had ventured that far. The impression of backwardness and poverty lodged deep in our imaginations.

Back in the U.S. a few months later, we learned that the archbishop of Tamale would be celebrating Mass in Baltimore. We went along.

Gregory Kpiebaye[5] is tall and thin, soft-spoken and gracious. He has a remarkable life story. At the age of nine, he was selected by foreign missionaries to attend their one school in the north. Twice a year he walked barefoot through the forest to get there. It was a two-day journey in each direction. After completing secondary school, he entered the seminary and then, as priest, progressed rapidly through the ranks, becoming bishop of Wa first, then archbishop of Tamale.

He tells amusing stories of his tangles with Roman authorities, including the time when, as one of the youngest bishops in Rome for a synod, he was reprimanded for wearing a skull cap of African cloth.

---

[5.] I write of the archbishop as he was then and as we knew him in the following years. Sadly, he passed away on May 31st, 2022.

"In Africa, it's hot and sweaty," he protested. "What use is a skull cap that can't be washed?" He wanted nothing of Vatican velvet and was chastised for his rebelliousness.

In Baltimore, the archbishop preached eloquently about the poverty of the people in northern Ghana.

"We visited Tamale last March," Clement told him when we gathered after the service. "We saw how poor the people are. We've been wondering how we could help." We agreed to stay in touch.

Then came the accident.

## Enter Mr. Amuzu

When Clement was on sabbatical at the University of Ghana, a car side-swiped his vehicle, badly denting the side door. Fortunately, he wasn't hurt. Rather than involve his insurance company, the other driver offered to loan him a car and pay for the repairs himself. "I know a guy who can do the job," he told Clement and took him to meet Mr. Amuzu.

Amuzu—short and stocky, dressed in oily work overalls— ran his car body repair business under a tree by the side of a busy road. "Can a guy like this really do the job?" Clement wondered. Given the driver's unqualified assurance, he agreed to take a risk; he was amazed by the result. Not only was the side of the car perfectly restored, but the paint color was matched exactly. There was no trace of the accident.

Always eager to promote local talent, Clement engaged Amuzu in conversation.

"Why are you working by the roadside?"

"I need a place," he told Clement. "But I don't have money."

"Hmm. That's too bad. I'll talk with my wife," Clement said, hinting we might be able to help.

On my next visit to Accra, Amuzu came to see us at Osu. As

we sat on the verandah in the fading afternoon light, I put on my business-owner hat. Amuzu was ill at ease, suspicious; he was probably not used to dealing with White people—let alone White women.

I started by asking about his current income stream. "If we give you a loan, we need to figure out whether you can earn enough to repay it in a few years. Can you tell us roughly how much you make each month right now?"

"Well, um," he hesitated. "I can't really say. Maybe it rains, and the place gets flooded."

"Let's take a good month. No floods. How many jobs do you do typically?" I asked.

"Maybe three."

"And roughly how much do you make from each job?"

"It depends. Maybe I need to go to Kumasi."

"Kumasi?"

"Yes—if I need parts."

I understood. There's a district in Kumasi where skilled craftsmen replicate auto parts they haven't been able to recover from broken-down vehicles. Almost anything needed for restoring a car body can be purchased there.

Gradually I got a rough idea of his monthly revenue, but lacking written records, Mr. Amuzu seemed to be pulling numbers from the air. The conversation got more difficult when I tried to figure out how he expected to grow his business if he took a loan. He was confident he could do it but couldn't explain himself in a way that made sense to me. There was a yawning gulf between his world and mine. This became even more apparent when it came to figuring out the expense side of his business.

"Let's think about your monthly expenses. If we gave you a loan, you would have a rent payment each month and a loan repayment."

He nodded.

"What else?"

"Oil, paint . . ." He hesitated as I wrote down each item. Then continued, "There's food, of course."

"Food?" I couldn't hide my surprise.

"I need to feed the apprentices," Amuzu replied indignantly. I could almost hear him thinking, "Doesn't she understand I need to feed the boys?"

"OK." I quickly regrouped and carried on. "What about wages? What do you pay your apprentices?"

I thought that would be a no-brainer, but it was Amuzu's turn to be surprised. "I only pay them if we have a job," he replied, sounding exasperated. His unspoken subtext seemed to be "White people certainly ask a lot of stupid questions! How can I pay them if there's no work?"

As the discussion continued, I realized that simple business practices such as tallying income and expenditures were quite foreign to Amuzu. We lived in different worlds. He showed no interest in learning from me, and—truth to tell—I didn't know what it would take to transform his ad hoc roadside activity into a business operating out of a secure, walled-in auto-body shop. Careful analysis of the costs and opportunities seemed doomed, but there was something alluring about his abundant self-confidence and machismo. We decided to take a chance and loaned him the money anyway.

For several years, Amuzu ran a successful business, repaying monthly what he owed. Whenever we visited the compound, it was chock-full of wrecked vehicles that in the West would have been consigned to the scrap heap. He was confident he could restore them all to working condition. We were amazed.

Over the years, we developed a warm relationship grounded in mutual respect and gratitude—on his part, for the opportunity we'd provided, and on ours, for the satisfaction of witnessing the results our small loan had achieved.

## A Small-Loan Scheme in Tamale

From three disparate events—a visit to Tamale, a meeting with an archbishop, and an accident in Accra—the idea for a more established loan scheme emerged. Maybe, with the help of the archbishop, we could replicate what we'd done for Amuzu in the north of Ghana. Maybe, by providing small-business loans, we could help lift a few people out of poverty. It would be an adventure outside the comfortable cocoon in which we lived in Accra. We floated the idea with the archbishop, and he agreed to help. He hardly knew us and may well have wondered what he was committing to, but he took a chance on us anyway. I was thrilled.

When we visited Tamale to launch the scheme in January 2006, Archbishop Gregory welcomed us warmly to his office at the Catholic Secretariat. I was impressed to find him simply dressed in a local tie-dye shirt and slacks, no clerical collar or purple shirt to designate his rank; he didn't cling to priestly authority or episcopal pomp. Later, as we traveled to different parts of the archdiocese, we recognized his influence in the many humble, hard-working priests we met. Even Clement— no lover of the church—was impressed.

The archbishop introduced us to Agnes, who would be working out the details with us. Agnes's main responsibility was running a peace-building and civic education program sponsored by a diocese in Germany. With her deep voice and brusque, forthright manner, she gladly embraced this addition to her workload. A former teacher and lay leader in the church, she is devoted to promoting the well-being of her fellow countrymen. We could tell right away she was someone who would get things moving.

"We'd like to invest in businesses that are producing a good or service. Not just selling things," we explained. We preferred not to fund the endless chain of buying and selling that is such a feature of Ghanaian commercial life.

Agnes seemed to understand. "Better we find people who will employ and train others—like apprentices," she added. "Then they, too, can benefit from the loans."

"Exactly," we said. "Also, we'd like the scheme to be self-sustaining. We won't take any money out. When a loan is repaid, the money can be recycled to another applicant."

"That's it," she agreed.

Glad to have a common vision, we quickly put together a plan and drafted a letter of agreement for the archbishop to sign. During the visit, we interviewed nine candidates the archbishop had identified and selected six to receive phase-one loans. It remained for us to send the funds. The scheme was up and running.

We returned to Tamale almost every year for many years. We interviewed numerous candidates and gave out more than fifty loans. The applicants represented human nature in all its variety: assertive and obsequious, honest and deceitful, serious and irresponsible, boastful and self-effacing. There were seamstresses and hairdressers and carpenters, poultry keepers and pig farmers, brewers and drug dispensers, printers and weavers, and, inevitably, some whose task was simply retailing in one of its many forms.

Millicent, a dressmaker, was one of the first to receive a loan. Tall and thin with a dignified bearing, she is always impeccably dressed. When we interviewed her, she was working out of a simple wooden stall close to the archdiocesan office. The sign over the shop read: "The Lord is my Shepherd," proclaiming her churchly allegiance. The priests passing by noticed how hard she worked and recommended her for a loan.

"I need an electric sewing machine," she told us. "And an embroidery machine if the money is enough."

Despite many setbacks, Millicent has succeeded beyond expectation. Now, several years and two loans later, she has a secure workshop in the center of Tamale. A tailor and a *joromi*[6] embroiderer, as well as several apprentices, work there. While the apprentices busy themselves sewing school uniforms—a bread-and-butter task for many dressmakers—her own expertise is fabricating high-end clothing using the narrow, woven strips of cloth that are the specialty of the region. She attracts orders from as far away as Accra.

We have witnessed her journey, both the ups and the downs, and rejoice in her success. When we visit, she tells us about her business and the current group of apprentices. But we know little of her personal life. We can only guess at the reason for the hint of sadness that often hovers behind her welcoming smile.

Justine—who spells his Christian name with an "e" at the end and will not be told that this spelling is normally used for women—is a carpenter. He, too, has come far. During the interview he sat on the edge of his seat, bursting with youthful energy. A wooden bench under a tree and a bag of hand tools were the extent of his business property. He wanted to put up a workshop and buy electric tools. Years later, he told us how scared he was when he received the loan—equivalent to about a thousand dollars—cash in hand. "I come from a poor farming family. I could never imagine handling so much money," he said.

Justine was levelheaded. He spent the money just as he had told us he would, and his business flourished. Every year, he achieved a new milestone to mark his progress out of poverty and into the middle class. First came a motorbike, then a Motorking,[7] then a truck. He went on to build a house for his

---

6. *Joromi* is the word used for the rich embroidery designs often used on shirts and other garments in Ghana.

7. A Motorking is a small motorcycle with a cart hitched behind it, making it possible for the owner to transport goods and materials. Motorkings are widely

family and even obtained a contractor's license. With only a trade school education, Justine has been able to send his children to secondary school and beyond.

The sign that Justine erected at the entrance to his workshop reads: "Wepia Carpentry Shop, Sponsored by Lutterodt." The sign is a testimony to his thoughtfulness and a lasting symbol of our connection to one small business in a dusty sub-Saharan city.

Herbert, also a carpenter and one of the first group of loan recipients, was as different from Justine as could be. At the interview, he presented us with an impressive business plan, and when we visited his shop we found it buzzing with activity. Older and more established than Justine, he already had a going business making furniture. "I made all the pews for the new Carmelite convent," he told us proudly. "I can take you to see them." He requested a loan so he could purchase a new molding machine. Accepting his application seemed like a no-brainer.

On a subsequent visit to Tamale, Agnes was out of town and Herbert offered to drive us around in his truck. It was a ramshackle affair but got us where we needed to go. As we drove, a recording of the rosary, recited in a very Irish accent, played continuously in the background.

When his payments were running late and the molding machine failed to materialize, we wondered whether his piety was spiked with a little deviousness. Had he used the loan to buy the vehicle? we wondered. This was something our loan agreements strictly forbade. He gave one excuse after another for late or missing payments. Then there was silence. Later we learned that Herbert was suffering from ill-health and had gone back to his village. His business decline was a big disappointment.

---

found in northern Ghana where they enable a steep increase in business activity. However, with only three wheels, they are not very safe, especially when balancing the large load they often carry.

Like Herbert, Angela's loan application had been compelling; fortunately, it had a better outcome. She maintained that young women in her town, Damongo, were being driven into prostitution for lack of gainful employment. A loan would help her establish a cosmetics store where she would sell hair extensions, pomades, and the like. It would have been hard to say no.

Angela's small business thrived. A few years after she had repaid the loan, we passed by her store on our way to Wa and stopped to say hello. She took a bottle of South African wine from a shelf and offered it to us as a gift. Wine! We were amazed at how far she—and Damongo—had come.

It was never easy to tell from the application and interview who would succeed and who would fail. Many applications were supported by parish priests who had little aptitude for predicting business success. Theo was quiet and courteous. He had been a leader in the charismatic movement and his mind seemed to dwell there still. He requested a loan to purchase equipment to start a small printing and copying business. Sadly, nothing quite worked out for him. "My copier broke down. It cost me to get it mended," he complained at first. Then, "I was sick in the hospital for two weeks and couldn't work." And finally, "I don't get people passing by. I need an office closer to the college." We sensed it was hopeless. He was always the victim. Eventually he had to close the business, leaving his wife to support the family.

The last time we saw Theo, he was standing at the door of his wife's sewing stall with his youngest child in his arms. When we stopped to say hello, he pressed Clement to accept a shirt his wife had made and offered me a small shopping bag. They were gifts he could ill afford, but we didn't feel we could refuse his generous gesture.

Success certainly didn't correlate with educational level.

Quite the reverse. Take Irene. She graduated from the University of Ghana, Clement's alma mater, and had worked for an NGO before setting out on her own. She wanted to model a poultry-rearing business for local women. After awarding the loan, we learned that she traveled frequently within Ghana and even overseas to attend meetings. When we warned her of the risk to her business while she was away from home, she assured us her maids could manage well in her absence. We were skeptical.

Sure enough, one day when she was out of town the coop caught fire and she lost all her birds. Unaccountably, she thought the loss absolved her of the responsibility to repay. "I don't know how you expect me to pay," she argued. "My birds are gone."

"If everyone thought like that, our loan scheme couldn't survive," Clement chided her. "When you took the loan, you accepted an obligation. You're a graduate of Legon; you should know better."

Irene chose to become arrogant and defensive. Agnes, who had recommended her for the loan, was embarrassed and would have none of her excuses. After a lot of blaming and shaming in the local community, Irene eventually repaid the loan in full, but the episode left us cautious about supporting graduate applicants in the future.

Andrew comes from a much simpler background. He also suffered multiple losses as he tried to develop a poultry business. We extended his repayment period many times, but he didn't try to walk away. Eventually he settled on a successful business hatching and selling day-old chicks and was able to pay back the loan. We were impressed by his tenacity.

Rita, too, is from humble origins. She runs a small hairdressing salon in Bimbilla, a market town some distance from Tamale. The salon has electricity but no running water. Rita applied for a loan to buy an electric hair dryer. Her husband, a policeman, was with her waiting to greet us when we visited.

"I want to thank you for the loan you gave my wife," he said. "It has really helped us." Policeman and hairdresser, husband and wife, were working together for a better future, simply, honestly, no excuses. We were touched by their commitment to a shared endeavor.

Philomena has only an elementary education herself but has supported her children through tertiary-level education thanks to her business brewing *pito*.[8] She had set up a mini ecosystem in and around her backyard: The mush left over from brewing was used to feed her pigs, and the manure from the pigs helped fertilize a small patch of corn. She asked for a loan to purchase a freezer.

"Then I can kill the pigs when they're ready and sell the meat at Christmas or Easter when the price is up," she explained. The idea made good sense to us.

When we visited her place, she took us to see her new pigsty and told us about the pigs as they grunted contentedly. "This one will give birth soon," she said, throwing a corn husk in the direction of a heavily pregnant sow. "Those over there are ready for market."

I was taken back to my childhood when my siblings and I would visit the cowsheds or pigsty with our dad. He would comment with his usual brevity on the animals or recent improvements to the buildings. I glimpsed an unexpected connection between these two experiences, so widely separated in time and space; there is an essential earthiness and integrity underlying all farming activity. Pigs are pigs everywhere!

During our trips north, we traveled to clients' places of business in Tamale and beyond: Yendi, Wa, Damongo, Chamba, Bimbilla. Most of the time we were safely ensconced in an air-conditioned SUV, but the road often took us along untarred or heavily potholed roads. If the road petered out, we walked

---

8. *Pito* is a local brew made from millet.

the final distance. Each visit was an opportunity to connect with different people, savor a new environment, stretch the boundaries of my world.

Yet, as I relive my experiences at a deeper level, I realize that I hadn't shed my tourist lens entirely. Each visit may have been a *kairos* moment—a pilgrimage, in a way—but each experience also gave me a satisfying sense of adventure and accomplishment; the remoter, the better. Amidst the many moments of genuine human connection, I still detect lingering traces of the apartness and entitlement that marked my childhood.

## A Meeting Called to Order

On our annual visits to Tamale, Agnes normally arranged a meeting for us to connect with current loan holders and interview new applicants. The meetings were high points of our visits.

Participants usually drifted in slowly. Most came by *trotro* and walked from the main road. A few came by motorbike. At one meeting early on, Justine came with his wife, who had applied for a loan for her hairdressing business. Their youngest son, a few months old, was on her back. Millicent was there, as were Herbert and Rita and many more. Meanwhile, Agnes was busy calling others to make sure they were on their way. "You need to be here," she told one. To another, "Come quickly, we're about to start. Don't give me excuses." Her familiar gruff tone belied her genuine concern for their well-being. She knew each of their stories and was committed to their success.

Eventually Agnes called the meeting to order and asked for a volunteer to open with a prayer. Most participants in the loan scheme are Catholics, recruited with the help of their parish priest. Their common beliefs and rituals, no longer regarded as an alien import, create strong bonds between them. Herbert volunteered. Business might be tough, but praying to

the Lord? That he could do. He stood up and invited everyone to do the same. Clasping his hands, he intoned a lengthy
prayer full of requests for divine help. After several minutes,
he invited everyone to join him in the Lord's Prayer. We concluded with a loud "Amen," and everyone took their seat.

Agnes opened the meeting with effusive thanks for our
presence, then invited Clement to speak: "Please, Prof, we all
need to hear the story about your first loan." He was happy to
oblige: the accident in Accra, the loan we gave Mr. Amuzu for
his auto body shop, the success of his business. They never
tired of hearing the story. White do-gooders like me are a dime
a dozen in Tamale, but for a fellow Ghanaian to venture from
Accra to lend a hand to his distant countrymen is rare indeed.
Appreciation for his presence was palpable.

After Clement, it was my turn to speak. I congratulated
those who were doing well but admonished those who had got
behind with their payments. "If you don't pay, it means there
are no funds for others to get loans," I said, gesturing to the
new applicants in the room.

My words were greeted with silence. They looked to Agnes
for translation. Agnes duly repeated what I had said, speaking
in English but in a way they could understand and adding a
few exhortations of her own.

"Auntie says that she and Prof want you to do well, but you
have to pay each month. No excuses." After carrying on for a
bit, her tone softened, "If you are having difficulty, come and
see me. We can work something out."

Clement picked up the theme. "Ghanaians need to be serious. It's no good thinking you can pay up when it suits you,"
he chided them. At such moments, Clement says it like it is,
appealing to aspirations he shares with his fellow countrymen.
I may have a better understanding of running a business, but
he's the one they listen to. Although he often grumbles about
our visits to Tamale, saying, "It's just a waste of money," he's
not unmoved by the way he is received by the small-business

owners. In an unguarded moment, he once told a friend in the U.S., "I am passionate about their success."

After droning on for a bit, the meeting came to life when it was time for participants to share their business difficulties. Several had problems with dishonest employees.

"One of my apprentices stole a piece of cloth," one said. "It was for a customer. I had to buy a new one."

"Tools went missing from my workshop," another volunteered.

"You can't trust people," Angela added. "When I go to Kumasi to get supplies, I close the shop."

Millicent told them how she dealt with the problem. "Sometimes I leave a five-cedi bill lying on the table when apprentices come for interview," she said. "I check if they pick it up. I only take those who are honest."

The conflict between family obligations and the needs of the business was another common concern. "I had to pay the school fees, or my children would have had to stay home," one person said. "My father was ill, and I had to take him to hospital," added another.

Hearing the many excuses, Agnes stepped in, "You need to separate business and family. If you take money from your business for family needs, you can never succeed." It was a principle we returned to again and again, yet it wasn't an easy one for them to follow. Personal lives and businesses are closely interwoven, especially for those living at the margin. Few have personal savings on which to draw in times of emergency or when a special need arises. (At least two of the loans were used to pay the dowry for a wife!)

Father Benet of the Wa diocese—always a wise and steady voice—had taken a loan to promote a small business he was modeling for the surrounding community. At the meeting, he strongly agreed with the principle of separating business and family interests. We were amused to learn later that he, too, had succumbed to the temptation to put his "family" first.

When churchmen from around the country gathered in Wa for the installation of a new bishop, he slaughtered the guinea fowl he had been keeping as breeding stock so that he could treat the dignitaries to the local delicacy. Who wouldn't have done the same?

From the discussion, we learned a great deal about the problems the business owners faced: the omnipresent threat of fire or disease for those raising livestock; the difficulty in collecting payments, particularly on government contracts; the dishonest agricultural extension officers who peddle inoculations that are diluted and ineffective; the effects of rapid inflation on the cost of raw materials, and so on. My own business situation was a walk in the park in comparison.

The meetings always closed on a high note. I felt reinvigorated by our connection to the people whose lives we'd touched, and they, in their turn, promised to be more regular with their payments. Despite their good intentions, however, the problem of collecting on the loans grew more challenging year by year.

## A Magical Moment

Because of the large number of defaults, we stopped issuing new loans in 2019, making very few exceptions. Memuna was one of them.

Memuna, the only Muslim among the loan recipients, runs a small printing business out of two kiosks in a scrappy market not far from Tamale city center. Across the lane from her shop is a butcher's stall. Flies are abundant, chickens run free. When we visited, children stared at us from behind their mother's skirt or the arms of whichever market-stall holder had rescued them from the path of a passing motorbike. An ancient baobab tree stands tall at the entrance to the crowded market lanes, unperturbed by the busy chaos below. Memuna radiates confidence and energy. Always dressed in traditional cloth, she has a stately presence.

Memuna had repaid an initial loan fully and on time and requested a second loan to purchase a cutting machine. "I have to pay someone outside to cut the paper," she had told us. "It's costly."

"If you can save half the price over the next year, we'll match it with a loan for the remaining half," we promised.

Now, one year later, we were ready to issue the loan. We were sitting in the courtyard of our hotel enjoying a cold drink when she arrived. Leocadia, who was now the coordinator for the loan scheme, was with us. After we had finished the business discussion, Memuna said, without any preamble, "I owe everything to you." I started to preen myself at the thought that our small loan had been so impactful, but soon realized she was speaking to Leocadia, not us.

"Without Mrs. Leocadia, I wouldn't have had an education," Memuna explained.

"Yes," Leocadia said. "Her family lived next door to us. She and her brothers and sisters used to play with our children."

"You've known each other a long time then?" I was curious.

"Since Memuna was a small girl," Leocadia continued. "When it was time for our children to go to school, their parents wouldn't send them. We felt so bad. Without an education they'd get left far behind."

Memuna interjected. "My father came from Niger. We're Muslims. He was traditional in his thinking. He didn't see the benefit of schooling, especially not for girls."

Leocadia picked up the thread. "My husband and I were both teachers, you know. We tried to talk to the parents. They weren't interested at first."

"What happened?" I was intrigued.

"We didn't give up. We kept going back to explain how the children would benefit from an education. We offered to pay their fees."

"My parents could afford to pay. They had money. They just didn't see the value of education," Memuna explained.

"Eventually they relented," Leocadia added.

"Yes, my father gave in—but not all the way. I could only go to school four days a week. On Fridays, I had to go to market and sell cassava." She paused. "Much later, my father realized the value of our education and was grateful."

Leocadia nodded. "When my husband died, Memuna's family came to the funeral. They came in their numbers. They brought many gifts. They understood how my husband had helped them."

Memuna's journey hadn't been easy. She told us of the hard road she had traveled, first to get a basic education, then to qualify as a teacher; how she had come to start her business; her determination to succeed; how she will always credit Leocadia and her husband for her start in life.

We listened, entranced. For us, it was a magical moment. In the hotel courtyard, in the fading afternoon light, learning the connection between the two women: how Leocadia and her husband had reached out to their Muslim neighbors, how they had enabled Memuna's success. For a moment the veil had parted, the borders that defined our separate lives seemed permeable; we were in what Barbara Holmes of the Center for Action and Contemplation in Albuquerque calls a "thin place." We were in awe.

## Farewell, Emeritus

On one of our last visits to Tamale, we went by road with friends from the U.S. who'd come to visit. The trip gave them an opportunity to witness scenes not available to the average tourist. On the last day of our visit, we made our customary courtesy call on Archbishop Gregory, then retired. Fondly known as Emeritus by the local people, he remains a revered figure. Emeritus's house is on a large tract of land that includes many other church buildings and residences. The massive mango trees in his yard were dripping with fruit. A few goats and chickens scratched about in the dust. A young girl ushered us into a back room. "Emeritus will be with you soon," she told us.

After a few minutes he glided in quietly. The same dignified man we had known for many years: no clerical garb, no bombast, but with a remarkable life story. Then in his late eighties, Emeritus was well but frail.

"I don't travel anymore," he told us. In the past, he had traveled almost every year, whether to shepherd the many priests he trained who now work in other countries or to raise funds for needy institutions in the diocese. (In his autobiography, he jokes about becoming a professional beggar.) He told us of a close encounter with death after one such visit.

"A few years ago, I went to see one of my priests in South Africa," he said. "He wanted to retire home to Ghana, but the local bishop wouldn't let him go. They have too few priests. I didn't realize the winters there are cold." He paused. "I didn't have any warm clothes with me and caught a bad chill. I was in hospital for a long time. I nearly died."

"I'm so sorry you had to go through that. Did they find out what was wrong?" I asked.

"The local doctors were useless. They didn't know what to do. It was a Cuban doctor who saved me." He smiled wistfully. The burden of his own people's lack of care seemed to weigh heavily on him, but he showed no trace of anger. He continued quietly, telling our visitors about his life and how he had been able to complete a lifelong ambition of translating the Gospels into his mother tongue, Dagaari. We asked him to retell the stories of his clashes with Roman authorities, and he was happy to oblige. He spoke quietly, peacefully. We were glad our friends had the opportunity to meet a man of such authenticity, so far from the stereotype of an African prelate.

We visited Emeritus at home one more time, after the COVID pandemic. He was sick but invited us to his bedroom to see him briefly.

"I'm not well," he told us. "Please pray for me."

We sensed it was the last time we'd see him. And it was. He died a few months later. But his spirit lives on, his memory undimmed. Archbishop Gregory Kpiebaya—Emeritus—forever friend!

An outing, an accident, and an archbishop. Agnes and a long line of small businesspeople in northern Ghana. Our gratitude is deep and lasting. For brief moments, we have been able to touch lives and livelihoods quite different from our own, to admire the grit and grace of people who face challenges that far outstrip any we have experienced. No longer "them" but "thou." People we have known and cared about, embraced and exhorted, admired and admonished. Justine and Millicent, Rita and Angela, Philomena and Memuna, even the laggards— Herbert, Irene, and the hapless Theo—are woven into the fabric of our lives. We are grateful to have walked with them for a time, to have witnessed close up their struggles and successes—and failures, too. They may live in a world very different from our own, the barriers to mutual understanding may be profound, but the place they hold in our affections can never be erased.

# Part VII

## And Then . . .

*We do not find our own center, it finds us.*

—*Richard Rohr,* Everything Belongs

# Bridges Not Boundaries

A t the start of the new millennium, I was my own boss
and, with the children away from home, had freedom to
pursue interests other than work and family. The local Catholic
parish provided me with a community in which I found purpose and belonging when at home in Columbia, while I was
also reimmersing myself in life in Ghana thanks to increasingly
frequent visits. Within the parish, I found both a need and an
opportunity to serve as a bridge between the two worlds I had
the privilege to know so well. It was a role that seemed ever
more appropriate and appealing.

## The Cultural Divide

The parish's Diversity Committee had already brought me
into contact with parishioners from many different countries as we showcased their various cultures at intercultural
liturgical celebrations and the social gatherings that followed.
But genuine acceptance of cultural differences was lacking.
In-depth cross-cultural communication was sorely needed.

Take the case of Comfort, a Liberian woman who was a
member of the parish. Comfort had managed to escape from
a country ravaged by civil war with the help of a Liberian doctor, Dr. Felicia, who engaged her as a domestic servant. When
I first met Comfort, she was looking for an opportunity to live
independently of her mentor. Her own entry to the U.S. was
just the first step; she was determined to ensure her seven

children would be able to follow.

The parish's social ministry helped her get subsidized accommodation and paid the airfares for her two youngest children to join her. So far, so good. A problem arose, however, when the younger daughter, Suzie, was in second grade and ready to receive her First Communion. Comfort didn't have Suzie's baptismal certificate. It is hard to imagine the drama involved. Liberia was still mired in violence, so obtaining the certificate from the cathedral in Monrovia where the child was baptized was out of the question.

"They tell me they need the certificate. How can I do that?" Comfort asked me, shrugging her shoulders and gesturing to indicate the impossibility of getting what the parish was asking for.

"Do you know anyone who was there to witness the baptism?" I asked.

"Her godmother is in Florida," she told me. "I'll ask."

Fortunately, the godmother was able to produce a photo of the baptism, which seemed to satisfy the authorities, and Suzie's First Communion went ahead as planned. I thought the matter was settled. Apparently not.

Several months later, Comfort came to me in high dudgeon. "Father W. ask Dr. Felicia if she can get Suzie's baptismal certificate," she complained. "Dr. Felicia know nothing about it. Why Father not ask me hisself? 'Cos I'm poor?"

Comfort was incensed. Now that she was living independently, the last thing she wanted was Dr. Felicia's involvement. She was insulted that Father W. hadn't spoken with her directly. Whatever was he thinking? I wondered. Was Comfort correct that he didn't know how to communicate with someone who was poor and came from a different cultural background? And why did he assume that Dr. Felicia would be able to help? Were all Liberians conflated in his mind?

I told Comfort I would speak with Father W. and caught up with him after Mass one Sunday; I was upset, and it must have shown. He mumbled an apology but didn't seem to understand the fuss. In his mind, he was just following church rules. Father W. is educated and well-meaning, but he had difficulty in recognizing the hurt he had caused. To me, the event highlighted the need for better cross-cultural understanding within our ethnically diverse parish.

Another incident occurred one Sunday morning. A Nigerian couple had arranged for their daughter to be baptized during Mass. They were longtime parishioners I knew quite well. When the service was about to start, the family was nowhere in sight. I approached the sacristan.

"Can we wait a few minutes until the family arrives?" I asked.

"We can't keep the whole congregation waiting," he responded. "We have to start on time."

About ten minutes into the service, I saw the family arriving at the back of the worship space. They were resplendent in matching gold-threaded Nigerian outfits: father, mother, two older brothers, and baby Jane. Surely, I thought, Father could pause the service briefly to welcome the family and invite them to the seats reserved for them up front.

I approached the sacristan again. "The family just arrived. Maybe Father could invite them to take their places."

The sacristan's reply was crisp and clear. "They have to wait. Father will do the baptism after Mass."

Couldn't we show a little flexibility here? I thought to myself. The failure to even recognize their presence seemed a harsh rebuff to a family whose very dress announced their respect for the solemn rite of baptism. I resonated with their humiliation.

The baby's father was more forgiving than I was. "We had difficulty getting the children ready in time," he told me when I spoke with him after Mass. I understood perfectly. For them, being dressed appropriately for the occasion counted for more than arriving on time. The same competing values had played out in my own life so many times. Neither the priest nor the sacristan had seen any need for accommodation.

These incidents and others like them made me wonder how I could be more effective in building bridges of under-standing between our White pastor and his African parish-ioners and—by extension—between our parishioners, most of whom had little or no experience outside the U.S., and the lives of the poor and marginalized in the developing world. I looked for opportunities.

## Confronting Global Poverty

As we spent more time in Ghana, I started to pick up the threads of my youthful concern for global economic develop-ment, a concern that had led me first to Congo then to Ghana but had lain dormant during our many years in the U.S. I won-dered whether I could leverage my long-term connection to the African continent to increase understanding of and con-cern for developing countries within the parish. What could I do to bring my two worlds together?

It was during Mass on Pentecost Day at the Church of Christ the King in Accra that the idea came to me. A breath of the Spirit maybe. Or an inspiration arising out of the beauti-ful celebration and rousing music. Maybe I could take some of the excitement I experienced in Ghana and my concern for the country's development back to my parish in Columbia.

The American public seemed largely ignorant of the U.S.'s outsize influence on developing countries and unconcerned about its accompanying responsibility. The church said a lot of good words about solidarity with the poor and marginalized—indeed, church institutions have for long been at the forefront in serving the poor across the globe—but not much was hap-pening at parish level. I saw an opportunity. Maybe I could start a group to bring issues affecting developing countries to the attention of our parish community. We had just started our loan scheme in Tamale. Though worlds apart, the two initiatives were deeply connected for me.

When I returned to the U.S., I broached the idea with the parish authorities, and they were supportive. A dozen or so people joined me, and we got off to an enthusiastic start engaging other parishioners in issues outside their normal field of vision: the consequences of climate change for coffee growers in Central America; the plight of the Palestinian people; the need to relax repayment requirements for highly indebted countries; and many other issues. We drew inspiration from the UN's Millennium Goals promulgated in 2000 and were guided by seminal texts such as Jeffrey Sachs's *The End of Poverty* and Paul Collier's *The Bottom Billion*.

Over the years, we attended rallies on behalf of Darfur and immigration reform, organized events to educate parishioners, and delivered hundreds of signed letters to our congressional representatives on Capitol Hill. At a meeting about the 2012 Farm Bill in Senator Barbara Mikulski's office, we protested the subsidies to cotton growers in the United States.

"These subsidies result in lower cotton prices worldwide. Farmers in Mali and elsewhere can't compete," we complained. "What's the good of providing 'aid' with one stroke of your legislative pen and undermining poor people's ability to earn a living with another?"

The staffers seemed surprised that this group of elderly women were so involved in the details of the legislation!

Catholic Relief Services (CRS) headquarters are close by in Baltimore, and their staff provided us with a wealth of valuable information. In 2010, we engaged the parish in CRS's Confronting Global Poverty campaign, adopting the same name for our own group for a while. We signed up more than two hundred parishioners and handed out "One in a Million" buttons they could be proud to display.

Hopefully our many activities had some impact on attitudes

within the parish, but it's difficult to know how far we moved the needle. Persuading Westerners to care about people across the globe can be a tough sell. Their natural tendency is to focus on the needs of people closer to home. During an annual fund-raiser for overseas charities, I approached a woman who'd once been a member of our group. Her response, "We're going local this year," spoke volumes. For many in the West, those living in poor countries are just too remote, not people like us in need of a helping hand. They are just "other."

The group's premise was that systemic change is essential if we are to address the root causes of poverty across the globe and that was our focus, but many parishioners were more concerned about individual instances of deprivation. "I understand when you ask us to contribute to CRS's work of helping poor farmers in Africa," a well-meaning parishioner—a professor of history, no less—told me once. "But asking me to sign a letter about the Farm Bill doesn't seem like something we should be doing at church. That's for the politicians." His comment reminded me of what Hélder Câmara, archbishop of Recife in Brazil, had said in the 1970s: "When I help the poor, they call me a saint. When I address the conditions that give rise to their poverty, they call me a communist."

Our message was generally better understood by parishioners who had spent time overseas, whether as Peace Corps volunteers, aid workers, or frequent visitors. Those who had visited developing countries briefly could also relate to the issues we discussed, even if their understanding often lacked depth and nuance. The "sightseer" lens—still lurking deep in my own unconscious—is an ever-present danger for Westerners, as is the tendency to think that a brief visit can make one an expert.

A retired parish priest of my acquaintance was very excited about an upcoming mission to Kenya; he would be in-country for one or two weeks. On his return, he enthused about all he had seen and done, happy to tell the world what he'd learned about Africa. I cautioned him to be careful in generalizing from his short experience.

Another friend tells of her journey to a remote hospital in East Africa. "My cousin is the only doctor at the hospital," she said, showing me photos from her trip. "It's in a farming village. She treats people who have nothing." The hospital remains her principal point of connection with the country. She has witnessed the desperation—and courage too—of the people her cousin serves. Her witness is important, but focusing on deprivation and backwardness in Africa can be a trap for Westerners seeking to understand the continent; it's one I have fallen into many times myself—until Clement has corrected me. It does not reflect the aspirations or traditions of the people, which is almost certainly how they would rather be known.

As it was, even among the most committed members of our global poverty group, it was difficult to convey an appreciation of Africa beyond easy stereotypes and tourists' impressions. A discussion during one of our planning meetings caused me to reflect on the reasons for this.

"Robbie has just come back from Africa," one of our long-term members told us, referring to a former parishioner many of us knew. "She had an amazing time. Maybe we could invite her to talk about it."

"Where in Africa did she go?" I asked. As a family, we are always sensitive to Westerner's undifferentiated reference to "Africa" and remind them it's a very large, diverse continent.

"She was in Malawi. She taught there for a semester."

"That's great," I said. I was playing for time, genuinely happy that Robbie had enjoyed her semester abroad, but a little surprised that our own member didn't seem to be connecting with the fact that I had taught for many years in "Africa" and visited frequently.

"If she comes, it would be good to have a Malawian come

with her," I ventured. "That way, we'll know we are getting a balanced picture. A visitor and a national would have complementary perspectives."

I was reminded of Clement's reluctance to let me tell friends what I knew of Ghana in the early days of our marriage. Although I had lived there for three years, he felt my knowledge of the country was too superficial. He was probably right.

One member of the group, Kathy, seemed to understand. "I agree with Sarah. A visitor may not get a full picture. A person from the country would provide a different perspective."

I was grateful for her contribution. Not for the first time, I questioned my ability to communicate my experiences even within a group of people as genuinely concerned about global solidarity as those in our tight-knit group. Could it be that someone with a short and vivid exposure to an African country can share their knowledge more effectively than I can? I wondered. Do I see less than they do because it's all so familiar? Maybe parishioners would find Sandra's stories more relatable than any I might tell. Even if the knowledge she conveyed was partial, it might be easier to grasp.

In an NPR *On Being* interview, the host, Krista Tippet, remarked, "Truth is not just about the thing that's said or the words that are used or the facts that are employed; it's about how those things land in [those who receive them]." However much I try to connect my two widely separated worlds, each with its own assumptions and ways of thinking, I cannot eliminate the distance. I have to figure out what are the points of connection and build from there. There's simply no way I can communicate my experience in all its particularity to those who haven't shared it. Nor, for that matter, should I presume to properly understand the experiences of those who are natives of other countries. Even much of Clement's early life is difficult for me to reach. Boundaries remain.

## On the Edge of the Inside

**W**hile distancing myself from the worst of church behavior, I have remained a Catholic, albeit on its liberal fringe. I am grateful for a church that is committed to the work of social justice, for its solemn rituals and deep mystical tradition, but I'm no longer in tune with the rigidity of Catholic dogma, its overly narrow moral teachings, and its self-important hierarchy. For many years, my relationship with the church was frayed and superficial. I remained nominally observant, unwilling to break the bonds that had been woven so tightly in my childhood. I knew there had to be more.

About the same time that our global poverty group was taking off, I started to read and reread the works of Thomas Merton, Bede Griffiths, and others who had accompanied me in my youth. Guided by Father Joe Kenna, who visited our parish often to say Mass and has become a dear and lasting friend, I enrolled in a course on biblical spirituality and a year-long program at the Shalem Institute based in Washington, DC. It was at Shalem that I encountered the work of Richard Rohr: a spiritual leader—a Franciscan priest, no less—who, though still within the church, was highly critical of many of its structures and traditions.

Rohr pointed the way to a transcendent, more inclusive spirituality such as is represented in the lives and teachings of Francis of Assisi, Teresa of Avila, and—yes—Gandhi and the Sufi mystics. He calls it the "perennial tradition." There is a common message at the center of all the world's great religious traditions. All religious truth is metaphorical. The most significant way of knowing is to admit one can never know. Doubt and dark night are par for the course. Here was a teacher who understood the ambiguity of the human condition yet found wisdom and inner strength in the biblical message. Rohr's teachings gave me permission to value community and experience over ritual and dogma, to embrace the idea that *Everything Belongs*—

as stated so aptly in the title of the first of his books that I read. No person or belief system is off-limits.

As rotund as the stereotypical friar but otherwise unassuming in appearance, Rohr articulated a message that was stunning in the simple truths it encompassed, truths that have largely been buried beneath the elaborate dogma and hierarchy of the church. He brought issues of connection and belonging to the center of attention, if only one had eyes to see. The "seeing," the new awareness, gave me a more inclusive frame for understanding the worlds in which I lived with their points of connection and inevitable barriers.

Wanting to go deeper, I enrolled in The Living School, a two-year program offered by the Center of Action and Contemplation that Rohr had founded in Albuquerque.

"Why Action and Contemplation?" people ask.

"Both are necessary," Rohr maintains. "But the word 'and' in the name is the most important. Good works are empty if not grounded in contemplative awareness; likewise, 'holier-than-thou' contemplation that does not lead to good works is a falsehood. It has to be 'Both-And.' Everything belongs."

"But why put 'action' first?" questioners continue.

"People arrive at 'Both-And' by different routes," Rohr likes to reply. "For many, action is the starting point. It is through action that many people come to recognize the need for contemplation."

That is how it had been for me. Concern for alleviating poverty in developing countries had been my way of affirming that everyone is important, but I knew how easily cynicism or hopelessness can prevail. Some form of internal searching—call it contemplation—is a necessary partner for effective, long-term action.

Paradoxically, my involvement in parish life was growing at the same time I was learning to live "on the edge of the inside" of the church, as Rohr likes to say. Greater spiritual depth, he asserts reassuringly, does not necessitate a formal break from the all-too-human institution of the church. It just means seeing it more clearly for what it is.

No longer entangled in—or should I say strangled by—the church's structures and certainties, I could remain in a liminal space while searching for a more inclusive way of being. I could take distance from the rigid (dare I say quasi-magical) protocol of attendance at Sunday Mass and the irrelevance of the typical homily while trying to build bridges within the church community in pursuit of a more holistic spiritual truth.

Bridge building is slow and arduous. The barriers to cross-cultural understanding— and thus to lasting empathy—are complex and multilayered. People only hear what they are ready to receive. Rohr's mantra of "Both-And" provides a key to cross-cultural understanding, prompting the ongoing search for empathetic understanding of other frames of reference: an attempt to reach beyond barriers and boundaries and enfold others' experiences in a unitive embrace, along with clear-eyed recognition that the task is never done.

# Connections

Clement and I both retired from professional life in 2016. It was a watershed moment for us, as it is for many couples. It meant a search for new meaning and purpose. Although we faced decisions about our retirement together, they presented themselves differently to each of us, reflecting not only our different places of origin but also differences in our interests and desires. Differences, too, in the places where we find community.

When I retired, leaving behind the struggles and successes that accompanied my immersion in the business life, I was able to let go in a way that many who knew me as a worker bee narrowly focused on my business venture didn't think possible. They may well have asked themselves, "Where will she turn? What will she do?" In the event, I surprised myself by how easily I was able to shed my business persona and embrace threads in my life I'd put aside when we moved to the U.S. Coordination of the parish's global poverty group and our loan scheme in Tamale had given new focus to my life; our monthslong visits to Ghana helped.

When Clement retired, he left behind a teaching load that had become increasingly laborious. Although he didn't leave mathematics entirely—he maintains contact with the mathematics department at the University of Ghana and still has a book to finish—his postretirement identity revolves around family in Ghana. He's become an avid researcher of Lutterodt family history and acquires new energy when conversing in Ga, surrounded by family and childhood friends. He, too, has picked up the threads of his younger days.

## A Soft Landing

As we considered our life in retirement, a key decision was where we would live. We knew part of our time would be spent in Ghana, but we also wanted a foot in the Western world, closer to our three children and with access to reliable healthcare. For a time, we thought seriously about moving our main residence from the U.S. to the UK. Justine was now living in London; my three siblings and their families all lived in the London area, as did one of Clement's brothers, not to mention the many nephews and nieces in our extended families. Moreover, the commute back and forth to Accra would be much easier from London than from the U.S.

We spent several weeks in London exploring housing, the cost of living, and other issues involved in relocating, but eventually decided against. Apart from the upheaval involved, and the difficulty in finding a suitable place to live, being in the UK would mean our two children on the West Coast of the U.S. would be half a world and eight time zones away. In the end, this concern took precedence over all others. We would stay in Columbia. No matter where we settled, we would be far from many people who were important to us; in Columbia, we would be more or less equidistant from each of our children. As long as we could withstand the rough and tumble of air travel, none of them would be more than a few hours away.

To avoid worries about snow-clearing and yard maintenance during our long absences in Ghana, we moved to a 55+ community. Conveniently close to our old house with familiar shops and medical facilities in easy reach, Snowden Overlook has a thriving social life; as always, we wondered how we would fit in. More than anything, Clement dreads the stereotype of Africa he suspects prevails in most Americans' minds. He's super-sensitive to anyone whose body language indicates the merest hint of negativity. My accent, my English upbringing—and above all the fact that I was married to a Black man—

meant it would take time for me to get to know our neighbors and for them to know me. Neither of us are big "joiners"— Clement less so than me.

Although the community is diverse in its ethnic composition, the clubhouse events, which I persuaded Clement to attend at first, were disconcertingly White. There was no escaping the fact that we were different. Even after living in the U.S. for half a lifetime, we had no immediate points of connection. I didn't sew, had no interest in learning to play bridge again, and wasn't drawn to Grill 'n' Chill 'n' Saturday evening events. After a couple of years, I joined a book club which brought me into more personal contact with other residents; that has been a definite plus. Unfortunately, Clement didn't find a comparable niche.

Early get-to-know-you conversations evoked in me the same feelings of "otherness" I had experienced when we first arrived in Columbia. I had no reason to assume that White members of the community were entitled in an unexamined sort of way. Yet, given my recent reading on racism, that was the thought that often came to mind, accentuating the distance between us if I wasn't careful. Fortunately, Rohr's teachings had given me a new lens through which to view the world. I was now more ready to see beyond what separated us. Both-And. When the conversation turned to school or college or childrearing, as it often did, I didn't remain silent as I had at the babysitter meetings all those years ago or when I sat alone on the bleachers during Isabelle's basketball practice. I felt more able to share my own rather different experiences.

Thankfully, many kind and generous neighbors reached out to us. Soon after we moved in, the editor of the community newsletter featured our life story in the monthly publication. When she read the piece, one of the residents recognized our last name as that of the landlady who had hosted her son when he stayed in Accra many years earlier. She wondered whether we were related. Of course! All Ghanaian Lutterodts are related and not more than four or five degrees of kinship apart. The landlady happened to be a quite distant cousin but one Clement knew well. There was an immediate connection.

Other residents reached out to us, too, among them the founders of a circle of Democratic activists formed when Donald Trump was inaugurated as president. Although the members were mostly White, Clement and I were well received and enjoyed the meetings with their focus on Democratic concerns.

At one of these meetings, Clement's presence was acknowledged in a quite unexpected way. It was during the COVID pandemic, and the meeting was on Zoom. Our county council representative, Dr. Opel Jones, joined us to answer questions about county policies. Clement and I were sitting together on the couch, sharing my laptop screen. It was shortly after the murder of George Floyd, and I had a question about police reform in the county. Dr. Jones started to answer my question when his voice trailed off as he peered intently at his screen.

"Is that Professor Lutterodt I see there?" he asked. "You taught me in grad school."

"Yes, that's me," Clement responded, his memory stirring. "I remember you." Normally a quiet, reserved presence, Clement was suddenly the center of attention.

"You taught me Analysis," Dr. Jones continued.

"I remember," Clement agreed.

"Good to see you, Prof."

After a brief exchange, the conversation reverted to issues of policing and other county matters, but there had been a shift in the dynamic. Clement's role as a professor of mathematics had been asserted. He was no longer an invisible Black man in a sea of White! He had a recognizable place within the group. It was a moment of connection.

Many members of the Snowden Overlook community are "snowbirds" who go south in the winter to escape the Maryland winter. They go to Florida; we go to Ghana! Most take a plane ride to get there. So do we—it just takes a few hours longer for us to arrive. While they are gone, they probably wear different clothes, mingle with different friends, shop in different grocery stores, and enjoy the local cuisine. So do we. But whereas our neighbors can easily relate to the annual decampment to Florida, our regular visits to Ghana are unusual, to say the least.

"You're going where?" our neighbors would ask in surprise when we first joined the community. They needed time to figure out where Ghana was and why we'd want to go there. Now, many ask, "When are you off to Ghana again?" I'm grateful they recognize this part of our identity.

Other than the inevitable jet lag, the transition between Washington and Accra and back again has become almost seamless for us. The two worlds are tightly stitched together in our singular experience. I belong—incompletely—in both places and live differently in each. In the U.S., I plan and look ahead and like to lead. I benefit from White privilege. I am one of a majority. In Ghana, I am one of a small minority. I observe and follow. I try to keep my mouth shut. But in both environments, in both worlds—or boxes, if you will—I have an opportunity to live in connection with the people around me, to build bridges, cross boundaries, however difficult that may be.

In Ghana, we attend a lot of funerals. Funerals are occasions for big social gatherings, times to visit with relatives and friends. I am often the only White—or one of a very few—in an all-Black environment. I still puzzle about what belonging really means in these situations. While I have a role as Clement's wife and value the opportunity to experience the funeral rituals up close, there is no escaping the fact that I'm different. After fumbling for many years, I have at last mastered—or so I hope—the dress code to be observed: *kaba and slit* styling in cloth that is black, black and white, or white as indicated in the funeral announcement (with red somewhere in the mix from time to time). But I can never carry myself with the poise and dignity of my Ghanaian counterparts. The extra length of fabric the local women toss elegantly over their shoulders just won't stay in place for me. And when the background music transitions from dirge to dancing, as usually happens toward the end of a long day of rituals and refreshments, I can only marvel at the joy and artistry with which the mourners turn to dance to process their grief. I would embarrass myself if I attempted to join in.

Although I often doubt if I can ever really belong in Ghana, there are multiple opportunities for connection in our daily comings and goings. Somehow, we are noticed.

The doorman at a hotel where we frequently go to change money or meet with friends smiles kindly as we leave. When I ask whether he remembers us, he responds, "Yes, M'm. I see you often."

When I call the local beauty parlor to ask about the availability of the stylist who knows how to cut "White" hair, the person answers, "Felicia will be here on Wednesday, but she doesn't have white hair."

"I'm the one with White hair," I respond, laughing at the misunderstanding.

A dressmaker who I see from time to time is worldly wise and tough in the tradition of Ghanaian market women. Her store is stacked floor to ceiling with elaborate fabrics from all over the world. As I entered the store one day, she asked, "Where's my boyfriend?" When I told her Clement was in the car, she immediately stepped outside to greet him. Although this may be her modus operandi with all customers, she makes us feel we have a special connection.

When I go to the internet company's office to prepay for some gigabytes, the girl at the help desk greets me with, "Last time you were here . . ."

"You mean you recognize me?" I have only been there once or twice before.

"I know who you are. We still need to connect up your husband's phone." I'm astonished that she remembers the details of our earlier conversation.

Whether in the U.S. or in Ghana, we are recognizably different. And yet, paradoxically, our very difference is sometimes an opportunity for connections. They may not be deep or intimate, but they are connections, nonetheless.

In my attempts at bridge building, my goal had always been to help Westerners understand Africa. It had never been my intention to help Africans understand Whites. During colonial times, Ghanaians had more than enough opportunity to observe and understand their oppressors. Yet, now sixty-five years after independence, there may be an opportunity to soften the image Ghanaians have of Whites. Maybe I can present a simpler, humbler image to the many people we encounter in our daily rounds, gratefully receiving the services they offer and patiently accepting the delays and misunderstandings that so often arise. (When it comes to patience, Clement has a lot to teach me still.) And with those who are in more senior positions, there may be scope for helping them understand, even pity, the deep-seated ignorance of White people that underlies the attitudes and behaviors they so rightly condemn. After all, each of us is some blend of good and bad, the person we would like to be and our shadow lurking in our unconscious: Both-And.

Despite the aches and pains and forgetfulness that accompany aging, retirement has brought many blessings: respite from the hassle of earning a living, freedom to travel and spend time in a more restful way, the opportunity to forge new connections.

Although we have lived half a lifetime in the U.S., we

remain something of a mystery to many Americans. In Ghana, our very presence provokes questions, inviting connection of a sort, albeit one that often lacks deep intimacy. In England, family stories prevail; there are also threads of shared experiences on which we can draw: Brewerstreet, our childhood, and the few times when family members visited Ghana.

Finding ways to build bridges between my different worlds will always be a challenge. It may be a mistake to try too hard. Simple presence may be enough. A presence in which my attention is focused not on cultural barriers but on whatever moments of connection present themselves. Black on White. White on Black. Both-And. Bridge building remains a work in progress.

# Epilogue

*Life must be lived forward, but it can only be understood backward.*

*—Søren Kierkegaard*

In my old age, blessed with freedom from material need and in relatively good health of mind and body, I am left with many unanswered questions, many uncertainties about my place in the universe and the meaning of my life's experiences. I am grateful for the time I have now to ponder the meaning of it all. Above all, I am grateful to be at ease with those uncertainties. I have learned to love the questions, as the poet Rilke famously advised his young friend.

I am content—with the Buddhists—to cultivate a "beginner's mind," to recognize that there are no easy answers; I try not to be impatient with the pastors and philosophers and pundits who seem to think there are, those who would like to assure us that there is a well-trodden path to nirvana or salvation or a transcendent truth. Maybe there is. I wouldn't know. I walk with them when it seems right and turn away when a deeper wisdom presents itself. I am content not to know, to sit with the mystery of it all. It is an immense liberation.

In setting out to write this memoir, I was searching for an underlying thread, a theme that could connect and bring unity to my diverse experiences, the different "containers" in which I have lived: the confined security of my childhood; the apparent freedom of my neocolonial years in Cape Coast; the challenge of raising a mixed-race family in racially traumatized America; the radical code-switching, not to say personality change, needed for survival—and eventual success—in the world of American business; the opportunity to spend time in a newly emerging Ghana and forge relationships across race, class, and culture; the search for purpose in retirement.

I have benefited from strong genes and a healthy self-image. They have allowed me to survive, even thrive, in the various environments where I have landed. But I cannot say I have found a clear underlying thread to my life; I'm not sure it matters. If there is such a thread, it's very different in kind and texture from what I first envisioned. Not easily described. It has little to do with where I've been or what I've done. It has more to do with the ways in which I have slowly come to understand and accept how the deep roots laid down in childhood have influenced whatever connections across cultures I've been able to make. In the U.S., I will always be the "woman with the British accent" (yes, that is where I'm *really* from!); in Ghana, I will always be a White woman—"the wife"; in England, I will always be family. I am who I am.

My connections are what I was able to make of them at the time, not what they might have been. If I have been able on occasion to build bridges, however fragile, I am grateful for that. If others find strands within my story that help them connect with worlds very different from those they've known—or survive in ones they know too well—I am grateful for that, too.

The boundaries between my separate worlds remain, but somehow they seem less important now. I am glad to recognize them for what they are, still defining my place in the world but not limiting or constraining me as once they did. As Richard Rohr says, everything belongs. I am grateful to have experienced moments when a boundary that separates my life from that of another has become porous, illumined by the bonds of our common humanity. Such moments are given, not found or created. My task is to remain open to them when they arise and savor the mystery that they hold. As Jane Hirschfield has said in relation to her poem "The Bowl" (the Buddhist symbol for humble receptivity), "The great gate to abundance is simply to feel yourself able to be porous, to be open to whatever is put in the bowl that is yours to hold." That is my task still. A task that requires me to quiet my restless mind. To heed my better angels. A task it has taken me a lifetime to understand.

# *Acknowledgements*

Many people have contributed in diverse ways to this memoir—not only those who have been at my side to help me bring it to its final published form but all those who have accompanied me on my life's journey, as captured in these pages.

There's my family of course. Not only have they encouraged and supported me in the writing, but they have accepted the fact that my memoir has exposed their lives in ways they didn't ask for and didn't necessarily want. The voice of my husband, Clement, can be heard throughout, advising, cautioning. Although it is my story, it is enriched by his insights into Westerners' sense of entitlement and Ghanaian sensitivities. Both in life and in this retelling, he has caused me over and over again to question my own presumptions. I owe my understanding of life at the intersection between races and cultures to him and to witnessing the experiences of our three children.

Justine advised on the overall structure of the book and on the reworking of a number of passages to ensure my message would reach a wider audience, while Isabelle has been an valuable partner in sharing her childhood experiences and in helping to arrive at a cover design to convey my theme. Toby's memories stretch back furthest. He provided helpful input on the years when we crisscrossed continents and adjusted gradually, and not without difficulty, to life in the U.S.

Many people who have been part of my journey have enriched it in ways they may not realize. Some are named; others, though unnamed, may recognize themselves in the stories I tell. In a few cases I have used aliases to protect people's privacy or prevent hurt. There are many more who have been important to me but do not appear in these pages, either for lack of space or because this book has been many years in the making. They include friends and relatives in the UK, Ghana, and the U.S.; fellow parishioners at St. Johns RC Church in Columbia, MD; teachers and fellow students of the Living School at the Center for Action and Contemplation in Albuquerque; and the many people who help us out in so many ways during our long stays in Ghana. Please forgive me if you do not find yourself here. You know who you are; I am grateful to you all.

I am immensely grateful, too, to the wonderful professionals in the literary and artistic world who helped bring this memoir to fruition. During my career I did a lot of writing, but I didn't realize how different writing a memoir would be! Rebecca de Santioge helped me get started with a series of lessons in creative writing. As soon as I saw her background on the web—Zimbabwe, Roehampton University, Thomas Merton—I knew we would hit it off, and we did. Later, when I went in search of a writing coach for the long haul, I found a lot of interesting options. Many offered a formula for success and the opportunity to participate in a host of on-line workshops. Although they had good advice to offer, I didn't feel that their boxed-in approaches would help me capture my rather unusual life experiences in a readable way. Bruce MacAllister seemed a better fit, with just the right mix of professional skill and eclecticism to give me confidence in his advice. He has been at my side (or, rather, at the other end of Zoom calls) for more than three years, forcing me to go deeper, find my inner voice—things that I found so difficult at first. Thank you, Bruce, for believing I would get there in the end and for being with me every step of the way. You often forced me to revisit a draft section and enliven the writing by adding theme or emotion or dialogue. When you applauded a passage, I felt as though I had been rewarded with a gold star for my homework! Without your encouragement I could not have persevered.

Along the way I benefited from the insight of many thoughtful readers. Thank you, Kathy Gross, Kathy Deal, Barbara Bordeleon for reading and commenting on early chapters and encouraging me to continue. An even bigger thank-you to Joyce Engmann and Geryl McClenney who read chapter by chapter, part by part as I worked my way through the third full draft . . . or was it the fourth? My friendship with Joyce dates back more than fifty years. She was a firsthand witness to many significant episodes in my life; her insights and feedback were invaluable. Geryl is a more recent friend, to whom much of what I wrote was new and unfamiliar. Her very different perspective provided an important counterpoint.

I was fortunate to find an editor who had lived in England and Ghana, who knew my "worlds," and could relate to my story. Brooke Goode helped me trim my stories, keep them interesting. Thank you, Brooke, for helping me sharpen my pen and cut unnecessary detail; it was a joy to work with you.

When I was almost done, several other people stepped in to read the manuscript cover to cover and provide input or suggestions: Geryl (again!), Vicki Cofield Aber, Caroline Pestieau, Joan Neal, Tom Eberle, Josephine Garmen and Frank Sasinowski. Even though it was too late to implement some of your excellent suggestions, your enthusiasm gave me a real boost during the final stages.

And then there's Aldo Puicón-Pérez, a consummate professional, who produced the cover design that you now see. Isabelle reintroduced me to Aldo when nothing seemed to be working. They suggested using different textiles as metaphors for my different "worlds" and organizing them in subtle ways to convey my theme of "uncertain belonging." It worked. Thank you, Aldo!

And finally, it was Atmosphere Press who took me over the

finish line. Thank you to Kyle McCord, Alex Kale, and the team of professionals at Atmosphere who helped me through the last steps to achieve a product I can be proud of.

# About the Author

**SARAH LUTTERODT** was born and educated in England, gaining a BA degree in physics from the University of Oxford, an M.Phil. in nuclear physics from the University of London, and a Ph.D. in Education from the University of Birmingham. She has spent most of her adult life outside England, working for two years at the University of Lovanium in the Democratic Republic of the Congo and subsequently for ten years at the University of Cape Coast in Ghana. Since 1980, she has lived in the United States, where she worked as a technical training consultant for General Physics Corporation before starting her own business, Quality Training Systems, in 1997.

She has celebrated fifty-two years of marriage to her husband, Clement, with whom she has three children, who pursue their careers in Seattle, Los Angeles, and London respectively. Now in retirement, she and Clement divide their time between their homes in Columbia, Maryland, and Accra, Ghana.

Printed in Great Britain
by Amazon